Y0-CPD-701

THE REEMERGENCE OF AN INNER CITY: THE PIVOT OF CHINESE SETTLEMENT IN THE EAST BAY REGION OF THE SAN FRANCISCO BAY AREA

BY WILLARD T. CHOW

San Francisco, California
1977

Published by

R & E RESEARCH ASSOCIATES, INC.
4843 Mission Street
San Francisco, California 94112

Publishers
Robert D. Reed and Adam S. Eterovich

Library of Congress Card Catalog Number

77-075492

I.S.B.N.
0-88247-457-X

Copyright 1977
by
Willard Tim Chow

PREFACE

This study is essentially my Ph.D. dissertation which was submitted to the Department of Geography, University of California at Berkeley in 1974. Most of the original maps have been redone by the cartography staff of the Department of Geography, University of Hawaii at Manoa. I am indebted to Everett Wingert and his students for their assistance in this project. I am also grateful to my colleagues and the secretarial staffs at the Department of Geography and the Pacific Urban Studies and Planning Program of the University of Hawaii at Manoa for their kokua and encouragement since my arrival in 1975.

The research and preparation of the study was conducted over a three year period from 1971 to 1974, during which I taught at Laney College in Oakland. I would like to thank Helen Logan and my students there for their insights, patience, and assistance during this period. Since then, several papers have emanated from this study. They include:

"Reviving the Inner City: the Lessons of Oakland's Chinatown," Public Affairs Report, Bulletin of the Institute of Governmental Studies, University of California at Berkeley, Vol. 16, No. 4 (August, 1975), pp. 1-7.

"Inner City Dynamics: the Case of Oakland's Chinatown," The China Geographer, No. 4 (Spring, 1976), pp. 1-17, reprinted by the Institute of Governmental Studies at Berkeley in 1977 (reprint number 61).

"Minorities in the Suburbs: the Promise of Growth," presented before the Annual Meeting of the Association of American Geographers, Salt Lake City, April, 1977.

This study will hopefully lay the foundation for what I hope to be a substantial body of research on urban ethnicity and the ways in which it is affected by public policies.

Many people made this study possible. I would like to thank the many families who responded to my survey of Chinese in the East Bay suburbs. Greg Mark, Gordon Yow, and Jane Yee Armstrong were most generous in sharing their papers and observations with me. I am grateful to George Linden of the California Department of Public Health, to Willie Chang of the Census Service Facility, to William Ides of the Alameda County Assessor's Office, and to Jerry Lew and Jack Keating of the Western Title Guaranty Company for giving me access to their data. Bert Bangsberg and William Bostwick of the Oakland Redevelopment Agency, John English of the Oakland City Planning Department, Ron Gee and Janet Sin York of the Chinese Community Council were extremely cooperative and helpful, for which I am most appreciative. I would like to express my thanks to the Reverend Frank G. Mar, Greg Chinn, Jean Vance, Nettie and Alfred Soo, the Reverend Ching Ming Lee, and Karen Chin for their assistance.

I am especially grateful to the members of my dissertation committee for their patience, stimulation, and comments. Lloyd Street not only broadened my horizons, guided me in the right directions, and sharpened the focus of my analysis, he has also been a good friend. I am extremely grateful to Clarence Glacken for his continuing inspiration, thoughtful criticism, and steadfast support. I am indebted to James E. Vance, Jr., the Chairman of my committee, who not only supervised my research but also advised me throughout my graduate program. His resourcefulness, invaluable suggestions, and confidence in me are profoundly appreciated. I would also like to extend my appreciation to Allan Pred, James Parsons, Dan Luten, and David Hooson for their support while I was at Berkeley.

I would finally like to thank Harriet Nathan of the Institute of Governmental Studies at Berkeley, who showed me how to write and rewrite, and Kathy Chow, whose editorial guidance, tolerance, and encouragement made this study feasible.

Willard Tim Chow
Honolulu, Hawaii
May 10, 1977

TABLE OF CONTENTS

TABLES

FIGURES

MAPS

Courtesy of Christopher Salter, Editor, CHINA GEOGRAPHER, for Maps 9, 10, 21, 24, 26, 34 and 35.

CHAPTER ONE

FOUNDATIONS FOR A NEW PERSPECTIVE

Closing the Theoretical Gap

Unlike previous research in urban geography, which had stressed the uniqueness of cities, the conceptual approach or "functionalist perspective" of many geographical studies during the 1960s emphasized the common functional and morphological character or urban places.[1] Urban geographers who joined the quantitative revolution in American geography viewed the city as an objective manifestation of knowledgeable, rational decision-making in pursuit of maximum tangible returns. Scholars schooled in the precision of scientific objectivity made sweeping middle class assumptions about the needs, capacities, and preferences of urban dwellers. Subjective variables, such as neighborhood sentiments, aspirations, and values, were seldom within the focus of their attention.

It is not surprising that the quantitative revolution shed little light upon the dynamics of inner city evolution, where middle class ideals did not prevail. In their rush to break with the idiographic tradition in urban geography, quantitative methodologists lost sight of the city as an institutional legacy, a political arena, and a physical symbol.[2] The persistence of communal tendencies among ethnic groups, which reached their fullest expression in the inner city, revealed the shortcomings of abstract quantitative approaches to the American city. The recent upsurge of geographical interest in behavioral models, social processes, and conflicting values was spawned by increasing disillusionment with the fruits of the quantitative approach.[3]

Misconceptions about how inner cities function as social as well as physical and ecological communities have yet to be resolved. The central city continues to be plagued by the pitfalls of unchallenged thinking.[4] This chapter will examine some of the conventional wisdom on the American city in hopes of closing the gap in our understanding. Geographers have long been interested in the process of environmental adaptation and in the organization and occupation of space.[5] Only with the past few decades, however, have urban geographers been willing to venture beyond Blanchard's hallowed ground of site and situation. Past studies have tended to treat cities as townscapes, population centers, concentrations of economic activity, or locations of historical events.[6] Behavioral studies in urban geography, which have questioned the validity of old assumptions, have much to contribute to our understanding.

Often uninformed, irrational, and satisfied with suboptimal returns, city folk do not always conform to theoretical expectations. Thunen's conclusion that competition would allocate land to its most suitable use was based on the assumption that collusion among land owners was a negligible force. Burgess' concept of ecological stability ignored the role of racial discrimination in perpetuating spatial patterns. Exogenous forces, outside the scope of community control, seem to exert several types of influence on inner city evolution. The factors which govern the process of urban settlement are illustrated in Figure 1.

The concepts in the above framework come from a wide range of time tested ideas. It is hoped that, as an organizing principle, the model will illuminate the gaps in our knowledge of cities. The literature on central cities in the United States can be sifted into different perspectives. Most studies have been critical and pessimistic about the role of the inner city as a viable ethnic community. Some have blamed its plight upon its residents; others have assigned the responsibility for its problems to society, to our technological economy, outmoded institutions, and dehumanized values.[7] The diversity of scholarly work done on the inner city by economists, political scientists, sociologists, anthropologists, psychologists, and historians suggests that its problems emanate from a diversity of exogenous sources as well as internal dysfunctional tendencies.

Geographical research, with its emphasis on form as an expression of function, has usually concentrated on what was most visible and distinctive.[8] Little attention has been devoted to the underlying process of inner city transformation or to the role of urban form as a constraint to functional adjustment. The physical layout and build of an area may of course be a determinant for future functions as well as a legacy of past functions. The dynamic and circular character of inner city settlement has yet to be fully explored. The direction of this chapter, which surveys the mainstream of scholarly thought, will be to muster support for such a perspective.

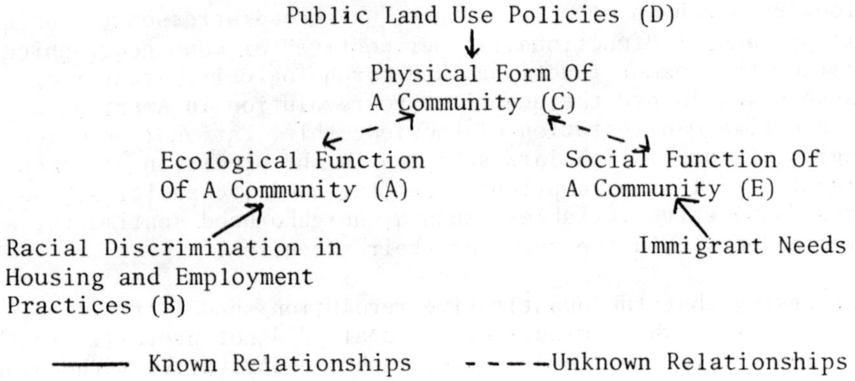

Public Land Use Policies (D)

↓

Physical Form Of
A Community (C)

Ecological Function
Of A Community (A)

Social Function Of
A Community (E)

Racial Discrimination in
Housing and Employment
Practices (B)

Immigrant Needs

———— Known Relationships   - - - -Unknown Relationships

Model of Inner City Evolution

Figure 1

The Ecological Function of a Community (A)

Inner cities do not develop "naturally," as is widely believed; they also reflect the institutional terms on which the competition for urban space is based. The conflict between inner city residents and outside interests for a greater share of urban power and resources has been a subject of enduring concern. Some writers have depicted the quest for community control as a struggle between local neighborhood and downtown interests.[9] Others insist on the complex nature of competition among local areas. Atshuler, for example, has argued that community control may be a mixed blessing for ghetto areas.[10] Still others adhere to the argument of colonial exploitation.[11] Alinsky's campaign for neighborhood control in the inner city shows signs of strength in many cities, if only as an index of frustration with "rational" economic solutions which have failed to work. The importance of ethnic institutions as a vehicle for solidifying political bonds seems clear.

Economic solutions likewise show little prospect for success unless accompanied by institutional changes in the means of allocating scarce resources. High rates of unemployment and the rising price of urban land constitute formidable obstacles to short-term programs of economic assistance. Sternlieb has argued that increasing the number of resident owners of slum tenements would go a long way toward improving living conditions in the inner city.[12] Smith contends that the urban land ratchet can only be made less regressive by giving inner city residents the credit they need to acquire ownership of community housing.[13] Although capital for housing improvements in the inner city is desperately lacking, banks and other financial institutions have found slum ownership to be profitable. Undermaintenance, condemnation, and lucrative returns apparently go hand-in-hand.[14] The stability of an inner city community may be rooted in its ability to secure economic control of the turf which it needs to support its residents.

The Role of Racial Discrimination (B)

The influence of racial segregation, de facto and de jure, on the evolution of inner city communities has yet to be systematically studied. Settlement patterns bear the imprint of values and attitudes which have been institutionalized into common practice.[15] The impact of racism on the dynamics of property values under conditions of filtering and

2

neighborhood change can hardly be denied.[16] The role of the real estate industry in perpetuating the practice of segregation likewise should not be overlooked.[17]

The effects of spatial isolation upon the social viability of inner city communities has been thoroughly examined by sociologists. Frazier, Drake and Cayton, Liebow, and Clark have all delved into the social environment which poor Blacks have created in their separate, subordinate status in American cities.[18] Lewis' research on the Puerto Rican community in New York has dramatized the ill-effects of crowded, confined environments on acculturation and problem-solving in the community.[19]

The ramifications of racial discrimination in hiring practices have definite implications for urban structure. Thurow has argued that the annual cost of discrimination to the average non-white worker is about $2100.[20] It is not surprising that minority families have not been able to share in the suburban expansion until employment opportunities opened to boost their mobility. The differential success of ethnic groups in creating a decent habitat for themselves in the inner city may be explained in large part by the degree to which they have been victimized by racism. The application of European immigrant models to the plight of non-white ethnic groups in the United States may indeed be limited.

The Physical Form of a Community (C)

The notion that changes in inner city form reflect the competition among ecological areas for capital is consistent with classic views on the evolution of urban structure. Burgess' transition zone pushes outward in response to immigration, social disorganization, and expansion by the Central Business District.[21] Changes in function lead to changes in spatial and physical form. The impetus for Hoyt's pull model of urban dynamics is filtering. The function of housing changes as it loses its attractiveness to older people and socially mobile groups.[22] The physical deterioration of structures depreciates its value to its residents, who tend to move into better accommodations in newer areas. In the multiple nuclei version of urban structure proposed by Harris and Ullman, land near the core is often kept vacant or retained in anti-social slum structures in anticipation of higher rent-paying activities, which would require rebuilding.[23] Form is related to the future as well as present functions of a community.

Inner city residential communities must compete with other areas of the city for resources to maintain and improve the structures which they have inherited. Subjected to the centrifugal and centripetal forces of invasion and succession by alternative land uses, the stability of inner city communities may be enhanced by their relatively unattractive physical setting. Usually nestled in the city's zone of discard, communities fortified by high rates of owner occupancy have managed to survive the threat of cell-by-cell exclusion. Public redevelopment of the inner city enabled planners to distort the process of competitive exclusion through eminent domain.[24] The increasing vulnerability of inner city communities, including those which are in good physical condition, is an outgrowth of institutional distortions in the competition for urban land.

Recent empirical studies seem to concur with this view. Davis has demonstrated that middle class housing in core areas is being replaced by lower and upper class housing.[25] Bourne has suggested that high density residential use may be simply an intermediate stage in the graduate conversion of low density residential use into vacant land, which can more readily be converted into warehousing, industry, retailing, or back again into new residential use.[26]

It is clear, however, that the process of land conversion is not regulated by purely economic incentives. Social ascription and sentimental values have made some sites more attractive, stable, and impervious to the social threat of proximity to lower class neighborhoods. The importance of sentiment and symbolism to lower class community stability in the inner city may be just as significant.[27]

An alternative argument is that physical deterioration is inevitable. Obsolescence in this view stems from changing ideals, styles, and techniques in the design, construction, and arrangement of buildings. The inner city, bounded by the "zone in transition," cannot help but embody such changes.[28] The complementary forces of invasion and succession on one hand and filtering on the other accelerate during periods of rapid growth. Differences in income, tastes, and needs constitute a built-in source of social obsolescence and an incentive for under-maintenance. In this sense, the crux of the problem is that physical structures may last too long, outliving their usefulness to their original residents and saddling their new residents with rundown and outmoded structures. The task of planning in this scheme would be to facilitate the redevelopment of the inner city as expeditiously as possible. In designing an inner city redevelopment project, planners would of course predetermine the functional character of the area--in stark contrast with the traditional idea that past form and private land owners would be the deciding factors.

The Role of Land Use Policies (D)

The implications of national shifts on structural changes in urban land use in the United States have been echoed in the work of numerous scholars. Some have argued that changes in technology and in corporate influence have undermined old notions of place-belonging.[29] Others contend that we have inner city problems largely because we are not a poor and immobile society, but rather because change is rapid and constant, and because economically and socially deprived groups are trying to expand their position in our society.[30] Greer, Mumford, and the Goodmans seem to be convinced that the plight of our cities is due to increases in societal scale.[31] Thompson asserts that sheer size has reduced communication among socio-economic groups and magnified the scale of slum segregation.[32] Vance's studies have shown that the separation of workplace from residence was the seminal force behind the social stratification of urban housing.[33] Unemployment rates prevailing in a city, which reflect regional shifts as well as local conditions, accentuate the process of inner city decay. Mooney insists that inner city unemployment is more closely related to city unemployment rates than it is to the relocation of jobs in the suburbs.[34]

The plight of inner city communities likewise cannot be divorced from cultural forces which have made urban problems a secondary priority in a nation of cities. Differentiated from the rest of the country by its social stratification, religious indifference, intellectual progress, and educational opportunities, the city has been a suspect institution in this country. Antagonistic attitudes toward the city have persisted in American thought and permeated our institutions.[35] Once aimed at big cities, the legacy of our cultural tradition has turned toward the core of these cities, which holds no place in the American Dream. Federal expenditures on the city have thus been directed at either renewing or creating suburban alternatives to the inner city.

Urban renewal projects and the interstate highway system have certainly done their part in helping to eradicate much of the inner city's housing stock. The Federal Housing Administration and the Veterans Administration have played a vital role in suburban growth and inner city decline.[36] Federal funding arrangements and state laws have also aggravated the problems of central cities.[37] Fiscal limitations, which insulate suburban areas from metropolitan taxation to support metropolitan activities, constitute a major obstacle to central city rehabilitation. Beset by national trends and national policies justified in the national interest, the abandonment of the central city and the physical deterioration of its facilities come as no surprise.

The Social Function of a Community (E)

A large volume of work has been done on the social dynamics of immigrant communities in American cities, most of it by sociologists.[38] Studies have found that radical physical changes which alter traditional perceptions or modify customary patterns of social interdependence often disturb the development of neighborhood institutions. The condemnation of inner city areas for municipal projects, educational facilities, and public transportation systems may destroy a community's churches, local commercial centers, and useful housing. Such projects tend to frustrate and divide neighborhoods, which were once tied together by the symbolic as well as functional aspects of neighborhood foci.

The search for physical solutions to urban ills by architects and planners continues, although widely criticized by advocates of social and economic reform.[39] The issue is by no means dead. Settlement patterns sometimes have an adverse effect on mental health, retarding the potential development of community institutions.[40] However, congested living conditions may mean different things to different people, depending on their perceptions.[41] Inner city dwellings which have been made physically attractive and socially exclusive appear to be in demand despite their compact living arrangements.

The location of community services may in actuality be more significant for an inner city community than the appearance of its structures. The location of neighborhood centers, such as schools, churches, and recreational facilities, have nevertheless received scant attention in geographical research.[42] Although patterns of social interaction are usually constrained by distance and social barriers, social geographers have shown little interest in the process by which "action spaces" are broken up by public policies.[43]

Advocates of ghetto dispersal point to the advantages of suburban living.[44] What may really matter to low income newcomers is not an abundance of privately occupied residential space but rather the availability of low rent accommodations close to friends and community institutions; not integrated housing but rather special educational facilities and community services; not wider awareness of urban opportunities but rather more intensive preparation for employment that will provide for their basic needs.

What they appear to need most are responsive community institutions. The maintenance of community housing and neighborhood vigilance depend on strong community ties.[45] The key to community development in the inner city is not to be found in the simplicity of urban villages.[46] Effective immigrant institutions, which can help newcomers acculturate, find jobs, assist them in times of need, and assure them of safe, decent, low rent housing, appear to be the missing link in the search for environmental stability.[47] Without them inner city communities have no means for self-direction.

Method of Study

Chinese settlement in the East Bay Region of the San Francisco Bay Area furnishes an ideal setting in which to test the validity of the above ideas. Three generations of inner city occupancy and community adaptation to over a century of immigration, racial discrimination, and urban growth provide varied conditions for historical analysis. Like many other American cities, Oakland is engaged in redevelopment of its inner city. The reemergence of this area into a middle class district has strong ramifications for Chinatown, which was located within the city's zone of discard until the past decade.

The Chinese in the East Bay still support a Chinatown in the inner city. Although much smaller and less impressive than San Francisco Chinatown, it is in many ways more typical of Chinese communities in the United States. Unlike San Francisco Chinatown, which serves a city within a city, Oakland Chinatown serves a widely dispersed and more completely acculturated Chinese population. The influx of foreign-born Chinese into Oakland during the 1960s placed new burdens on the community. Many of San Francisco's problems have spilled over into Oakland, where attempts to resolve them have been complicated by redevelopment.

A considerable amount of research has been done on Black inner city life. An increasing amount is being done on Mexican-American settlement in the inner city. Little has thus far been written on the experience of Asians in the American city.[48] Most studies of inner city settlement have focused on European ethnic communities in this country. Non-white ethnic groups of course encounter discrimination based on racial and not just cultural differences. Since racial discrimination against the Chinese in the United States has tapered off since World War II, their experience in the inner city seems to be a good example of how racism has affected the evolution of ethnicity in the American city.

Cross-sectional surveys of inner cities have been less than satisfying. Comparative analysis tends to miss the importance of processes and ethnic distinctions. Case studies seem to be more fruitful even though their findings may not have general application. The work of Spear on Chicago, Osofsky on Harlem, Firey on Boston, Chombart de Lauwe on Paris, and Handlin on New York exemplify the kinds of in-depth investigation lacking in comparative approaches.[49]

This dissertation will inquire into the relationship between inner city form and function, and the degree to which form and function are expressions of outside forces during different periods of Chinese settlement in Alameda and Contra Costa Counties. Specific attention will be paid to the impact of racism and public land use controls on the physical and spatial evolution of Chinese settlement and to the effect of physical and spatial change in the community. What is needed now is not better data or more sophisticated analytical techniques but rather more insight into the social consequences of public policies.[50]

Footnotes to Chapter One:

1. Sister Annette Buttimer, "Values in Geography," Resource Paper No. 24, Assn. of Amer. Geographers (1974) pp. 19-23.

   Clyde Kohn, "The 1960's: A Decade of Progress in Geographical Research and Instruction," Annals, Assn. of Amer. Geog., Vol. 60 (1970) pp. 211-219.

   Placido Lavalle, Harold McConnell, and Robert G. Brown, "Certain Aspects of the Expansion of Quantitative Methodology in American Geography," Annals, Assn. of Amer. Geog., Vol. 57 (1967) pp. 423-436.

2. Harold Brookfield and George Tatham, "The Distribution of Racial Groups in Durban," Geog. Rev., Vol. 47 (1957) pp. 44-65.

   G. Hamden, "The Growth and Functional Structure of Khartoum," Geog. Rev., Vol. 50 (1960) pp. 21-40.

   Richard Hartshorne, "The Twin-City District: A Unique Form of Urban Landscape," Geog. Rev., Vol. 22 (1932) pp. 431-442.

   Akim Mabogunje, "The Growth of Residential Districts in Ibadan," Geog. Rev., Vol. 52 (1962) pp. 56-77.

   Rhoads Murphey, "Boston's Chinatown," Econ. Geog., Vol. 28 (1952) pp. 244-255.

   Warwick Nelville, "Singapore: Ethnic Diversity and Its Implications," Annals, Assn. of Amer. Geog., Vol. 56 (1966) pp. 236-253.

   Robert Novak, "The Distribution of Puerto Ricans on Manhattan Island," Geog. Rev., Vol. 46 (1956) pp. 182-186.

   Edward Price, "Viterbo: Landscape of an Italian City," Annals, Assn. of Amer. Geog., Vol. 54 (1964) pp. 242-275.

   Peter Scott, "Capetown: A Multi-Racial City," Geog. Journ., Vol. 121 (1955) pp. 143-144.

   F. Van Der Leeden, "Puerto Ricans in New York City," Geog. Rev., Vol. 44 (1954) pp. 143-144.

                                    Versus

   Robert Adams, "Residential Structure of Midwestern Cities," Annals, Assn. of Amer. Geog., Vol. 60 (1970) pp. 37-62.

   Lawrence Bourne, "Physical Adjustment Processes and Land Use Succession: A Conceptual Review and a Central City Example," Econ. Geog., Vol. 47 (1971) pp. 1-15.

   J. Tait Davis, "Middle Class Housing in the Central City," Econ. Geog., Vol. 41 (1965) pp. 248-251.

   Truman Hartshorn, "Inner City Residential Structure and Decline," Annals, Assn. of Amer. Geog., Vol. 61 (1971) pp. 72-96.

   Richard Morrill, "The Negro Ghetto: Problems and Alternatives," Geog. Rev., Vol. 55 (1965) pp. 339-361.

   Harold Rose, "The Development of an Urban Subsystem the Case of the Negro Ghetto," Annals, Assn. of Amer. Geog., Vol. 60 (1970) pp. 1-5.

----"The Spatial Development of Black Residential Sub-Systems," Econ. Geog., Vol. 48 (1972) pp. 43-65.

3. Shane Davies and Gary Fowler, "The Disadvantaged Urban Migrant in Indianapolis," Econ. Geog., Vol. 48 (1972) pp. 153-167.

   Daniel Doepers, "The Globeville Neighborhood in Denver," Geog. Rev., Vol. 57 (1967) pp. 506-522.

   Robert Elgie, "Rural Immigration, Urban Ghettoization, and Their Consequences," Antipode, Vol. 2 (1970) pp. 35-60.

   Roger Kasperson and Myra Breitbart, "Participation, Decentralization, and Advocacy Planning," Resource Paper No. 25, Assn. of American Geographers (1974).

   Harold Rose, "Social Process in the City: Race and Urban Residential Choice," Resource Paper No. 6, Assn. of American Geographers (1969).

   David Ward, "The Emergence of Central Immigrant Ghettos in American Cities," Annals, Assn. of Amer. Geog., Vol. 58 (1968).

   Julian Wolpert, Anthony Mumphrey, and John Seley, "Metropolitan Neighborhoods: Participation and Conflict Over Change," Resource Paper No. 16, Assn. of American Geographers (1972).

   Two recent monographs on this topic:

   Harold Rose, The Black Ghetto: A Spatial Behavioral Perspective (N.Y., 1971).

   David Ward, Cities and Immigrants: A Geography of Change in Nineteenth Century America (London, 1971).

4. Preston James, "The Origin and Persistence of Error in Geography," Annals, Assn. of Amer. Geog., Vol. 57 (1967) pp. 1-24.

5. M. Aurousseau, "Recent Contributions to Urban Geography," Geog. Rev., Vol. 14 (1921) pp. 444-455.

   For clarification see:

   M. R. G. Conzen, "The Scandinavian Approach to Urban Geography," Norsk Geografisk Tidscrift, Vol. 12 (1949) pp. 1-5.

   Robert Dickinson, "The Scope and Status of Urban Geography," Land Econ., Vol. 24 (1948) pp. 221-238.

   Jack Eichenbaum and Steven Gale, "Form, Function, and Process: A Methodological Inquiry," Econ. Geog., Vol. 47 (1971) pp. 525-544.

6. R. E. Pahl, "Trends in Social Geography," in Chorley, Frontiers in Geographical Teaching (London, 1965).

   For an exceptional perspective see:

   James E. Vance, Jr., "City and Super City: Complex Structure of the Bay Area in the Seventies," Papers, Assn. of Amer. Geog. (1970) pp. 11-40.

7. Compare, for example, Edward Banfield, The Unheavenly City (N.Y. 1968) with Report of the National Advisory Commission on Civil Disorders (N.Y. 1968).

8. Nevin Fenneman, "The Circumference of Geography," <u>Annals, Assn. of Amer. Geog.</u>, Vol. 9 (1919) pp. 3-11.

    Richard Hartshorne, <u>Perspective on the Nature of Geography</u> (N.Y. 1959).

    Preston James, "The Field of Geography," in Preston James and Clarence Jones, <u>American Geography: Inventory and Prospect</u> (Syracuse, 1956).

    Carl O. Sauer, "The Education of a Geographer," <u>Annals, Assn. of Amer. Geog.</u>, Vol. 46 (1956) pp. 287-299.

9. Martyn Bowden, "Downtown through Time: Delimitation, Expansion, and Internal Growth," <u>Econ. Geog.</u>, Vol. 47 pp. 121-135.

    Milton Kotler, <u>Neighborhood Government</u> (N.Y., 1969).

    David Ward, <u>op. cit.</u> (see Note 3 above).

10. Alan Atschuler, <u>Community Control: The Black Demand for Participation in Large American Cities</u> (N.Y. 1970).

    George Becker, <u>The Economics of Discrimination</u> (Chicago, 1957).

    Terry Clark, <u>Community Structure: Decision-making Budget Expenditures, and Urban Renewal</u>," in Frederick Wirt, <u>Future Directions in Community Power Research</u> (University of California, Berkeley, 1971).

    Norton Long, "The Local Community as an Ecology of Games," <u>Amer. Journ. of Soc.</u>, Vol. 54 (1958) pp. 251-261.

    Wallace Smith, "Class Struggle and the Disquited City," in <u>Land Using Activities</u>, CREUE (University of California, Berkeley, 1970).

11. Robert Blauner, "Internal Colonialism and Ghetto Revolt," <u>Social Problems</u>, Vol. 16 (1969) pp. 398-408.

12. George Sternlieb, "Slum Housing: A Functional Analysis," <u>Law and Contemporary Problems</u>, Vol. 32 (Spring, 1967).

13. Wallace Smith, <u>Housing: The Social and Economic Elements</u> (Berkeley, 1970).

14. Ira Lowry, "Filtering and Housing Standards: A Conceptual Analysis," <u>Land Econ.</u>, Vol. 36 (1960) pp. 362-370.

    Arthur Sporn, "Empirical Studies in the Economics of Slum Ownership," <u>Land Econ.</u>, Vol. 36 (1960) pp. 333-340.

15. Charles Abrams, "The Uses of Land in Cities," <u>Scientific American</u>, Vol. 213 (1965) pp. 150-156.

    Charles Haar, "The Social Control of Urban Space," in Lowdon Wingo, <u>Cities and Space</u> (Baltimore, 1965).

16. Luigi Laurenti, "Theories of Race and Property Value," in <u>Property Values and Race</u> (Berkeley, 1960).

    David McEntire, "The Housing Market in Racially Mixed Areas," in <u>Residence and Race</u> (Berkeley, 1960).

David Meyer, "Interurban Differences in Black Housing Quality," Annals, Assn. of Amer. Geog., Vol. 63 (1973) pp. 347-352.

Harold Rose, "Social Processes in the City: Race and Urban Residential Choice," Resource Paper No. 6, Assn. of American Geographers (1969).

Wallace Smith, Filtering and Neighborhood Change, CREUE (University of California, Berkeley, 1964).

Robert C. Weaver, "Race, Class, and Urban Renewal," Land Econ., Vol. 36 (1960) pp. 235-251.

17. William H. Brown, Jr., "Access to Housing: The Role of the Real Estate Industry," Econ. Geog., Vol. 48 (1972) pp. 66-78.

Gilbert Osofsky, Harlem: The Making of a Ghetto (N.Y. 1963).

Allan Spear, Black Chicago: The Making of a Negro Ghetto, 1890-1920 (Chicago, 1967).

Karen Walby, "Residential Segregation and Housing Prices," Proceedings, Assn. of Amer. Geog. (1972) pp. 104-108.

For a summary see:

John Denton, ed., Race and Property (Berkeley, 1964).

18. Kenneth Clark, Dark Ghetto (N.Y., 1965).

St. Clair Drake and Horace Cayton, Black Metropolis (N.Y., 1945).

E. Franklin Frazier, The Negro Family in the U.S. (Chicago, 1939).

Elliot Leibow, Tally's Corner (Boston, 1967).

See also:

John Adams, "The Geography of Riots and Civil Disorders," Econ. Geog., Vol. 48 (1972) pp. 24-42.

19. Oscar Lewis, "The Culture of Poverty," Scientific American, Vol. 215 (1966) pp. 19-25.

20. Lester Thurow, Poverty and Discrimination (Washington, D.C., 1969).

21. Ernest Burgess, "The Growth of the City," in Park, Burgess, and McKenzie, The City (Chicago, 1925).

22. Homer Hoyt, The Structure and Growth of Residential Neighborhoods in American Cities, U.S.F.H.A. (Washington, D.C., 1939).

23. Chauncy Harris and Edward Ullman, "The Nature of Cities," Annals, Amer. Acad. of Pol. and Soc. Sci., Vol. 242 (1945) pp. 7-17.

Edward Ullman, "The Nature of Cities Reconsidered," Papers and Proc., Reg. Sci. Assn., Vol. 9 (1962) pp. 7-23.

24. Charles Colby, "Centrifugal and Centripetal Forces in Urban Geography," Annals, Assn. of Amer. Geog., Vol. 23 (1933) pp. 1-20.

Bernard Frieden, The Future of Old Neighborhoods (Cambridge, 1964).

James E. Vance, Jr. "Focus on Downtown," Community Planning Review (Summer, 1966) (Ottawa, Canada).

David Ward, op. cit. (see Note 3 above).

25. J. Tait Davis, op. cit. (see Note 2 above).

26. Lawrence Bourne, op. cit. (see Note 2 above).

Truman Hartshorn, op. cit. (see Note 2 above) likewise envisages the decline of Cedar Rapids to be a sequential process.

27. Walter Firey, Land Use in Central Boston (Cambridge, 1947).

Jane Jacobs, The Death and Life of Great American Cities (N.Y., 1963).

Suzanne Keller, The Urban Neighborhood: A Sociological Perspective (N.Y., 1968).

Edward Laumann, Prestige and Association in an Urban Community (Indianapolis, 1966).

Kevin Lynch, The Image of the City (Cambridge, 1960).

28. For zone in transition concept see:

Paul Griffing and Richard Preston, "A Restatement of the Transition Zone Concept," Annals, Assn. of Amer. Geog., Vol. 56 (1966) pp. 339-350.

Richard Preston, "The Zone in Transition: A Study of Urban Land Use Patterns," Econ. Geog., Vol. 42 (1966) pp. 236-260.

----"A Detailed Comparison of Land Use in Three Transition Zones," Annals, Assn. of Amer. Geog., Vol. 58 (1968) pp. 461-484.

29. John Dyckman, "Changing Uses of the City," Daedalus (Winter, 1961).

30. Nathan Glazer, "Introduction," Cities in Trouble (Chicago, 1970).

31. Paul Goodman and Percival Goodman, Communitas (N.Y., 1947).

Scott Greer, The Emerging City (N.Y., 1962).

Lewis Mumford, The City in History (N.Y., 1961).

32. Wilbur Thompson, "Urban Economics, in H. Wentworth Eldredge, Taming Megalopolis, Vol. 11 (Garden City, 1967).

----"Urban Economic Growth and Development in a National System of Cities," in Philip Hauser and Leo Schnore, The Study of Urbanization (N.Y., 1967).

33. James E. Vance, Jr. "Housing and the Worker: The Employment Linkage as a Force in Urban Structure," Econ. Geog., Vol. 42 (1966) pp. 294-325.

----"Housing and the Worker: Determinative and Contingent Ties in Nineteenth Century Birmingham," Econ. Geog., Vol. 43 (1967) pp. 95-127.

See also:

Frederick Boal, "Technology and Urban Form," Journ. of Geog. (April, 1968) pp. 229-236.

David Ward, "A Comparative Historical Geography of Streetcar Suburbs in Boston, Massachusetts, and Leeds, England," Annals, Assn. of Amer. Geog., Vol. 54 (1964) pp. 447-489.

34. J. D. Mooney, "Housing, Segregation, Negro Employment and Metropolitan Decentralization: An Alternative Perspective," Quart. Journ. of Econ., Vol. 83 (1969) pp. 299-311.

35. Carl Bridenbaugh, Cities in the Wilderness (N.Y., 1938).

E. Gordon Ericksen, Urban Behavior (N.Y. 1954).

Charles Glaab, The American City: A Documentary History (Homewood, Ill., 1963).

Morton White and Lucia White, The Intellectual vs. the City (N.Y., 1962).

Robert C. Wood, Suburbia: Its People and Their Politics (Boston, 1958).

36. Charles Abrams, The City is the Frontier (N.Y., 1965).

Martin Anderson, The Federal Bulldozer (Cambridge, 1964).

James Q. Wilson, Ed., Urban Renewal: The Record and the Controversy (Cambridge, 1966).

37. John Lindsay, The City (N.Y., 1969).

38. Roland Warren, The Community in America (Chicago, 1963) outlines their major concerns.

39. William Alonso, "Aspects of Regional Planning and Theory in the U.S.," Working Paper No. 87, Center for Planning and Development Research (Berkeley, 1968).

Nathan Glazer, "Slum Dwellings Do Not a Slum Make," in Cities in Trouble (Chicago, 1970).

40. Leonard Duhl, "The Human Measure: Man and Family in Megalopolis," in Lowdon Wingo, Cities and Space (Baltimore, 1963).

Herbert Gans, "Planning and City Planning - for Mental Health," in H. Wentworth Eldridge, Taming Megalopolis, Vol. 11 (Garden City, 1967).

Daniel Wilner and Rosabell Walkley, "Effects of Housing on Health and Performance," in Leonard Duhl, The Urban Condition (N.Y., 1963).

41. Nathan Glazer, "Housing Problems and Housing Policies," The Public Interest, (Spring, 1967).

Nathan Hare, "Black Ecology," The Black Scholar (April, 1970).

Melvin Webber and Carolyn Webber, "Culture, Territoriality, and the Elastic Mile," Papers, Reg. Sci. Assn., Vol. 13 (1964) pp. 59-70.

42. George Carey, Lenore Macomber, and Michael Greenberg, "Educational and Demographic Factors in the Urban Geography of Washington, D.C.," Geog. Rev., Vol. 58 (1968) pp. 515-537, is a recent exception.

Shane Davies and David Huff, "Impact of Ghettoization on Black Employment," Econ. Geog., Vol. 48 (1972) pp. 421-427, illustrates the role of community informational services in job placement.

43. Frank Horton and David Reynolds, "Effects of Urban Spatial Structure on Individual Behavior," Econ. Geog., Vol. 47 (1971) pp. 36-48.

R. J. Johnston, "Activity Spaces and Residential Preferences," Econ. Geog., Vol. 48 (1972) pp. 199-211.

R. E. Pahl, "Sociological Models in Geography," in Chorley and Haggett, Models in Geography (London, 1967).

James W. Simmons, "Changing Residence in the City: A Review of Intraurban Mobility," Geog. Rev., Vol. 58 (1969) pp. 622-651.

James Wheeler and Frederick Stutz, "Spatial Dimensions of Urban Social Behavior," Annals, Assn. of Amer. Geog., Vol. 61 (1971) pp. 371-386.

44. Anthony Downs, "Alternative Futures for the American Ghetto," Daedalus (Fall, 1968) pp. 1331-1378.

John Kain and Joseph Persky, "Alternatives to the Guilded Ghetto," The Public Interest (Winter, 1969).

45. Jane Jacobs, op. cit. (see Note 27 above).

46. Herbert Gans, The Urban Villagers (N.Y., 1962).

Lewis Mumford, The Urban Prospect (N.Y., 1956).

47. Michael Aiken and Robert Alfred, "Community Structure and Innovation: The Case of Public Housing," Amer. Pol. Sci. Rev., Vol. 64 (1970) pp. 843-864.

----"Community Structure and Innovation: The Case of Urban Renewal," Amer. Soc. Rev., Vol. 35 (1970) pp. 650-655.

Charles Stokes, "A Theory of Slums," Land Econ., Vol. 38 (1962) pp. 187-197.

48. Rose Hum Lee, "The Decline of Chinatowns in the U.S.," Amer. Journ. of Soc., Vol. 54 (1948-49) pp. 422-432, is one of the first studies on the subject to be published.

49. P. H. Chombart de Lauwe, Paris et l'Agglomeration Parisienne, Vol. I (Paris, 1952).

R. P. Dore, City Life in Japan: A Study of a Tokyo Ward (Berkeley, 1958).

Walter Firey, op. cit. (see Note 27 above).

Gilbert Osofsky, op. cit. (see Note 17 above).

Allan Spear, op. cit. (see Note 17 above).

50. James E. Vance, Jr. "Land Assignment in the Precapitalist, Capitalist, and Post-capitalist City," Econ. Geog., Vol. 47 (1971) pp. 101-120.

CHAPTER TWO

THE LEGACY OF CHINESE EMIGRATION

Poems from Angel Island
(date unknown)

A sudden scene in mid-autumn
The moon outside the window illuminates with penetrating force.
I stand in front of the cold window and bored.
Sadly I realize it's already mid-autumn.
We should celebrate the Autumn moon festival.
But how shameful, we don't have anything for celebration.

Chinese in America come because they are poor.
Selling their fields and lands
Sighing, they come to America
Families at home. . . .
Who knows it is difficult here beyond belief.

Three wooden cells in this island,
    barely covering our bodies.
My misery is piled as high as the K'un Lun mountains.
So full I can't express.
Waiting for the opportune day.
I'll wipe out the Immigration customs
    without mercy.

Asian Horizon, Vol. 1, No. 2 (Nov./Dec. 1973), a journal published by the Asian Student Union, the Philippino Youth Development Council, and the Chinese Student Association of Laney College, Oakland, California.

Introduction

The experience of ethnic groups in American cities has varied widely, depending upon how rapidly they have been acculturated, assimilated, or adapted to the mainstream of American life. Immigrants arrive with their own blend of values, customs, expectations, and institutions. They also bring anxieties, handicaps, limitations, and myths. The interaction between immigrants and local residents is constrained by linguistic, educational, and occupational differences as well as by restrictive laws and practices.

The social geography of the central city is an outgrowth of inherent differences and imposed restrictions on social interaction. This chapter will show how such differences developed to shape the fate of Chinese immigrants in the United States. Chapter 3 will focus upon the growth and impact of restrictions on Chinese immigration. The experience of the Chinese in California, and more specifically in Alameda and Contra Costa counties, cannot be understood without some inquiry into the origins of their plight.

Most studies on the Chinese in the U.S. have emphasized the uniqueness of their problems and achievements. Few have suggested that the myriad of obstacles which the Chinese have encountered have also been faced to varying degrees by other ethnic minorities. Although the saga of the Chinese immigrant emanates from the colorful history of his struggle, the causes of his predicament are rooted in the same kind of community problems which continue to plague other newcomers in the American city.

China in Transition

Chinese emigration was a desperate response to an untenable situation. The stability of Kwangtung Province in Southern China had been undermined by war, famine, and foreign intrusions. The Chinese peasant perceived the prospect of employment overseas as a means of perpetuating traditional values and institutions in an increasingly chaotic world. The problems of the "Middle Kingdom" were transplanted overseas, where adherence to obsolete values and institutions impeded the process of Chinese acculturation in the inner city for almost a century.

In rural China, only devotion to family was even stronger than ties to the land and the village. Overseas emigration was neither a quest for easy riches nor a search for new adventures. It was one of few remaining options open to those whose unyielding obligation to family made no task too burdensome, even if it meant many years away from friends, relatives, and ancestral grave.[1] Remittances insured that the clan would survive and perhaps even prosper in the face of domestic upheaval.

Although civil strife usually accompanied the transition from one dynasty to the next, it was not until the 19th century that Chinese peasants as well as political refugees and merchants really began to emigrate.[2] The first 150 years of Manchu rule (1644-1911) were characterized by peace and prosperity. However, by 1800, population pressure and internal conflict were becoming so severe that tens of thousands emigrated from Kwangtung and Fukien provinces to Formosa, Southeast Asia, and Latin America.[3]

Population pressures were especially acute in the Pearl River Delta, which had one of the highest rates of land tenancy in China.[4] The introduction of the Irish potato to Southern China during the 18th century paved the way for deforestation, the cultivation of hillsides, soil erosion, and severe flooding. The population of China rose from less than 150 million to 430 million between 1700 and 1850.[5] The movement of Chinese peasants toward the tropics in search of economic opportunities intensified the conflict between local peasants and "alien" peoples from the north.

Incompetance and abuse by the Ch'ing (Manchu) Government provoked over a decade of civil war. The Taiping Rebellion (1851-1864), which almost toppled the dynasty, resulted in more than 20 million deaths and left more than 600 cities and towns in ruin.[6] Century-old animosities erupted between the native, or Punti, people of the Pearl River Delta and the Hakka, or guest people, from the northeast. While the Hakkas allied themselves with the Ch'ing regime, many of the oppressed Puntis joined the revolt. Retribution against the Hakka minority by the defeated Punti rebels drove thousands of embittered Hakkas into the rugged hills of Kwangtung Province during the 1850's.[7] Other Hakkas sought refuge in Southeast Asia.

Divided by civil war, feuding clans, and district rivalries, the peasants of the Pearl River Delta were also victimized by pirates and bandits. The Tanka (Tan-chia) or boat people of the delta, treated as outcasts for centuries, seized opportunities to profit from the increasing turbulence. Occupied as ferrymen and smugglers, they prospered from the growth of "coolie" traffic along the coast. Kidnapping became a lucrative enterprise with the emergence of an overseas market for Chinese "slave labor."

One of 98 districts in Kwangtung Province, Toishan provided about 60 percent of the Chinese immigrants to the U.S.[8] Toi, which means plateau or elevated place, and shan, which means mountain, suggest that Chinese emigrants were "pushed" overseas. Unlike the rich lowland regions of the province, the Toishan district did not practice paddy cultivation. Many Toishanese turned to trade, dealing with large cities like Hong Kong, Canton, and Macao, which handled most of China's foreign trade during the 19th century (see Map 1). "There was nothing to do in the village, nothing but farm. Plant yams, plant taro, gather wood--work all day in the sun just to get two meals from somebody else."[9]

Opportunities Abroad

Chinese contact with the West and with Southeast Asia dates back at least 2000 years. Chinese expansion during the T'ang Dynasty (618-906) had attracted mercantile entrepreneurs into Indochina long before European colonial penetration into that area.[10] Macao had become a Portuguese trading post by 1557. Chinese trade with the Philippines

District Grouping	1855		1866		1868		1875	
	No.	%	No.	%	No.	%	No.	%
1 Sze Yup & assoc. dist.	16,107	41.6	32,500	55.8	35,900	58.8	124,000	82.0
2 Heungshan (Chungshan) & Assoc. dist.	14,000	36.2	11,500	19.7	11,800	19.4	12,000	7.9
3 Sam Yup	6,800	17.6	10,500	18.0	10,000	16.4	11,000	7.3
4 Hakkas	1,780	4.6	3,800	6.5	3,300	5.4	4,300	2.8
	38,687	100.0	58,300	100.0	61,000	100.0	151,300	100.0

District Grouping	Ca. 1926-28		1950		1960
	No.	%	No.	%	%
1 Sze Yup & assoc. dist.	23,000	82.5	37,000	74.0	57.0
2 Heungshan (Chungshan) & Assoc. dist.	2,500	9.5	7,000	14.0	30.0
3 Sam Yup	1,500	6.0	5,000	10.0	8.0
4 Hakkas	500	2.0	1,000	2.0	5.0
	27,500	100.0	50,000	100.0	100.0

Sze Yup = People belonging to the Ning Yeun, Hop Wo, Kong Chow and Shiu Hing Association.
Heungshan (Chungshan) = People belonging to the Young Wo Association.
Sam Yup = People belonging to the Sam Yup Association.
Hakkas = People belonging to the Yan Wo Association.

Source: Thomas Chinn, A History of the Chinese in California, Chinese Historical Society of America (San Francisco, 1969) p. 20.

TABLE 1

TOTAL CHINESE IN CALIFORNIA BY DISTRICT OF ORIGIN
IN DIFFERENT CENSUS YEARS

heightened by the end of the 16th century with the establishment of Spanish trade routes between Acapulco, Cebu, and Manila. Chinese settlers had arrived in Mexico City by 1635.[11] European entrepreneurs, having expanded into Southeast Asia during the 17th and 18th centuries, provided increasing opportunities for immigration by Chinese laborers as well as merchants.

Foreign trade in China was restricted by imperial decrees, strengthened to stem the flow of rowdy foreigners and British opium into China from India which had escalated during the 18th and 19th centuries. Commercial contacts with foreign "barbarians" were finally confined to Canton in 1757. China's humiliating defeat in the Opium War (1839-1842) made Hong Kong a British port and opened the ports of Canton, Shanghai, Amoy, Foochow, and Ningpo to English and then to all Western traders. It was thus not until the 1840's that Western contact with China had finally expanded enough to provide a systematic means of social mobility.[12]

Thousands of Chinese laborers headed for plantations in Cuba and Peru and for gold fields in California and Australia during the 1840's. News of employment opportunities overseas diffused through the Pearl River Delta, the Han Valley, and the hinterland of Amoy. Hong Kong, declared a free port in 1841 with no duties or bills of health required, became the major embarcation point for Chinese emigrants. The Cantonese, having

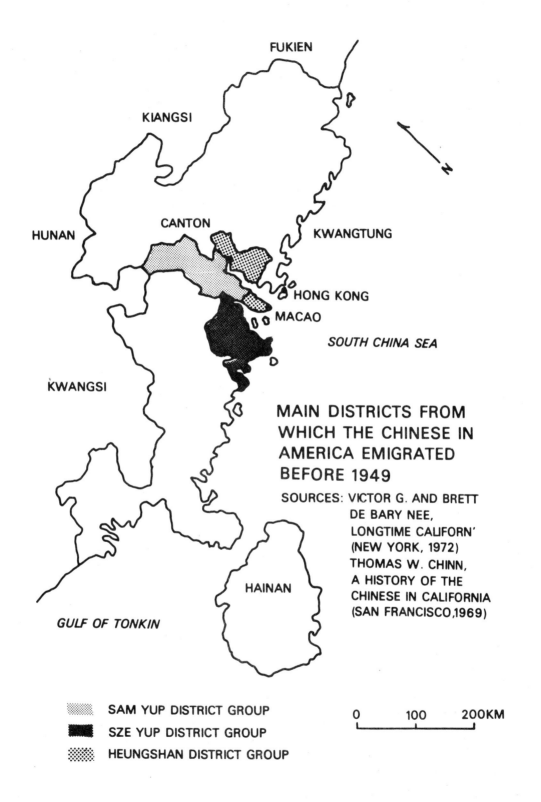

FUKIEN

KIANGSI

CANTON

HUNAN   KWANGTUNG

                         HONG KONG

                         MACAO

                    SOUTH CHINA SEA

KWANGSI

**MAIN DISTRICTS FROM
WHICH THE CHINESE IN
AMERICA EMIGRATED
BEFORE 1949**

SOURCES: VICTOR G. AND BRETT
         DE BARY NEE,
         LONGTIME CALIFORN'
         (NEW YORK, 1972)
         THOMAS W. CHINN,
         A HISTORY OF THE
         CHINESE IN CALIFORNIA
         (SAN FRANCISCO,1969)

HAINAN

GULF OF TONKIN

SAM YUP DISTRICT GROUP

SZE YUP DISTRICT GROUP

HEUNGSHAN DISTRICT GROUP

0   100   200KM

been exposed for over a century to Western customs and products, were less reluctant to emigrate than the Chinese in other regions of Kwangtung Province.

The demand for cheap labor rose after the abolition of slavery by the British in 1834, which paved the way for similar acts by other governments. Chinese laborers were brought to Cuba by 1845, to Peru by 1849, to Hawaii and Panama by 1850, to New South Wales by 1851, to British Guiana and Trinidad by 1853, to Jamaica by 1854, and to India and Tahiti by 1865.[13] Gold discoveries drew thousands of Chinese into Australia, California, and British Columbia. The Chinese now comprise the largest minority in all of Southeast Asia, except in Burma, where Indians are the largest minority group.[14]

TABLE 2

Chinese Emigrants Resident Abroad in 1922 (Source: Ta Chen, Chinese Migrations, With Special Reference to Labor Conditions, U.S. Department of Labor, Bureau of Labor Statistics, Bulletin No. 340, Washington, D.C., 1923, p. 15.

Anam	197,300	Java	1,825,700
Australia	35,000	Korea	11,300
Brazil	20,000	Macao	74,560
Burma	134,600	Mexico	3,000
Canada	12,000	Peru	45,000
Cuba	90,000	Philippines	55,212
East Indies	1,023,500	Siam	1,500,000
Europe	1,760	Siberia	37,000
Formosa	2,258,650	Straits Setlmts.	432,764
Hawaii	23,507	South Africa	5,000
Hong Kong	314,390	Continental U.S.	61,639
Japan	17,700	TOTAL	8,179,582

From Defiance to Dependence

Resistance to the indifference and oppression of the Ch'ing government had surfaced long before the outbreak of the Taiping Rebellion. Political brotherhoods, or secret societies, traced their origins back to 1674 with the founding of the Triad Society. Chinese secret societies thrived as people's faith in the efficacy of the traditional clan obligations and class distinctions was shaken. Brotherhoods spread into Southeast Asia and then into California in search of political refuge. They offered an alternative to further submission at the hands of those in power. The Taiping Rebellion was an expression of their desperation.

In California secret societies or tongs also provided an alternative for oppressed Chinese laborers, whose fate was sealed in racism and exploitation. The tongs turned to illegal business activities and secret compacts in order to expand their influence in already divided Chinese communities that stood surrounded by a hostile world. Despite the legitimacy of their ends, societies often resorted to high-handed means of coercion and "tax" collection in order to support themselves. They linked together revolutionary groups, fraternities bent on righting alleged or real injustices, and gangs of criminals which controlled gambling, prostitution, and opium smuggling.[15] Their role as a benevolent association was nevertheless formidable in the bachelor society of pre-World War II Chinatown.[16] The tongs took care of those whose needs were not being met by authoritarian district and clan organizations.

The Manchu regime, steeped in its own self-righteousness, was not favorably disposed to supporting emigration. Overseas Chinese communities were regarded as a source of both political unrest, as evidenced by tong ambitions, and embarrassment to the world's most "civilized" country. The government looked upon those going abroad as stupid,

unpatriotic, unworthy of protection, and guilty of treason.[17]   Section 225 of the Fundamental Laws of the Ch'ing Dynasty outlawed emigration until 1860.

Although difficult to enforce, the ban gave local officials an instrument of
moral and legal leverage. It permitted them to exact payments from the overseas emigrant
and his family in China.[18]   In addition, it left the emigrant without the help of his
country in a turbulent overseas environment. It was not until 1869, with the signing of
the Burlingame Treaty, that the Ch'ing Dynasty finally began to demonstrate some concern
for the welfare of Chinese citizens abroad. Consulates were not established in America
until 1878, after the destiny of the newcomers had already been sown.

The problems of the Chinese countryside were simply carried overseas, where emigrants encountered even more severe obstacles. Handicapped by linguistic limitations, burdened by debts, unaccustomed to the ways of the West, harrassed by anti-emigration laws,
and obligated to support his family at home, the Chinese laborer was in many ways doomed
before he departed. The foundations of self-reliance were undermined from the outset. The
antagonism with which these men were greeted in effect made the sojourners even more dependent upon help from merchants in the Chinese community, whose power was derived from their
early opportunism and special status as merchants in a country eager to expand its Far East
trade. Unencumbered by linguistic, financial, cultural, or political constraints, merchants continue to dominate overseas Chinese communities, even today.

Immigration into the United States

Chinese immigration into the United States was fraught with the same anxieties
and handicaps which beset their countrymen in other lands. Their experience in the
American West, however, was exceptionally traumatic. Assimilation into the "melting pot"
proved to be more of a myth than a reality for non-white ethnic groups. Institutionalized
racism compounded their plight and distorted their adaptation to American society. For a
considerable time, the Chinese remained the only people to be barred from further immigration to the New World.[19]

It is unclear when the first Chinese settled in the United States, though
Chinese sailors probably visited colonial ports during the 18th century. It is known,
however, that Chinese servants were living in Philadelphia by 1796 and in San Francisco by
1848.[20]   Immigration records claim that only 43 Chinese entered the United States before
1849, but this figure does not include those on the Pacific Coast, which was under Spanish
and then Mexican rule until 1846. The earliest Chinese were employed almost invariably as
servants, seamen, or merchants. Of the 300 Chinese in San Francisco in 1849, most were
engaged in commerce, having paid their own way to California from the Sam Yup districts
surrounding Canton.[21]   The influx of large groups of Chinese laborers into the United
States did not commence until 1852, on the heels of the Gold Rush in California.

American contacts with Chinese began in 1784 with the arrival of the Empress of
China at Canton. The forced termination of American trade with the British West Indies in
1773 turned the newly independent nation's attention to China as a new market. The British
East India Company's monopoly on trade with China, which had been an obstacle to American
mercantile ambitions, was no longer applicable after 1776. Yankee ships, owned and financed by venturesome merchant families from New England and the Atlantic seaboard, exchanged
their cargo of "trade goods" for seal and sea otter furs with the Indians of Vancouver
Island and the coast of the Oregon Country, for sandalwood in Hawaii, and for sea cucumber
in the East Indies--all of which were in tremendous demand in Canton. After more than a
year at sea, American sailing ships returned across the Atlantic with a fortune in tea,
silk, porcelain tableware ("chinaware"), and furniture.[22]   American dependence on the
Chinese market established a basis for long-term contact between Chinese and American merchants. Increasing reliance by Chinese peasants on the expanding market for cheap labor
in the United States during the 1850's provided merchants in Hong Kong an opportunity to
capitalize on these long-term contacts.

According to Shirley Sun, there were three ways to finance the sojourn abroad.[23]

The first was the coolie system, widely used in Latin America after the British abolished slave trade in 1834. The victims of civil war, clan battles, piracy, and gambling debts were often kidnapped or tricked into signing contracts indenturing them to work overseas. Smuggled abroad on foreign ships, they were often sold to the highest bidder upon disembarcation. Crimps recruited coolies and delivered them to barracoons or depots, where recruiters received $7 to $10 per head. The word ku-li, which means "bearer of burden" in the Tamil or Bengali language, means "bitter strength" in Cantonese. The coolie system flourished in Peru and Cuba until 1874, when the Chinese government finally became alarmed over their treatment.

The contract labor system involved voluntary agreements but still obligated the laborer to a specific period of service for a given wage under non-negotiable working conditions. Fares were automatically deducted from wages by agents of the creditor. American employers would arrange to hire laborers through a foreign or Chinese contractor, who recruited emigrants in the Pearl River Delta. The Central Pacific Railroad, for example, obtained thousands of Chinese laborers through Sisson and Wallace of San Francisco, a company owned by one of the Crocker brothers. Sisson and Wallace in turn arranged with a Dutch mercantile firm, Koopmanschap & Company, to bring over 30,000 Chinese beginning in 1865.[24] Chinese firms in Honolulu engaged in the acquisition and transport of laborers from both China and the United States mainland to work on Hawaiian sugar plantations.[25] Enforcing these contracts required an elaborate system of control, which often proved ineffective in California.

The credit-ticket system was by far the most flexible arrangement. The cost of passage and expenses were paid back out of the laborer's earnings, but he was not bound to serve a definite period, at a specific wage, under particular conditions. Merchant-contractors in Hong Kong advanced laborers passage money and arranged for transport. Agents in Sacramento, Marysville and Stockton were responsible for finding the newcomers jobs and for collecting debts.

In order to purchase passage back to China, the laborer had to clear all debts through his district association or company. British and American ships cooperated in order to win the favor of district companies, on whose business they thrived. The power of the merchant-creditors who dominated their district associations, was further enhanced by the advent of more reliable and less expensive steamship service on the Pacific in 1866, first by the Pacific Mail Steamship Company and then by the Occidental and Oriental Steamship Company. Reduced competition among shipping companies was accompanied by more assurance that compliance would be complete and that merchant investments would be less risky.

The credit-ticket system evolved to meet the needs of employers, financiers, and carriers of immigrant Chinese labor. Overseas emigration was a boon to the impoverished villages of the Pearl River Delta, to opportunistic California investors in search of cheap labor, and to the Chinese and American middlemen who made it all feasible. Whether or not the system benefited the sojourner, himself, is a separate issue.

Immigrant Aspirations

The Chinese called America gum shan or mountain of gold and considered themselves to be gum shan hok or guests of the golden mountains.[26] They arrived as young men who had come to work, if necessary until the age of 50 or 60, and to save money. The sojourners hoped to return to their villages, admired and venerated by relatives, who depended upon remitted earnings for their survival.

> Sometimes, if too many children had been born, the parents would have to sell the youngest one to keep the family going. Usually, it was a girl child, sold as a servant to a wealthier family or into prostitution. For many peasants, sending a boy to Hong Kong or abroad, wherever there was a labor market and money to be earned, was the only way to survive.[27]

Duty to family gave meaning to their toil and eased their suffering. Longing for treasures and a happy family, they left their rural villages for the "golden hills," where they expected to be treated as "guests."

The prospect of returning to their villages with two or three hundred dollars was inducement enough for men whose total annual income at home amounted to one-tenth that sum; no venture was deemed too arduous.[28] Working for someone else had long become a way of life in Kwangtung Province. Dreams of returning with enough money to retire as a landlord kindled their imaginations. In some villages, as many as 80 percent of the men were at least periodically resident overseas.[29]

Few laborers managed to realize their ambitions. In an increasingly competitive labor market, most were able to save just enough for a short trip back to China about once every five or ten years. The rumor of easy riches in California had inflated their expectations. Peasants were encouraged to migrate by those who had prospered. Those who failed never returned to document their frustrations. Sons followed fathers and nephews followed uncles in hopes of success through hard work and filial piety. Merchant-creditors in Hong Kong provided them with the opportunity of a lifetime.

The Chinese laborer's first introduction to gum shan was Angel Island:

Angel Island, now a 720-acre State Park in San Francisco Bay, is far from indicative of the island's recent history. It was once used as a prison for rebellious American Indians; during World War II the island was a prisoner-of-war camp and from 1909-1949, the island was an immigration detention center. In 1920 alone, the immigration authorities processed over 20,000 travelers. Nominally a "quarantine station" to clear all immigrants from the Pacific, the island, in fact, served to detain Chinese travelers for indefinite periods behind bars.[30]

Wall inscriptions from Angel Island (from the 1910's and 1920's) help to reveal the laborer's suffering:

(1) I have admired America as a place of
    opportunity and happiness.
  Right away, I got some money and started
    my journey.
  After months of traveling in wind and waves,
    I ended up in this prison suffering.
  Oh, to return to my motherland and be a
    farmer again!
  My breast is filled with grievance that I can't
    sleep.
  Therefore, I write a few lines to express
    my mind.

(2) Staying on this Island, my sorrow increases
    with the days.
  My face is growing sallow and my body is
    getting thin.
  Cooped up here, my difficulties are unending.
  Now, I dare to give up all, and go back.

(3)   I left my village behind me and now I miss
           the bridge and flowers of my hometown.
       I stare at the faraway clouds and mountains,
           with eyes full of tears.
       A wanderer longing for treasures and a
           happy family.
       Who can know that I was imprisoned on this
           Island?
       Thinking of China reminds me of the story of
           Juan-Chi.
       China is shamed by giving away her rights
           to foreign powers.
       My fellow countrymen should realize this crisis
           and strive together.
       I vow to take over America to right
           earlier wrongs.

Source: Shirley Sun, Three Generations of Chinese-East and West (Oakland, 1973), pp. 27-29.

Merchant's World

The immigration of Chinese laborers into California was motivated more by the lingering possibility than by the rising probability of success. The prospect of long-term employment, even at less than competitive wage levels, diminished with each decade of Chinese immigration. Domestic conditions nevertheless provided continued impetus for migration until outlawed in 1882. The influx of Chinese labor lined the pockets of their creditors. Merchants whose retail businesses and employment agencies depended on the newcomer market were among those who stood to benefit from increased immigration. Chinese merchant-creditors quickly assumed control of both the clan and district organizations as they began to prosper.

The newcomers regarded their merchant leaders as a source of strength and support. This faith in the viability of clan and district obligations and loyalties continues until the present time as an outgrowth of Chinese ideals and values. Mutual patronage and assistance among clansmen and members of the same district was supposed to benefit the whole group. Prosperity would be shared and needs would be met. Rooted in the stability and intimacy of Chinese village life, traditional institutions were transplanted to overseas Chinese communities. In the face of growing hostility, periodic unemployment, and widespread uncertainty about their future in the United States, the sojourners had little choice but to resort to mutual assistance for security.

Merchant-contractors located in San Francisco established working agreements with recruiting agents in Hong Kong, who arranged for the financing, lodging, and shipment of prospective overseas laborers. Local merchants based in Sacramento, Stockton, Marysville, and other towns kept track of the newcomers, collected debts, and provided goods and services for their use. These merchants, representing the district from which the laborers originated, found their comrades employment and shelter, supplied them with Chinese food, clothing, herb medicines, and an assortment of services from barbers to prostitutes. They served an essential function, providing necessities and opportunities which could not be supplied in the "normal" marketplace of anti-Chinese California.

From the time of their arrival on the docks of San Francisco to the purchase of return passage, the newcomers remained under the wing of their clan and district associations or companies. Retail merchants in San Francisco, representing their respective clans or districts, greeted the sojourners, furnished them with temporary housing above their stores, assisted them with their mail, banking, travel, medical, language, employment, and even burial needs. In turn, the merchants earned prestige as elders of the clan or district and profited from loyal patronage. Clan and district ties established the foundations

22

of commercial and social interdependence in Chinese California. Competition among Chinese merchants in San Francisco and among smaller merchants in other towns reflected clan and district rivalries.

The merchant's ability to communicate in both English and in the dialect of his district gave him an advantage as a middleman, especially as a wholesaler-importer or as a labor contractor. Previous contact with American and English merchants in Hong Kong or Canton, and with San Francisco residents in the late 1840's and early 1850's, enabled the merchants to learn the English language and Western customs much more readily than was possible for the rural laborers who arrived later. The newcomers relied upon the merchants in their clan, or from their district, as spokesmen as well as backers in time of need. The more threatening and violent conditions in California became, the more the newcomers turned to their merchants for help. The Cantonese word for Caucasions--bok gai, or foreign devils--was a crystallization of their experience at home and overseas.

Immigrant Values and Institutions

Raised in a society based on the maintenance of family solidarity, the Chinese abroad found themselves without the security of family relations. As strangers in an unfriendly world, they needed to establish new grounds for mutual assistance and collective responsibility. Clan associations evolved as an extension of the Confucian extended family system. Common surnames symbolized common ancestral origins, no matter how indirect or superficial. The clan system was adapted to meet the peculiar situation of overseas Chinese communities, where newcomers had few direct relatives. Respect for elders, both living and deceased, shaped the manner in which the immigrants tried to broaden their risks in an increasingly hazardous milieu.

Clan organizations provided newcomers with protection, arbitration, employment references, a meeting place, and burial arrangements. Excluded from schools, hospitals, the courts, better occupations, insurance, and public services in general, the Chinese had little choice but to depend upon clansmen for support.[31] The shortage of Chinese women in California remained striking until after World War II. Clan lodging and meeting quarters functioned as centers of social interaction in a predominantly male society as well as a place for members in time of need. Disputes between clan members could easily be settled by elders, whose power to ostracize the party at fault was sufficient to insure widespread compliance. To be banned from the hospitality, security, and support of one's clan association was comparable to social exile in which the lone man found himself bereft and destitute.

Clan loyalties also prevailed over economic activities. The practice of hiring and patronizing clan members provided the vehicle by which certain clans began to dominate at the expense of other clans. Prosperity for one member meant more jobs for other members and a wider economic base from which to finance clan programs and investments. Immigrants often preferred to work where their clansmen had already become established. The Fongs of Sacramento, the Yees of Pittsburgh, the Moys of Chicago, the Lees of Washington, D.C., the Ah-Tyes of Stockton, the Ginns and Halls of Santa Barbara, and the Ongs of Phoenix grew in number as clansmen began to dominate in each respective city. Clan elders were accorded responsibility for the honor, harmony, and well-being of the clan. Due to their status and influence in the immigrant community, the merchants usually reigned as elders. The absence of nobels and the scarcity of scholars, who would have prevailed under the Confucian class system, legitimized their "grass roots" position in overseas Chinese clan associations.

District organizations were established as early as 1852, when the influx of large numbers of Chinese laborers began. Clan associations emerged at about the same time.[32] More powerful than the clans, district companies developed to promote district interests in certain industries or sectors of economic activity. Clans, on the other hand, were organized to enhance the welfare of individuals. Clan elders represented clan interests in district enterprises, further solidifying the role of the merchants in the community. Like the clans, which often settled disputes among clan members, the district organizations provided an effective means of expanding the economic base of group interests, as perceived by district elders.

District loyalties stemmed from regional rivalries in the Pearl River Delta. Centuries of antagonism among the more "refined" Sam Yup speaking city residents of the Canton area, the more "aggressive" Sze Yup speaking mountain folk to the west, the Heungshan speaking "country peasants" to the south, and the alienated Hakka speaking "guest" people of the region were carried overseas. Historic differences in language dialects and in life styles were institutionalized into district company rivalries. Newcomers naturally preferred to work for and patronize those with whom they felt most comfortable and to whom they could turn in times of need. The practice of selective patronage and discriminatory hiring allowed a district organization to prosper at the expense of others.

District associations supported social programs, such as the first Chinese language schools and temples. For the most part, however, they functioned as guilds, concerned with the economic security of district occupations. Profits, as in the case of clan income, were supposed to be invested to expand economic and social opportunities for all district members. In San Francisco Sze Yup firms controlled most of the laundries, small retail shops, and restaurants. Sam Yup members dominated the tailoring, repair, mending, and butcher businesses. Heungshan people monopolized fish retailing, ladies garment manufacturing, and Peninsula horticulture.[33]

District companies, dominated by business interests, maintained working agreements with large American labor contractors. The Pacific Chinese Employment Company (King and Merritt, proprietors), for example, claimed to have special arrangements with principal Chinese companies in their advertisements. They asserted until 1877 that they were better prepared to send out laborers of all kinds at shorter notice than any competitor on the Pacific Coast.[34] The role of merchant-contractors in district companies nevertheless remains elusive. One argument is that they exploited newcomers under the guise of mutual aid. Another is that outside oppression by Californians forced them to resort to questionable means of finding jobs for increasingly desperate laborers.

By the 1860's violent confrontation among district companies had subsided into a policy of cooperation, at least in areas of common interest. Formation of the Chinese Consolidated Benevolent Association, known as the Chinese Six Companies, reflected the pressing need for settling community disputes in an increasingly disorderly world.[35] Still governed by a "power elite" of merchant-businessmen, the Six Companies continue to adhere to ideals and values which may no longer be appropriate.[36] Continued dependence by newcomers on the merchants' world of Chinatown can no longer be justified on the basis of outside oppression.

Alternative Institutions

In San Francisco the formation of the Chinese Consolidated Benevolent Association in 1854 solidified the community from the outset. At first composed of four and then five district associations, the "Five Companies" settled inter-district disputes, coordinated resistance to the anti-Chinese movement, spoke for the Manchu government, and provided for the welfare of the Chinese community as a whole. The Association made special hospital, educational, ceremonial, legal, burial, and police services available to Chinese newcomers excluded by local, public and private agencies. Governed until the turn of the century by scholars from China hired by each district company, the Chinese Consolidated Benevolent Association was regarded as the legitimate representative of the Chinese in the city. In the 1860's, the Hop Wo Association broke away from the Sze Yup Association and joined with the Yee clan to form a sixth company. Ensuing factionalism resulted in further schisms in the 1890's. The Six Companies are now composed of seven district associations.

Conflict among the tongs, or secret societies, over jurisdiction of illicit activity first erupted during the 1850's. Despite concerted efforts by the Six Companies to curtail their influence, the tongs had managed to infiltrate and seize control of several district companies at the height of their power during the 1880's.[37]   Based upon profits from the opium, gambling, prostitution, and protection rackets, the tongs challenged the authority and undermined the effectiveness of the district associations. Tong struggles continued to disturb the security and tarnish the image of the community until 1931, when the last "tong war" was fought.[38]   Accounts of their exploits have been well-publicized.[39]

Yet "tong," which means association or fraternal lodge, refers to other groups besides the infamous secret societies whose "hatchetmen" and "highbinders" operated so notoriously in San Francisco. The tongs furnished newcomers with an alternative to the three-tiered clan-district-benevolent association system of community organization which had become so firmly implanted in San Francisco. Immigrants alienated by their clan or district needed some place to turn. Having no surname or linguistic restrictions, the tongs became a popular recourse. Tong lodges or fraternal halls were established in many Chinatown communities. The tongs provided their members with the kind of social security and group leverage that had made the clans so appealing and the district companies so powerful. In the case of the tong, however, members shared common fears and interests, not a common faith in traditional values. Following the "tong wars," most fraternities changed their names to avoid guilt by association. The On Leong Tong, for example, which once dealt in slave girls, is now called the On Leong Merchants.[40]   The Chee Kung Ton has become the Chinese Freemasons.[41]   Disagreements among tongs have been settled by arbitration through the "Peace Society" established by the Six Companies in 1931. The tongs now exert little influence in community decision-making.

Although firmly entrenched in San Francisco, the Six Companies were not able to dominate the smaller Chinese communities. Each Chinatown in the United States developed its own benevolent association which evolved in response to its own needs.[42]   Independent communities composed of relatively small Chinese populations encountered less factionalism. Immigrants in these cities claimed fewer clan or district origins. The Chinese in Honolulu, for example, were mainly from the Heungshan district. In contrast to San Francisco Chinatown, which was inundated during the tumultuous decade of the 1870's, many of the smaller Chinatown communities were beset by dwindling numbers. Opportunities for employment and social mobility were wider in smaller Chinatown communities, at least for those willing to brave the onslaught of racial violence.

Widening Geographic Alternatives

Smaller centers provided the newcomers with an alternative to the regimentation and confined quarters of San Francisco Chinatown. Although also under the leadership of merchants, the smaller Chinatown communities were threatened more by external than internal exploitation. They furnished newcomers with less security but more opportunity. Those who recognized that they had a future in America tried to save enough to establish families in these communities.

The founding of the Native Sons of the Golden State in San Francisco in 1895 signalled the dawn of a new period of Chinese settlement in the United States. Organized by native-born Chinese-Americans who rejected the policies and the authority of district association leaders, it was dedicated to defending and securing the civil rights of Chinese-American citizens. Unlike the other institutions embraced by overseas communities, the organization pressed for assimilation and political activism. In 1915, the Native Sons of the Golden State expanded into a national organization, headquartered in San Francisco, and changed its name to the Chinese American Citizens Alliance. Chapters were established in Chicago, Detroit, Pittsburgh, Boston, Houston, San Antonio, Albuquerque, Los Angeles, Fresno, San Diego, Salinas, Portland, and Oakland. Its daily newspaper, The Chinese Times, was founded in 1921 and enjoys the largest circulation of all Chinese language newspapers in the country. Profits support the organization's extensive legislative lobbying, civic actions, educational, and political programs.[44]   The C.A.C.A.'s Republican orientation stems from its membership, which is comprised mainly of businessmen and professionals.

Once a forceful organization, the alliance has weakened as Chinese-Americans have acquired more of their rights. Discontinuation in 1947 of the group's death benefit fund, a form of life insurance granted when the discriminatory practices of insurance companies excluded most Chinese from coverage, undermined its viability. The formation of the Chinese-American Democratic Club in San Francisco in 1954 further eroded its strength, especially among the younger generation who never experienced the racism of the pre-World War II era.

In contrast to the clan-district-benevolent association institutions, which were geared to serve the temporary needs of the sojourning "guests" and their creditors, the Chinese American Citizens Alliance recognized that the future of the Chinese in the United States could only be secured through legislative reform. Clan and district rivalries, tong battles, and other internal community conflicts were recognized as futile under the prospect of continued discrimination. Neither clan nor district nor tong loyalties would suffice for Chinese without civil rights. American-born Chinese, having more at stake, pressed for assimilation. Many were children of successful merchants who had pioneered in the smaller Chinese communities.[45] Unlike most of the Chinatown merchants of San Francisco, merchant families in smaller towns relied more on the patronage of city residents in general. They did not depend so heavily on the labor and purchases of Chinese laborers. Many Chinese families intent on settling permanently in America tended to disperse away from Chinatown by the turn of the century, after the threat of racial violence finally began to simmer down. Obligations and responsibilities in smaller Chinese communities shifted from district, clan, and tong to family and community ties. The demographic implications of this distinction are shown in Figure 2.

In the words of Bette Lord, author of Eighth Moon: "Americans think you must make every sacrifice for your children. The Chinese think you must make every sacrifice for your parents." Traditional Chinese values, perpetuated in the larger Chinatowns, under the direction of clan and district institutions, began to lose their significance in smaller Chinese communities where immediate family responsibilities were more pressing.

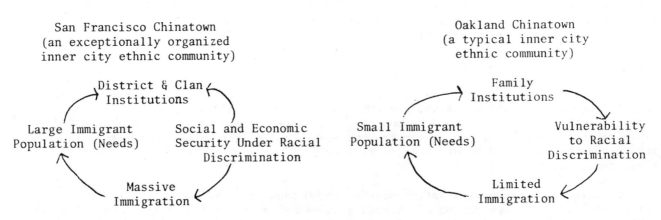

San Francisco Chinatown
(an exceptionally organized
inner city ethnic community)

Oakland Chinatown
(a typical inner city
ethnic community)

FIGURE 2

TWO TYPES OF AMERICAN CHINATOWNS

Footnotes to Chapter Two:

1. Gunther Barth, Bitter Strength: A History of the Chinese in the U.S., 1850-1970 (Cambridge, 1964) p. 29.

2. S. W. Kung, Chinese in American Life (Seattle, 1962) p. 6.

3. Sen-Dou Chang, "Distribution and Occupations of Overseas Chinese," Geog. Rev., Vol. 58 (1968) p. 91.

4. Chen Han-Seng, Landlord and Peasant in China (New York, 1936).

5. Yi-Fu Tuan, China (Chicago, 1969), p. 144.

6. C. H. Lowe, The Chinese in Hawaii: A Bibliographic Survey (Taipei, 1972) p. 2.

7. Gunther Barth, op. cit., p. 24.

8. Betty Lee Sung, Mountain of Gold: The Story of the Chinese in America (New York, 1967) p. 11. See also Ta Chen, Chinese Migrations with Special Reference to Labor Conditions, U.S. Depart. of Labor, Bureau of Labor Statistics, Bulletin No. 340, Washington, D.C., 1923, pp. 5-27.

9. Victor G. Nee and Brett de Bary Nee, Longtime Californ': A Documentary Study of an American Chinatown (New York, 1972) p. 16.

10. S. W. Kung, op. cit., p. 5.

11. Thomas W. Chinn, A History of the Chinese in California (San Francisco, 1969) p. 6.

12. Sen-Dou Chang, op. cit., p. 89.

13. Ibid., pp. 91-92.

14. See Victor Purcell, The Chinese in Southeast Asia (New York, 1951).

15. Gunther Barth, op. cit., p. 107.

16. Victor G. and Brett de Bary Nee, op. cit., Part I, pp. 13-60.

17. C. H. Lowe, op. cit., p. 1.

18. Gunther Barth, op. cit., p. 66.

19. Ibid., p. 9.

20. Thomas W. Chin, op. cit., p. 8.

21. Ibid., p. 9.

22. Daniel Chu and Samuel Chu, Passage to the Golden Gate (Garden City, 1967) pp. 3-6.

23. Shirley Sun, Three Generations of Chinese-East and West (Oakland, 1973) pp. 3-4.

24. Alexander Saxton, The Indispensable Enemy: Labor and the Anti-Chinese Movement in California (Berkeley, 1971) p. 65.

25. C. H. Lowe, op. cit., p. 11.

26. Betty Lee Sung, op. cit., p. 16.

27. Victor G. Nee and Brett de Bary Nee, op. cit., p. 16.

28. Gunther Barth, op. cit., p. 68.

29. Victor G. Nee and Brett de Bary Nee, op. cit., p. 16.

30. "The Chinese Family in San Francisco," Group Research Project, School of Social Welfare, University of California, Berkeley, June 1966, pp. 60-64.

31. Ibid., pp. 65-66.

32. Thomas W. Chin, op. cit., pp. 2-4.

33. Ping Chiu, Chinese Labor in California (Ann Arbor, 1963) p. 127.

34. See William Hoy, The Chinese Six Companies (San Francisco, 1942) p. 7.

35. For more on "power elite," see Anita Yao and Rose Chew, "Chinese Community in San Francisco," International Institute of S.F., Sept. 1960, p. 2.

36. "Chinese Family in San Francisco," op. cit., p. 72.

37. Betty Lee Sung, op. cit., p. 137.

38. See Charles C. Dobie, San Francisco's Chinatown (New York, 1936).

39. Ibid., pp. 154-155.

40. Betty Lee Sung, op. cit., p. 138.

41. Ibid., pp. 136-137.

42. "Chinese Family in San Francisco," op. cit., pp. 120-122.

43. Ibid., p. 123-124.

44. Rose Hum Lee, The Chinese in the U.S.A. (Hong Kong, 1960) p. 186.

45. Quoted in the San Francisco Chronicle (August 27, 1974) p. 29.

CHAPTER THREE

CHINATOWN IN THE MAKING: RACISM AND MIGRATION

Introduction

The pervasiveness of restrictive laws and practices imposed against the Chinese in the United States has been well documented.[1] Although there seems to be little agreement about the cause of racial prejudice, the role of racism in the anti-Chinese movement was clearly outlined.[2] Discriminatory laws and practices, even though no longer unquestionably accepted, provide ample opportunity for racist attitudes to surface. This chapter will delve into the effects of racism on Chinese migration and settlement at both the national and regional levels. The impact of racism on Chinese settlement in the East Bay Region, which will be the focus of Chapter Four, may be regarded as an example of systematic forces operating at the local level.

Racism, according to Pierre Van Den Berghe, is a belief that genetically transmitted differences between groups are intrinsically associated with the presence or absence of certain socially relevant abilities or characteristics. He maintains that "objective" physical differences among groups are by definition based upon the presumption that such differences are socially significant or relevant.[3] Most race relations scholars have been inclined to attribute the anti-Chinese movement to the peculiarities of the newcomers without emphasizing the cultural roots of majority sentiments. Stuart Creighton Miller, however, has shown that anti-Chinese attitudes were national in scope, antedated the beginning of labor recruited immigration by at least a generation, and reflected a clash between extremely contrasting cultures.[4] The importance of social sanctions and norms in fostering racist behavior cannot be overestimated. Although racism is for some people a symptom of psychological problems (e.g., scapegoating), it is for most a convenient rationalization for rewarding or self-serving behavior.[5]

The benefits and costs of racial discrimination have been difficult to ascertain, despite its obvious impact upon purchasing power and land values. Gary S. Becker, in his pioneering attempts to conceptualize discrimination in terms of international trade theory, concluded that while both majority and minority groups lost from such practices, the losses are especially great for minorities.[6] Lester Thurow has found that the cost of discrimination borne by the average non-white worker is $2100 per year (based on econometric analysis of poverty factors) which represents a subsidy or transfer to the average white worker of $248 per year.[7]

The negative effects of racism upon interregional minority migration has yet to be fully recognized. Andrei Rogers has revealed from the results of his regression model of migration flows in California that variations in unemployment rates, wage rates, and distance between origins and destinations accounted for only 27 percent of the total variation in non-white movements, compared with explaining 80 percent of the variation for white movements.[8] Non-economic forces, such as discrimination, continue to impede the movement of non-whites to economic opportunities. The racial turbulence which governed the first 50 years of Chinese settlement in the United States shaped the course of their migration and restricted the range of their residential opportunities.

The aftermath of violence left the newcomers antagonized by American ways, pessimistic about their future in this country, and even more dependent on traditional values, customs, and institutions. Racial agitation and restrictive laws encouraged the emergence and perpetuation of Chinatown communities. The problems of bondage and alienation, covered in Chapter Two, were aggravated by racial hostilities which offered little recourse but to seek refuge in the Chinese quarter.

"The Chinese Must Go!"

Like other non-white immigrants, the Chinese were victimized by racist practices which impeded their social and economic progress in this country. After a century of welcoming the tired, the poor, the huddled white masses yearning to be free, national immigration policies began to register a clear anti-color bias. Indicative of changing attitudes, both national parties included anti-Chinese measures in their platforms by 1876. Six years later, the Chinese became the first ethnic group to be formally excluded from immigration to the United States. The Exclusion Act was not repealed until 1943.

The Chinese became convenient scapegoats during the Reconstruction period, with its attendant financial, social and political problems.[9] The failures of industrial capitalism in California were blamed on the Chinese. Cascading through the mainstream of American journalism was the image of the "utterly heathen, treacherous, sensual, cowardly, cruel Chinamen."[10] One of the most influential writers of his time, Henry George echoed fears that the shores of America would be deluged by "swarms of Chinamen." "Uniquely enslaved to an idolatrous ancient tradition, politically servile, morally depraved, and loathsomely diseased," the Chinese were viewed as singularly impervious to the 19th century ideas of progress, liberty, and civilization, to which an emergent modern American was fervently committed.[11]

Free market competition, once proclaimed by Adam Smith to be the invisible hand which would automatically regulate the economy, had already begun to tarnish by mid-century. The underpinnings of corporate irresponsibility had been laid long before the arrival of Chinese laborers.[12] The conflict between capitalists and workers was inevitable. Labor organizers seized the Chinese issue as a rallying point for dramatizing their cause. In the words of Samuel Gompers, founder of the American Federation of Labor, "the Caucasions are not going to let their standard of living be destroyed by Negroes, Chinaman, Japs, or any others."[13]

Although considered a threat to white labor in general, the Chinese actually solidified the position of skilled white laborers in California at the expense of other white laborers. Excluded from the skilled occupations, the Chinese in fact depressed the wage rate only in the market for unskilled or semi-skilled labor. According to Alexander Saxton, the presence of Chinese in the Far West served to inhibit the immigration of unskilled white workingmen to the Pacific Coast, thereby securing the dominion of established groups of laborers against the threat of young, aggressive competition for the East.[14] What might appear to stem from the simplicity of Marxian dialectics was in fact spawned by exploitation and fragmentation within the labor movement. Clashes between small employers and larger firms, which could afford to hire Chinese laborers, were also inflamed during the last three decades of the 19th century.[15]

Ruled ineligible for naturalization in 1867, the Chinese were regarded as "unassimilatable" in the eyes of most Americans. Burgeoning unemployment, arising from the national Panic of 1873, heightened fears and deepened moral convictions. Workers blamed the Chinese, the Negroes, the railways, the corporations and the banks.[16] Political victories often accrued to incumbents and office seekers who espoused the cause.[17] Despite the ban on Chinese immigration in 1882, the nation's economic woes continued. Recessions during the periods 1882-85 and 1893-96 provided the fuel for recurrent violence and a groundswell of resentment, especially where the Chinese were employed in large numbers.

According to Victor and Brett Nee, passage of the Exclusion Act seemed to mark the beginning, not the end, of racial agitation against the Chinese. The objective, they argued, was not merely exclusion but also extermination.[18] Wives of Chinese laborers were excluded in 1884. Anti-miscegenation laws prevented intermarriage between Chinese men and white women in most states with substantial Chinese populations. Anti-miscegenation laws remained in force in California until 1947, in Montana until 1953, and in Oregon until 1951. Not until a Supreme Court ruling in 1967 were anti-miscegenation laws in Arizona, Georgia, Louisiana, Mississippi, Missouri, Nebraska, South Dakota, Utah, Virginia, and Wyoming finally overturned.[19]

California: Land of Promise?

In spite of popular beliefs that California was a land of promise for immigrant groups, it is clear that ethnic conflicts prevailed throughout the history of the state.[20] Racial agitation against the Chinese was exceptionally intense. Mary Roberts Coolidge, in her pioneering study of Chinese immigration, traced the source of racist legislation to Southern Democrats, who rose to power in California between 1852 and 1875 often at the expense of the Chinese.[21] Gunther Barth, on the other hand, pinned the blame on middle class disdain for the "immoral" aspects of Chinese conduct.[22] Yet the crux of anti-Chinese sentiment centered upon labor unrest. Denis Kearney's Workingmen's Party, the Knights of Labor, and local anti-coolie clubs mobilized thousands of unemployed and embittered Californians against the Chinese. The precarious political balance between the state's Democratic and Republican parties enabled organized labor to wield tremendous political power.

Forbidden from testifying in court by an 1854 State Supreme Court decision, the Chinese were victimized almost at will. When they stood their ground, they were chased out of town or even lynched; personal insults and brutality were common, especially in the Western part of the country--historically the seat of anti-Chinese, and later anti-Japanese, prejudice and discrimination.[23] Assault, robbery, and murder, to say nothing of lesser crimes, could be perpetrated against them with impunity, as long as no white person was available to witness in their behalf.[24]

By 1853, a foreign miners tax was established in California to curb the influx of Chinese immigration and the outflow or remittances. Enforced almost exclusively against the Chinese, collectors received about 50 percent of their revenue from the Chinese in the first four years, but 98 percent of their revenue from Chinese miners in the last 16 years of operation.[25] The abusive methods by which these taxes were collected by officials and by those impersonating tax collectors have been well-documented.[26] Robbery, assault, and fraud were common practices. Similar legislation was passed in California against Chinese fishermen in 1860. A Chinese "police tax" was enacted in California in 1862 "to protect white labor against competition with coolie labor and to discourage the immigration of Chinese to the state."[27] The roots of racism were institutionalized into fiscal policies.

The emergence of a national market threatened the growth of the state's infant industries by 1873. The reduction of westbound freight rates in 1876 ushered in a new wave of lower priced goods from Eastern factories, compelling many firms in California to resort to Chinese labor. The railroads, corporations, and Chinese appeared to be responsible for the state's economic collapse during the last few decades of the century. However, this concept has been challenged. For example, Ping Chiu has emphasized that westbound tonnage to California imported by rail never exceeded that by ship, even in the peak year of 1880.[28] According to James E. Vance, Jr. the prime cause of California's economic distress was structural. He observed that once the Gold Rush was over, California found herself over-populated and underemployed. The decline of prospecting left laborers in the state dis-satisfied with a return to their former "cow country" employment but without any real sub-stitute.[29]

The adjustment from extractive to manufacturing activities proved painful for the stranded workingmen caught in the transition. California, as Vance has concluded, was set-tled after the Gold Rush mainly by those searching for a more desirable lifestyle.[30] Economic opportunities, limited by high rates of unemployment, played a much less signifi-cant factor in California's growth from 1860 to 1940 than is generally believed. This rise of racial agitation in the 1860's, provoked by rising unemployment, drove thousands of Chinese out of California into eastern states, against the flow of white migrants into the state.

31

TABLE 3

STATES WITH THE LARGEST CHINESE POPULATIONS
1870-1900

Rank	1870	1880	1890	1900
1	California 49,277	California 71,132	California 72,472	California 45,753
2	Idaho 4,274	Oregon 9,510	Hawaii 15,301	Hawaii 25,767
3	Nevada 3,152	Hawaii 5,916	Oregon 9,540	Oregon 10,397
4	Oregon 2,330	Nevada 5,416	Washington 3,260	New York 7,170
5	Montana 1,949	Idaho 3,397	New York 2,935	Washington 3,629
6	Hawaii 1,938	Washington 3,186	Nevada 2,833	Massachusetts 2,968
7	Utah 445	Montana 1,765	Montana 2,532	Pennsylvania 1,927

The Impetus for Urbanization

The dispersal of Chinese settlement in the American West was prompted by diminishing opportunities and expanding hostilities in California. In 1860, almost all of the Chinese in the country resided in California. But by 1870, the portion of Chinese in the nation had fallen to 77 percent. Our of 17,000 Chinese miners listed in the Census of 1870, California had only about 9000, with the remaining 800 scattered in Idaho, Oregon, Nevada, and Montana, and smaller numbers in Utah, Wyoming, and Washington.[31]

The eruption of racial violence in California during the late 1860's and early 1870's forced thousands of Chinese to return to China. Those who could not afford to return sought opportunities in other states or in the larger Chinatowns of the state. Although the Chinese had become the largest single racial or national group of miners in California by 1873, the number of Chinese miners in the state had been decreasing for a decade.[32]

Placer mining brought thousands of Chinese into central Idaho in the late 1850's. Idaho, second only to California in Chinese population in 1870, dropped to number five in 1880 as opportunities opened in neighboring states. Even though excluded from the lucrative Comstock Lode in 1859, many Chinese railroad workers and miners settled in Virginia City to service the boom until violence broke out in 1869. Gold mining and service opportunities at Butte, Montana, attracted nearly 2000 Chinese into the state by 1870. Chinese railroad workers discharged in Colorado turned to gold mining in the 1870's. Anti-Chinese riots in 1880 curtailed the growth of Denver's Chinatown. Gold discoveries in the Black Hills of South Dakota were followed by the establishment of a small Chinese settlement at Deadwood by the 1870's. The influx of Chinese coal miners into Wyoming in 1875 was terminated by the massacre of 30 Chinese and the burning of the Chinese quarter at Rock Spring in 1885. Although Chinese laundries, tailors, restaurants, and domestic servants were in great demand in frontier towns, the threat of Chinese competition in the mines escalated as mining became more capital intensive. Ethnic competition on the rails has been well-known.[33]

The shift from hand-operated to mechanized techniques witnessed the emergence of company mining and organized labor in the mines. Forced out of mining by local laws and union regulations, the Chinese turned to service occupations in the cities.[34] Frustrated by structural changes within the industry which undermined their hopes for success, many white miners took out their anxieties on the Chinese. Rarely did law enforcement along the mining frontier provide security for Chinese minorities beseiged by angry white workers. Hostility was especially vicious and deep-rooted at mining sites and railroad towns in Wyoming, Colorado, Nevada, Montana, and California.

Gold mining, canning, and railroad construction in the 1850's and 1860's sent thousands of Chinese laborers to Oregon, which from 1880 to 1910 remained second only to California in its Chinese population. Fishing and canning opportunities in the Puget Sound Area of Washington supported several thousand Chinese by 1880. But by 1885, bands of terrorists, led by the Knights of Labor, had expelled the Chinese from Tacoma as well as from Pierre, King, Kitsap, Snohomish, Skagit, and Watcom counties. Attempts to oust the Chinese from Seattle in the same year were unsuccessful.[35] The anti-Chinese movement in the Northwest, as in the Mountain region, was a product of racial unrest and labor competition. Completion of the Canadian Pacific Railway left many white workers unemployed and embittered.

Chinese settlement in the Southwest followed the construction of the Southern Pacific Railroad, which reached Arizona in 1877 and San Antonio, Texas, in 1883. The Chinese often settled in towns along the route, like San Antonio and Tuscon, where they established laundries, groceries, and vegetable gardens. Other Chinese moved to Phoenix and Houston, where postwar growth had been rapid enough to provide ample employment opportunities, especially in the grocery business. In contrast to the Pacific Northwest and the Mountain states, labor unrest in the Southwest has been negligible.

Although the Chinese have fared relatively well in the South, Mary Roberts Coolidge has argued that the anti-Chinese movement in California was an outgrowth of Southern racism. A deal was struck by Congressmen in which anti-Black votes from the West would be exchanged for anti-Chinese votes from the South.[36] Stanford Lyman contends that violence did not occur in the Confederacy, because the Chinese were perceived not as a threat but rather as an exploitable element in the labor force, to be used as a club against recalcitrant Negro laborers.[37] Another view is that, due to their small numbers and wide distribution, the Chinese remained "socially invisible."[38] Equally plausible, however, is the absence of agitation by organized labor in the region. Although racism was certainly present, the catalyst for igniting racial fears was missing. Industrialization, unlike racism, was limited to certain regions of the country.

Chinese immigration to Hawaii by contract laborers began in 1852. Efforts to organize workers against the "planters' pets" were instigated by the Workingmen's Union by 1884. An Anti-Asiatic Union was formed in 1888 and in 1892 the Chinese were restricted from further immigration. With the annexation of the Islands to the United States in 1898, federal immigration laws became effective.[39] Yet the violence and hatred which greeted the Chinese in so many areas on the mainland of the United States were not as common in Hawaii. Although organized labor played a catalytic role in prohibiting Chinese immigration, racism was not pervasive enough to fuel the spread of hostilities. Traditional Hawaiian values and customs helped to counter the racist sentiments of the Islands' white population.

> The Hawaiian tradition of treating strangers, foreigners, outsiders, and even intruders with tolerance and good-will immensely facilitated the economic and social advancement of the Chinese, and for that matter, all groups in the state. . . . The (native) Hawaiians married the Chinese and found them to be good providers; they gave and sold land to the Chinese; they traded with the Chinese on the basis

of equality; and they showed an eagerness to learn from the Chinese; in short, the Chinese who decided to stay in the Islands had little trouble in getting along with the Hawaiians.[40]

News of anti-Chinese violence throughout the West during the last three decades of the century prompted thousands of Chinese miners, railroad workers, and laborers to seek opportunities in the East. By 1900, only 75 percent of the Chinese in the country lived in the Western states, compared with 90 percent in 1890. New York, Massachusetts, Pennsylvania, and Illinois had attracted substantial Chinese populations. Chinatowns had sprouted in New York City, Boston, and Chicago by 1900 to accommodate the needs of increasing numbers of Chinese newcomers.[41]

The arrival of Chinese in the Midwest and Atlantic Coast states did not go unchallenged by eastern residents. According to Miller, the importation of Chinese strikebreakers at a shoe factory in North Adams, Massachusetts, and the influx of Chinese laundrymen at Belleview, New Jersey, ignited protests among labor leaders and journalists in 1870.[42] The use of Chinese cigar makers in Ohio and Chinese strikebreakers by employers at a cutlery factory in Beaver Falls, Pennsylvania, in the 1870's seemed to confirm Easterners' fears that they, too, would be "swamped."[43]

The decade of the 1890's marked the first decline in the Chinese population of San Francisco, from 25,833 in 1890 to 13,954 in 1900. However, this drop was accompanied by the growth of Chinatowns in the eastern part of the country. Chinese populations doubled in New York City (2048 to 4874), Brooklyn (600 to 1206), and Newark (127 to 261) and trippled in Philadelphia, Boston, Chicago, Baltimore, Washington, D.C., and New Orleans.[44] The shifting pattern of Chinese settlement is shown in Table 3.

Excluded from manufacturing occupations, the Chinese in the East soon tended to concentrate in larger cities, where the demand for laundries, restaurants, and curio shops was larger and more diversified.[45] Efforts to restrict the Chinese from occupations dominated by organized labor proved more successful in the East, where the conflicts between capitalist and laborer were much more pronounced. Miller revealed that almost every labor newspaper and organization in the country opposed Chinese immigration after 1870. He disclosed that even the Negro delegates at the first Colored State Labor Convention in Baltimore in 1869 passed a plank in favor of Chinese exclusion.[46]

The Chinese, according to Elmer Clarence Sandmeyer, were neither the first nor the last group of newcomers to meet such hostility. It was said of the Irish, a generation before this agitation, that "they do more work for less money than the native workingman and live on a lower standard, thereby decreasing wages."[47] Prodding the Chinese eastward into the heartland of American labor interests was not the attractiveness of its labor conditions but rather the increasing scarcity of opportunity in the Far West. Migration had after all brought them across the Pacific. Many with no place else to turn headed east in the wake of mounting racial agitation. Others sought refuge in Chinatowns of the West, where the uncertainties of personal and job security could be minimized. Those who could afford to do so returned to China, sustaining the myth of the "mountain of gold."

The Dynamics of Chinatown Formation

The development of Chinatowns in large cities like San Francisco and New York during the period of racial hostility, 1870 to 1910, was more than coincidental. According to Stanford Lyman, Chinatowns were neither solely creatures of white racism nor products of congregative sentiments. Instead, he insists, they must be seen as a complex produced by the two elements acting simultaneously.[48] In the face of increasing agitation, the Chinese quarter acquired new functions. As long as the Chinese were free to live, work, and travel without fear for their personal safety, Chinatown remained essentially a place to visit, shop, and do business. By 1880, however, it became a place to reside for thousands of refugees" displaced from rural areas and small towns in the West. Unlike the Irish, the Chinese found themselves hemmed in by legal restrictions and racial violence.

It was in Chinatown that the lonely Chinese laborer could find fellow-
ship, companions, social familiarity, and solace. Chinatown acted as
a buffer against the prejudices, hatreds, and depredations of hostile
whites. Chinatown included the offices and hostelries of the various
Chinese benevolent and protective associations, places where one could
get a bunk for the night, some food, a stake, and knowledge of the
numbers, kinds, and conditions of available jobs. Chinatown also
housed the Chinese elite--the merchants of the ghetto--who acted as
spokesmen for and protectors of the laborers and who held the latter
in a state of political dependence and debt bondage.[49]

The ghetto, which originally referred to the Jewish quarter in 16th century
Venice, has always been a place where ethnic groups have been confined for extended periods.
Chinatown San Francisco proved to be no exception by 1880. In his penetrating study of
Harlem, Kenneth Clark asserted that the invisible walls of the dark ghetto have been erected by white society, by those who have the power both to confine those who have no power
and to perpetuate their powerlessness.[50] Robert Blauner contends that Asian-Americans,
although victimized by racism, have not been colonized by whites as Blacks have been. He
insists that when immigrant ghettos persist, as in the case of San Francisco's Chinatown,
it is because they are a big business for the ethnics, themselves, and because there is a
new stream of immigrants.[51]

This view suggests that ghettos, in the United States, which emerge because of
racism, are sustained by exploitation, whether from within or without. More often than not,
however, both white and ethnic individuals are involved in perpetuating the dependency of
ghetto living. The significance of traditional Chinese institutions in reinforcing obligations has been emphasized in Chapter Two. The role of white interests in exploiting and in
maintaining this dependence has yet to be documented, although research on this topic has
been expanding. Lyman, for example, claims that in place of the political machine and
wardheeler, the Chinese were protected and represented by their own ethnic associations,
which kept them in a state of unofficial colonial dependence.[52] In the words of Kenneth
Clark:

> The ghetto is ferment, paradox, and dilemma. Yet within its pervasive
> pathology exists a surprising human resilience. The ghetto is hope,
> it is despair, it is churches and bars, it is aspiration for change,
> and it is apathy. It is vibrancy. It is stagnation. It is courage,
> and it is defeatism. It is cooperation and concern, and it is suspic-
> ion, competitiveness, and rejection. It is the surge toward assimila-
> tion, and it is alienation and withdrawal within the protective walls
> of the ghetto.[53]

From Chinese Camps to Chinese Quarter

The impact of racism on the growth of Chinatowns in California has not been fully
recognized. Barth, for example, blames the victims: "Compressed into narrow confines,
filth and immorality persisted, endangering the health and virtue of the growing state
(California), and soon came to be regarded by Americans as part of their second nature."[54]
Barth failed to recognize that the physical conditions of the quarter were reflections of
American exclusion and control.

San Francisco, which supported only 7.8 percent of the state's Chinese in 1860,
did not even become the leading Chinese county in California until 1870, when it accommodated 24.4 percent of the state's Chinese population (see Table 4). The sojourners, the
name given to Chinese laborers, most of whom dreamed of eventually returning to their villages in China to retire, were mainly employed in rural communities. They resided in small
camps until forced out of mining by racial agitation. The portable rocker made it feasible
for Chinese miners to migrate from place to place and to avoid persecution without abandon-
ing their initial investment.[55] Henry George observed in 1869 that "every town and hamlet
had its Chinatown--its poorest, meanest, and filthiest quarter and wherever the restless

Rank	1860	1870	1880	1890	1900
1	El Dorado 4,762	San Francisco 12,022	San Francisco 21,745	San Francisco 25,833	San Francisco 13,954
2	Calvares 3,657	Sacramento 3,595	Sacramento 4,892	Los Angeles 4,424	Sacramento 3,254
3	San Francisco 2,719	Nevada 2,627	Alameda 4,386	Sacramento 4,371	Los Angeles 3,209
4	Amador 2,568	Placer 2,410	Butte 3,793	Alameda 3,311	Alameda 2,211
5	Placer 2,392	Yuba 2,337	Nevada 3,003	Fresno 2,736	San Joaquin 1,875
6	Sierra 2,208	Butte 2,082	Santa Clara 2,695	Santa Clara 2,723	Fresno 1,775
7	Butte 2,177	Alameda 1,939	Placer 2,190	San Joaquin 1,676	Santa Clara 1,738
8	Nevada 2,147	San Joaquin 1,629	Yuba 2,146	Monterey 1,667	Placer 1,050
9	Tuolemne 1,962	Amador 1,627	San Joaquin 1,997	Butte 1,530	Kern 906

Note: Numbers refer to Chinese population in the county in those years.
Source: Thomas Chinn, A History of the Chinese in California (San Francisco, 1969), Table VI, p. 21.

TABLE 4

CALIFORNIA COUNTIES WITH THE LARGEST CHINESE POPULATIONS

prospectors opened a new district, there, singly (sic) or in squads, appeared the inevitable Chinaman."[56]

Chinese quarter in the mining towns of California served the needs of white and Chinese miners. Chinn reported that Chinese laundries, restaurants, boarding houses, and general stores appeared in Weaverville, Shasta, Yreka, Goodyear's Bar, Coloma, Placerville, Dutch Flat, Nevada City, Grass Valley, Auburn, Bear Valley, Sonora, Coulterville, Mokelumne Hill, Angel's Camp, Hornitos, Knight's Ferry, and Columbia. He wrote that Oroville, Marysville, and Chinese Camp boasted Chinese populations that once rivaled that of San Francisco.[57] Labor shortages in the small towns provided opportunities for those willing to do "women's work" and other menial tasks.

Moreover, the Chinese comprised a lucrative market for second-hand mining claims, which benefited white miners anxious to liquidate and move to more attractive discoveries by the late 1850's.

The outcome was a tacit regularization of status of the Chinese in the camps. They could come in and stay. They could work at tasks other than mining, especially if these were menial or unskilled; and they could comb out low yield or worked over sites.[58]

More than two-thirds of the Chinese in California resided in the mining regions by 1860 (see Map 2). They constituted about one-fourth of the miners in the state and were generally tolerated, at least until the turbulence of the 1870's.

Although Chinese stores were the focus of sojourner life in mountain villages and mining towns, laborers from isolated settlements, craving for greater diversions than the country store offered, frequently visited larger Chinatowns.[59] Chinatown San Francisco served as a point of debarcation and embarcation, a corporate headquarters, a wholesale center, and a place to visit during the 1850's and 1860's. Chinatown provided lonely sojourners an ingeniously supervised outlet for pent-up emotions and suppressed desires and environs with the illusion of home for a few fleeting hours.[60]

According to Thomas W. Chinn, Chinatown San Francisco had become a bustling commercial hub by the mid-1850's. In 1853, the Chinese were occupying buildings on Dupont Avenue between Sacramento and Jackson Streets and on Jackson from Kearney to Stockton Streets. He assessed that by 1856 the quarter had 33 general merchandise stores, 15 apothecaries, five restaurants, five butchers, five barbers, three tailors, three boarding houses, three wood yards, two bakers, five herb doctors, two silversmiths, one wood engraver, one curio carver, one broker for American merchants, and one Chinese interpreter.[61] According to Sandmeyer, the increasing number of Chinese engaged in trade and other independent business in San Francisco was also exhibited in Sacramento, San Jose, Stockton, and Marysville in 1876.[62]

The arrival of the Chinese was first looked upon favorably by Californians. According to H. H. Bancroft, they were considered to be clean, industrious, desirable, and in the days when workmen were scarce, they filled the need for laborers, cooks, and domestic servants. Mark Twain described the Chinese as "quiet, peaceable, tractable, free from drunkeness, and they are industrious as the day is long." [63] Residential segregation, which dominated the pattern of Chinese settlement in 1885, did not apply to the scattered pattern of Chinese occupancy in San Francisco in the 1850's.[64] Chinn cautioned that the segregated arrangement which so marked Chinatown San Francisco in the later years of the 19th century was not evident in the early years. A Chinese candle factory was at Third and Brannan, the Ning Yung Company was on Broadway, the Young Wo Company was on the slopes of Telegraph Hill, the Yan Wo Company was in the vicinity of the present Sheraton-Palace Hotel, and a Chinese fishing village was at Rincon Place.[65]

Attempts to expel the Chinese from placer mining did not become a common practice until 1858.[66] Thousands of Chinese, victimized by the rise of capital intensive company mining between 1854 and 1864 and by the Foreign Miners Tax, sought employment in other sectors of the transforming economy. Railroad construction kept some 10,000 Chinese at work on the Central Pacific alone from 1866 to 1869.[67] Reclamation projects provided work in the Central Valley until the mid-1870's.[68] The mining districts had lost half of their Chinese residents between 1860 and 1870, while the Chinese population of the Valley counties soared.[69] According to Carey McWilliams, after having comprised only about one-tenth of the farm labor supply in 1870, the Chinese made up about one-third of the state's farm workers in 1880 and one-half in 1884.[70] Restrictive laws, passed under pressure by Italian, Greek, and Dalmatian fishermen, undermined Chinese fishing activities in the 1880's.[71]

Anti-Chinese riots at Los Angeles and Martinez in 1871, at Truckee in 1878, and at Eureka in 1885 paved the way for agitation in other small towns through the Central Valley, along the foothills of the Sierra Nevada and on the coast. Between January and April of 1886, expulsions were reported in 35 California communities.[72] The Chinese were pushed from rural into urban areas. Protection was confined to large cities, where employers of Chinese domestic and factory labor enlisted in their defense.[73] Secretary of State Bayard announced in 1886 that a concerted movement was in progress to drive the Chinese from all cities and towns in California, except San Francisco, and that the Governor and the county sheriffs evinced no disposition to protect their rights. Bankrupt Chinese were said to be pouring into San Francisco from all over the Pacific Coast, increasing the city's oriental population by 20,000 in 3 months.[74]

CALIFORNIA COUNTIES WITH THE LARGEST CHINESE POPULATIONS IN 1860 AND IN 1900

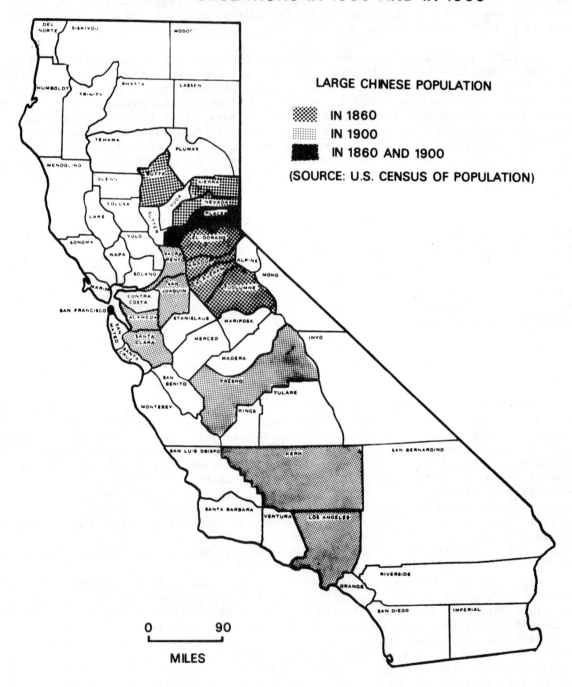

LARGE CHINESE POPULATION

IN 1860
IN 1900
IN 1860 AND 1900
(SOURCE: U.S. CENSUS OF POPULATION)

0   90
MILES

San Francisco: The Makings of a Ghetto

Although housing in San Francisco Chinatown had become overcrowded, unsanitary, and dilapidated, the quarter furnished the Chinese with relatively secure accommodations. Special police or "specials" hired by the Six Companies to guard against racial violence in the quarter kept the peace. Vigilance and round-the-clock activities made what would have otherwise been the city's worst fire trap into one of its least flamable districts.[75] Mayor Phelan's efforts to oust the Chinese by quarantining the entire quarter and removing indigent Chinese to detention barracks on the basis of unconfirmed reports of bubonic plague were held to be unconstitutional by a Federal court in 1900.[76] The threat of abatement remained but never materialized until the earthquake and fires of 1906.

Chinatown was much too profitable to be demolished. Dillon emphasized that the Chinese owned only 10 of the 153 major pieces of real property in Chinatown in 1873 and only 25 of the 316 major parcels listed in 1904.[77] Expensive leases to the Chinese were a source of both high rents for tenants and exorbitant profits for white landowners. Confinement and overcrowding had become a means of exploitation, made possible by racial agitation.

Expansion was not even needed until the mid-1870's, after the Chinese had occupied what had been the French quarter for almost two decades. Martyn Bowden observed that the eastern and southern boundaries of Chinatown in 1876 were not very different from those in 1868.[78] By 1874, he reported that the Chinese were finally buying land along Dupont across California and along Sacramento across Kearney.[79] According to Cather, there were 25,000 to 30,000 Chinese living in an area of two by six blocks by the beginning of the 1880's.[80] Roughly bounded by California, Stockton, Broadway, and Kearney Streets, the quarter had become a teeming ghetto by 1885.[81] Even as late as 1906, Chinatown only occupied 15 blocks, all below Mason and north of Sacramento.[82] Most parcels were owned by French, Italians, and Germans.

Chinese labor became essential to San Francisco's many industries, especially those with national markets. As late as 1869, the Chinese in California were engaged in a wide variety of economic activities:

> Woolen factories, knitting mills, railroad building, highway and wharf construction, borax beds, farms, dairies, hop plantations, small fruit farms, kitchens, wood cutting, land clearing, potato digging, salt works, liquor manufacturing, cigar and cigarette making, the manufacture of slippers, pantaloons, vests, shirts, drawers, overalls, and shoes, tin shops, shoe blacking, fishing, gardening, poultry and pig raising, peddling, cabinet making, washermen, house servants, coal heavers, deck hands, cabin servants, sailors, mining, vineyard laborers, and laborers in the tule lands.[83]

Chinatown San Francisco provided shelter and information vital to maintaining this supply of low wage labor, which kept many of the Bay Area's infant industries in business. In the words of Frank M. Pixley, an opponent of Chinese immigration testifying in the mid-1870's:

> Our Chinese quarter, as it is called, is their place of residence. If they go to a wash house in the vicinity, to a suburban manufactory, to gardening near town, or if to build railroads in San Bernadino or on the Colorado, or to reclaim tule lands in the interior, their departure there is temporary, and their return here is certain. Therefore the number in San Francisco depends upon seasons and the contract labor market.[84]

Restrictions against the use of Chinese labor minimized conflicts in the building, maritime, and metal trades. Confrontations within the consumer goods sector, on the other hand, remained bitter and involved small cigar-making, shoe-making, and tailoring shops, which attempted to differentiate their products by means of white stamps and labels.[85] By 1880, the unemployed gathered daily in San Francisco to listen to speeches, march across Market and Mission Streets into the industrial district, call en mass at factories and workshops, demanding dismissal of their Chinese employees, and return to hear reports of the day's events.[86]   Attacks against the Chinese were sanctioned by politics as well as by laws prohibiting them from testifying against whites. According to Governor Frederick Low, "you cannot get a police court here for beating a Chinaman today, before an elected judicial, because the hoodlums and his friends will have the vote and the Chinaman has not, and cannot."[87]

Contrary to widespread beliefs, overcrowding in San Francisco Chinatown during the last two decades of the 19th century did not emanate from increased immigration. Passage of the Exclusion Act and economic distress stemmed the influx of newcomers. The Chinese population of the country actually shrank from 105,465 in 1880 to 89,863 in 1900. Conditions in San Francisco Chinatown during this period reflected flagrant racial violence in California, which had forced a previously dispersed population to seek the protection of concentrated urban settlement.

Unemployed workingmen, victimized during the depression years from 1893 to 1896, drifted in search of jobs and handouts, terrorizing towns in the San Joaquin Valley and in the new fruit-growing region surrounding Los Angeles, where the Chinese had found employment in the 1880's and 1890's. Anti-Chinese demonstrations were reported during August and September of 1893 in Riverside, San Bernadino, Redlands, Compton, Bakersfield, Tulare, Fresno, Madera, Calistoga, and Vacaville.[88]   The depth of racial hatred by Californians for the Chinese had its most stark and tragic manifestations only after passage of the Exclusion Law.[89]

Racism in the Perpetuation of Chinatown

The Geary Act, passed in 1892, not only extended the Exclusion Act for another decade but also required all Chinese to register within one year or face deportation as criminals. Advised by their American lawyers that the law would be held unconstitutional, the Six Companies told the Chinese not to register. In sustaining the Geary Act, the Supreme Court turned most of the Chinese in this country into criminals. Agitators bent upon removing the Chinese took the law into their own hands during the 1890's.[90]   Chinatown San Francisco became a city of refuge, as it had in previous periods of racial hostility.

A Federal court ruling in 1884 forbidding the entry of the wives of laborers already in the United States marked only the beginning of legislation aimed at extermination of the Chinese in the country. In 1898, the Secretary of the Treasury broadened the Exclusion Act, which banned the entrance of Chinese "laborers" in 1882, to include as many categories of work as possible. The only Chinese exempted from the ban were merchants and their families, students, travelers, and American-born Chinese and their children.[91]   The Immigration Act of 1924, upheld by a Supreme Court decision, continued to permit American citizens of Chinese ancestry to bring their children but not their wives to America.

It is no accident that Chinatown remained a bachelor society until World War II, when immigration restrictions were finally eased. Dispersal into single family residential neighborhoods was not only constrained by this lack of Chinese families. Restrictive covenants also hindered the movement of Chinese away from Chinatown until ruled unenforceable by the Supreme Court in 1947. Asian land laws, passed in Oregon, Washington, and California in 1906 prohibited both the Chinese and Japanese from owning agricultural lands. Eligibility for agricultural ownership was based on eligibility for citizenship.[92]   Alien-born Chinese did not become qualified for naturalization until 1943. Rural employment thus offered the Chinese little promise of success under existing rules.

Attempts to circumvent the restrictions on Chinese immigration only served to tighten the web of ghetto life. Efforts to purchase "legitimized" status to gain entry into the United States turned Chinatown into a clandestine community. Occasionally, the owners of laundries, restaurants, or even hired laborers (all of whom were subject to exclusion) managed to bribe wealthier merchants to list them as partners in a business and thereby bring their wives to this country.[93]

The earthquake and fires of 1906, which destroyed immigration records as well as the Chinese quarter in San Francisco, allowed many to claim that they were American-born citizens. Sojourners returning to China for a visit who registered a son born there created a "slot," which could be sold to brokers in Hong Kong. "Paper sons" with ages corresponding to their "slots" could gain admission for several thousand dollars.[94]

The immigration of "paper sons" maintained the supply of low wage labor in China-town, despite the implications of the Exclusion Act. "Paper sons" often became indentured servants until they paid off their debts to brokers.[95] Harrassment, extortion, and black-mail against the "father" and especially the "son" prompted many to seek the security of clan and tong retributions. Rose Hum Lee argues that the "slot" market was a major source of social disorganization and an obstacle to acculturation for those ashamed of their duel surnames and afraid of being exposed.[96]

Residential confinement became a way of life, not only for the illegal immigrants, but even for those who had nothing to hide. The rights of Chinese people in this country were obscured by the enforcement of racist legislation.

> In Oregon, Washington, and California, practically all residential
> districts were restricted to Caucasions. College training in en-
> gineering or other technical subjects did not guarantee decent posi-
> tions to the Chinese. If one should go out, dressed casually for a
> walk, or go to a club, or even to church, he was liable to be
> picked up by the immigration officers on suspicion of illegal resi-
> dence. . . . Such arrests were reported to be very common, especially
> in the late 1920's. It was up to the Chinese to prove that he was
> not an illegal alien or even an illegal citizen.[97]

Racism made Chinatown a city of refuge. Racial violence was responsible for the emergence of the ghetto. Racist laws and exploitation insured its perpetuation, long after the agitation of the 19th century had subsided. Chinatown persisted, because the rules of the game made the quarter a profitable operation for land owners, employers, politicians, public officials, and organizations whose power was derived from Chinese dependency. The Exclusion Act actually helped thousands of Chinese, Americans, and Europeans to make mil-lions of dollars by engaging in smuggling as a regular and profitable business.[98]

The mainsprings of Chinese settlement in the United States stemmed from the ex-ploitation of Chinese dependency and powerlessness in a period of intense racism. Institu-tionalized racism provided the justification, the rationalization, the moral "climate" for sustaining the confinement of ghetto life, which had become so lucrative for so many interests. To believe that "the Chinese take care of their own" is tantamount to accept-ance of this confinement and the blighted, crowded, and deprived conditions which it formen-ted.

Footnotes to Chapter Three

1. See Cheng Tsu-Wu, ed., Chink! Anti-Chinese Prejudice in America (New York, 1972).

2. Stuard Creighton Miller, The Unwelcome Immigrant (Berkeley, 1969), pp. 3-15.

3. Pierre Van Den Bergh, Race and Racism (New York, 1967) p. 11.

4. Miller, op. cit., p. vii.

5. Van Den Berghe, op. cit., p. 21.

6. Gary S. Becker, The Economics of Discrimination (Chicago, 1971) p. 6.

7. Lester C. Thurow, Poverty and Discrimination (Washington, 1969) p. 137.

8. Andrei Rogers, "A Regression Analysis of Interregional Migration in California," Review of Econ. and Stat., Vol. 44 (May, 1967) p. 216.

9. Rose Hum Lee, The Chinese in the U.S.A. (Hong Kong, 1960) p. 13.

10. Henry George, New York Tribune (May 18, 1869)

11. Miller, op. cit., p. vii.

12. John Kenneth Galbraith, Economics and the Public Purpose (Boston, 1973) pp. 12-19.

13. Alexander Saxton, The Indispensable Enemy (Berkeley, 1971) p. 265 (quoted from a speech by Gompers in the St. Paul Union Advocate), American Federationist, Vol. XII (Sept. 1905) pp. 636-637.

14. Ibid., p. 263.

15. Ibid., p. 212.

16. S. W. Kung, Chinese in American Life (Seattle, 1962) p. 69.

17. Rose Hum Lee, op. cit., p. 13.

18. Victor G. and Brett de Bary Nee, Longtime California': A Documentary History of an American Chinatown (New York, 1972) p. 55.

19. Betty Lee Sung, Mountain of Gold (New York, 1967) pp. 254-256.

20. Charles Wollenberg, ed., Ethnic Conflict in California History (Los Angeles, 1970) p. viii.

21. Mary Roberts Coolidge, Chinese Immigration (New York, 1909) p. 20.

22. Gunther Barth, Bitter Strength (Cambridge, 1964) pp. 4-6.

23. Rose Hum Lee, op. cit., p. 13.

24. Elmer Clarence Sandmeyer, The Anti-Chinese Movement in California (Urbana, 1939) p. 45.

25. Stanford Lyman, "Strangers in the Cities, the Chinese on the Urban Frontier," in Wollenberg, Ethnic Conflict in California History (Los Angeles, 1970) p. 72.

26. See Henry George, op. cit. and Thomas W. Chinn, A History of the Chinese in California, Chinese Historical Association of California (San Francisco, 1969) pp. 31-32.

27. Cheng Tsu-Wu, op. cit., pp. 26-31.

28. Ping Chiu, Chinese Labor in California: An Economic Study (Ann Arbor, 1963), p. 50.

29. James E. Vance, Jr., "California and the Search for the Ideal," Annals, Assn. of Amer. Geog., Vol. 62 (June, 1972) p. 195.

30. Ibid., pp. 202-203.

31. S. W. Kung, op. cit., p. 42.

32. Thomas W. Chinn, op. cit., p. 33.

33. See Saxton, op. cit., p. 62 and Chinn, op. cit., pp. 43-47.

34. Rose Hum Lee, op. cit., p. 58.

35. Cheng Tsu-Wu, op. cit., pp. 201-205.

36. See Chester Lloyd Jones, "The Legislative History of Exclusion Legislation," Annals, Amer. Acad. of Soc. and Poli. Sci., Vol. 34, No. 2 (July 10, 1909). See also Roger Daniels, Concentration Camps, U.S.A. (New York, 1971) p. 11.

37. Stanford Lyman, op. cit., p. 70.

38. S. W. Kung, op. cit., p. 168.

39. C. H. Lowe, The Chinese in Hawaii: A Bibliographic Survey (Taipei, 1972) pp. 10-12.

40. Ibid., pp. 19-20.

41. S. W. Kung, op. cit., p. 42.

42. Miller, op. cit., p. 175.

43. Lyman, op. cit., p. 77.

44. Rose Hum Lee, op. cit., p. 36.

45. Rose Hum Lee, "The Decline of Chinatowns in the U.S.," Amer. Journ. Soc., Vol. 54, (1948-1949) p. 428.

46. Miller, op. cit., p. 196.

47. Sandmeyer, op. cit., p. 38.

48. Lyman, op. cit., p. 78.

49. Ibid., p. 78.

50. Kenneth Clark, Dark Ghetto: Dilemmas of Social Power (New York, 1965) p. 11.

51. Robert Blauner, "Internal Colonialism and Ghetto Revolt," Social Problems, Vol. 16 (Spring, 1969) pp. 107-108.

52. Stanford Lyman, Asian in the West (Reno, 1971) p. 44.

53. Clark, op. cit., pp. 11-12.

54. Barth, op. cit., p. 4.

55. Ping Chiu, op. cit., p. 25.

56. Henry George, op. cit.

57. Chinn, op. cit., p. 31.

58. Saxton, op. cit., p. 53.

59. Barth, op. cit., p. 111.

60. Ibid., p. 3.

61. Chinn, op. cit., p. 10.

62. Sandmeyer, op. cit., p. 20.

63. Mark Twain, Roughing It.

64. Barth, op. cit., p. 110.

65. Chinn, op. cit., p. 10.

66. Lyman (1970), op. cit., p. 72.

67. Saxton, op. cit., p. 4.

68. Chinn, op. cit., p. 56.

69. Saxton, op. cit., p. 4.

70. Carey McWilliams, California the Great Exception (New York, 1949), p. 152.

71. Chinn, op. cit., p. 38.

72. Saxton, op. cit., p. 207.

73. Henry George, op. cit.

74. Saxton, op. cit., p. 209.

75. Ibid., p. 149.

76. Ibid., pp. 243-244.

77. Richard H. Dillon, The Hatchet Men (New York, 1962), p. 47.

78. Martyn J. Bowden, "The Dynamics of City Growth: An Historical Geography of the San Francisco Central District, 1850-1931," unpublished Ph.D. dissertation, University of California, Berekeley, 1967, p. 58.

79. Ibid., p. 308.

80. Helen V. Cather, "History of San Francisco's Chinatown," unpublished M.A. thesis, University of California, Berkeley, 1932, p. 44.

81. Barth, op. cit., p. 110.

82. Coolidge, op. cit., p. 411.

83. Sandmeyer, op. cit., p. 21.

84. Lyman (1970), op. cit., p. 78.

85. Saxton, op. cit., p. 168.

86. Ibid., p. 147.

87. Dillon, op. cit., p. 47.

88. Saxton, op. cit., p. 230.

89. Nee, op. cit., p. 54.

90. Saxton, op. cit., p. 231.

91. Nee, op. cit., p. 56.

92. Eliot Grinnell Mears, Resident Orientals on the American Pacific Coast (Palo Alto, 1927) pp. 138, 166.

93. Nee, op. cit., p. 148.

94. "The Chinese Family in San Francisco," A Group Research Report, University of California, Department of Social Welfare, Berkeley, 1966, p. 15.

95. Rose Hum Lee (1960), op. cit., p. 303.

96. Ibid., pp. 305-306.

97. S. W. Kung, op. cit., p. 89.

98. Nee, op. cit., p. 148.

CHAPTER FOUR

RACIAL CONSTRAINTS ON THE STRUCTURE
OF CHINESE SETTLEMENT

Introduction

Early Chinese settlement in the East Bay Region of San Francisco was the result of an unrelenting search for new economic opportunities. The pioneer Chinese in the East Bay, unlike their countrymen in San Francisco, wished to extricate themselves from the crowded confines and web of obligations which had turned San Francisco Chinatown into a city within a city during the 1870's. The experience of the Chinese in the East Bay is at least in this respect more indicative of Chinese settlement patterns in other cities in the United States where communities functioned mainly as social and commercial centers. San Francisco Chinatown, the largest concentration of Chinese settlement outside of Asia, has functioned uniquely as a symbolic center and city of refuge and is thus an interesting but not representative case of settlement patterns.

This chapter will examine the impact of racism on the structural evolution of Chinese settlement in the East Bay. Like their countrymen to the east, the Chinese in the East Bay had to adapt without the security of a large Chinatown in order to survive in the face of racial violence and restrictions. Their adaptation reveals the kinds of barriers which other minorities, as well as other Chinese communities outside the San Francisco Bay Area, had to confront in their efforts to settle beyond the security of the ghetto. Although racial discrimination against Asian-Americans is now more covert, racism in California has historically been aimed squarely at Asians who constituted the largest racial minority in the state until World War II.

Pioneer Chinese in the East Bay Region

The Chinese first arrived in the East Bay during the 1850's when labor shortages developed due to the Gold Rush. Buildings in San Francisco were erected quickly and carelessly, resulting in many fires. Sawmills were established across the Bay in Brooklyn or what is now East Oakland as early as 1849 and stores emerged to serve the lumbermen's needs. [1] Chinese loggers and mill operators were among the first to populate the town's wooded hills. Opportunities in the thriving orchards, vegetable gardens, and shrimp fisheries attracted Chinese farm laborers and fishermen into Alameda County, which supported 193 Chinese by 1860. [2] The tremendous growth of the county population from only 8741 in 1860 to 62,171 in 1880 widened the market for Chinese labor during this period.

Chinese railroad workers helped to turn Oakland into the principal rail terminus in the state during the 1860's. Temescal Dam, completed in 1869 to supply Oakland's burgeoning population with water, was built by armies of Chinese workers. [3] Chinese domestic servants (house boys) were employed by many of the well-to-do suburbanites of Berkeley, Alameda, and Piedmont. Most of the fresh fruit, vegetables, and fish sold in Oakland during the 1870's and 1880's was peddled by members of the Chinese "Basket Brigade." Chinese peddlers arrived early each morning at the wharf and proceeded in single file toward their various routes, carrying their produce in two 100 lb. baskets suspended by a pole. [4] Chinese operatives proved indispensable to the manufacturing of cotton bags in East Oakland (Brooklyn) during the 1870's. [5] By 1870, the Chinese population of Alameda County had soared to 1939, of which less than half (906) resided in Oakland. The early Chinese were widely dispersed, because jobs were widely scattered.

Oakland, which did not even become the county seat until 1873, managed to support a small but viable Chinatown by 1880, when the Chinese population of Alameda County reached 4386. Chinese laundries were established in Oakland and Berkeley by the 1870's. [6] Retail stores, employment offices, and community service agencies emerged to serve the surging Chinese population of the county. [7] Centrally located and readily accessible by ferry and

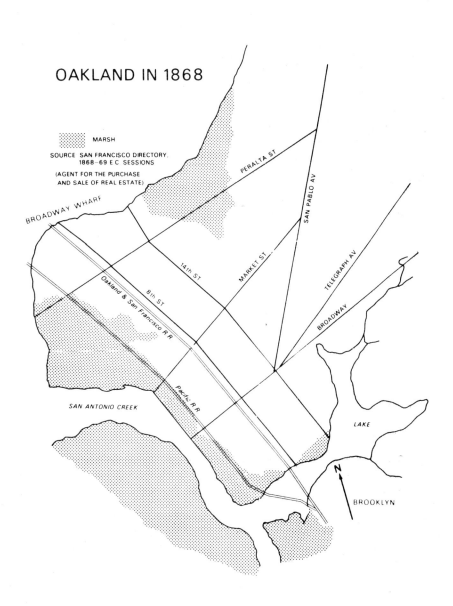

OAKLAND IN 1868

MARSH

SOURCE SAN FRANCISCO DIRECTORY,
1868–69 E C SESSIONS

(AGENT FOR THE PURCHASE
AND SALE OF REAL ESTATE)

BROADWAY WHARF

PERALTA ST

SAN PABLO AV

MARKET ST

TELEGRAPH AV

14th ST

8th ST

Oakland & San Francisco R R

BROADWAY

Pacific R R

SAN ANTONIO CREEK

LAKE

N

BROOKLYN

rail to employment opportunities in different areas of the East Bay, Oakland Chinatown functioned as the major commercial and social center of the Chinese population in the region.

Jobs in agriculture provided new opportunities for Chinese laborers out of work with the decline of gold mining and the completion of the Central Pacific Railroad in 1869. Hundreds of Chinese were attracted to the vegetable gardens and fruit orchards of Fruitvale, Hayward, San Leandro, Castro Valley, and Alvarado, where the demand for low wage labor was most acute. According to Ping Chiu, 359 Chinese farm laborers and 109 gardeners worked in Alameda County in 1870. Although the number of Chinese gardeners dropped to 72 by 1880, the number of Chinese farm laborers in the county rose to 825--more than any other county in the state! The number of Chinese farmers in Alameda County in 1880 was 244.[8] Seven percent of the county's population was Chinese in 1870, ranging as high as 14.2 percent in Brooklyn Township (Fruitvale).[9] The Chinese thus played a vital role in labor intensive farming.

Opportunities in rural Contra Costa County were much less inviting. Employment in the infant hide and tallow industry, grain farming, and coal mining during the 1860's and 1870's remained closed to Chinese workers. Although almost every community in northwestern Contra Costa County, except Clayton, had at least one Chinese in 1875, only a few towns had more than a few Chinese. San Pablo with 19, Pacheco with 17, and Antioch with 14 Chinese were the leading centers of Chinese settlement in the county.[10] Only 160 Chinese resided in the county in 1870, comprising less than 2 percent of the total population. Without railroad connections until 1878, the county suffered a late start.

Thousands of acres of reclaimed tule lands in the northern part of the county, near the Sacramento Delta, were leased to Chinese and Italian gardeners, who supplied San Francisco with vegetables.[11] By 1880, the county supported 128 Chinese gardeners and 162 Chinese farmers.[12] Chinese laborers and a Chinese cook were employed at the Martinez fruit ranch of Dr. John Strentzel, father-in-law of John Muir and widely regarded as a pioneer in California horticulture. Chinese shrimp fishermen, who camped just south of Point Molate, fished the waters of San Pablo Bay and peddled their catch in Richmond long before the turn of the century.[13] Of the 2500 fishermen in the Bay Area in 1893, about one-quarter were Chinese.[14] Chinese factory workers were employed in Martinez fish canneries during the late 1870's. By 1880, 732 Chinese resided in Contra Costa County, comprising 5.8 percent of the total population. They helped to initiate the county's horticultural growth.

Racial Agitation in the East Bay

The wave of racial violence which had uprooted thousands of Chinese in California during the late 1870's also spread to the East Bay. Although the total population of the two counties nearly doubled between 1880 and 1890, the Chinese population declined by 45 percent during the same period, after decades of steady growth. The Chinese in Oakland, many of whom decided to brave the turbulence, were admired by their brethren who had taken refuge in San Francisco.[15] The "men of Oakland" were typical of Chinese in other cities and towns in California who were determined to make the urban "frontier" their home.

Riots and assaults upon the Chinese in the Bay Area had become so numerous in the 1870's that they were advised to stay out of sight, "lest they be massacred in cold blood."[16] The unemployment, labor strife, bankruptcies, and general unrest which followed the Panic of 1873 also erupted into anti-Chinese demonstrations in Oakland.[17] Anti-coolie clubs paraded in Oakland in 1876 and threatened the residents of Chinatown.[18] Several uproarious meetings held by Dennis Kearney's Workingmen's Party at Oakland in 1878, ignited racial tensions.[19] Secret societies, like the Central Pacific Anti-Coolie Association, capitalized on the Chinese issue to further the economic interests of employers. By 1880, unemployed demonstrators had forced Pacific Jute Mills in Oakland to discharge 800 Chinese workers.[20]

Local politicians likewise exploited the Chinese to their advantage. The election

EARLY RESTRICTIONS AGAINST CHINESE LAUNDRIES IN OAKLAND

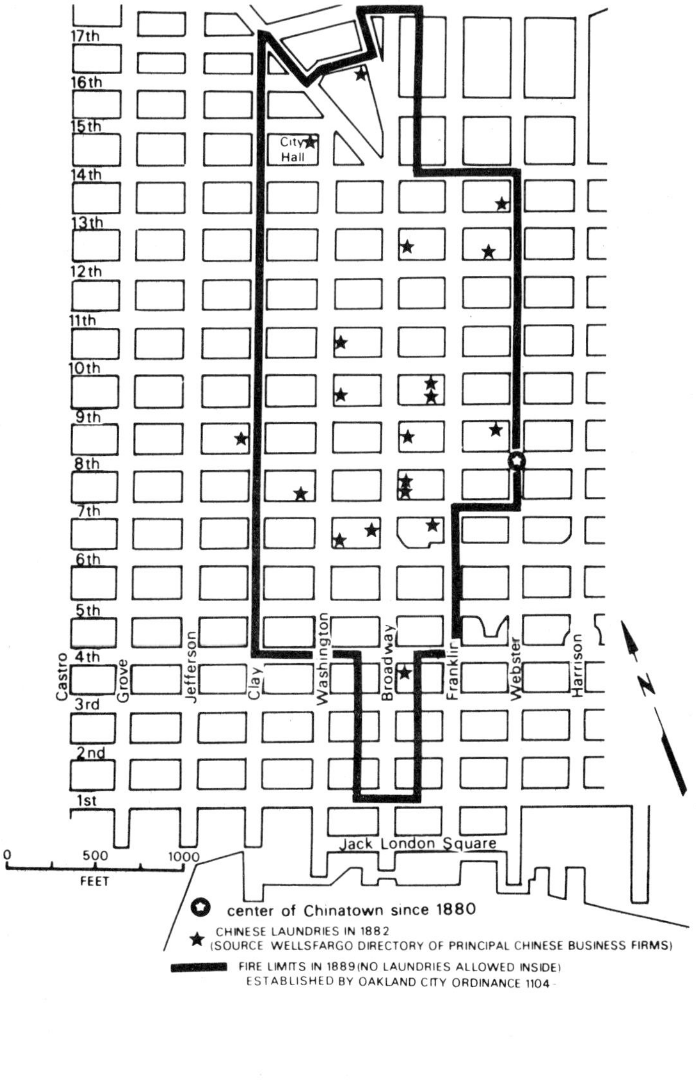
17th
16th
15th
14th
13th
12th
11th
10th
9th
8th
7th
6th
5th
4th
3rd
2nd
1st
City Hall
Castro
Grove
Jefferson
Clay
Washington
Broadway
Franklin
Webster
Harrison
N
Jack London Square
0
500
1000
FEET
center of Chinatown since 1880
CHINESE LAUNDRIES IN 1882
(SOURCE WELLSFARGO DIRECTORY OF PRINCIPAL CHINESE BUSINESS FIRMS)
FIRE LIMITS IN 1889(NO LAUNDRIES ALLOWED INSIDE)
ESTABLISHED BY OAKLAND CITY ORDINANCE 1104

of J. W. Bones as State Senator from Alameda County in 1878 paved the way for victories by other Workingmen's Party candidates throughout the state, including San Leandro and Berkeley.[21] Oakland's Mayor, J. E. Blethen, called a big mass meeting in 1882 to protest against Chinese immigration.[22] The Chinese were in the words of Alexander Saxton an "indispensable enemy."

The Chinese in Contra Costa County fared no better. Resentment against Chinese competition in manufacturing and in fishing was long standing. Anti-Chinese riots had broken out at Martinez as early as 1871.[23] Unprovoked assaults against Chinese employees of a salmon cannery in Martinez in 1882 by large numbers of boys and Greek and Italian fishermen drove the Chinese out of the industry.[24] Attempts by Greek, Italian, and Dalmatian fishermen to legislate the Chinese out of shrimp fishing by regulating the size of nets in the 1870's and requiring monthly fishing licenses in the 1880's were less effective than violence. The Chinese shrimp industry survived until it became a victim of water pollution at the end of World War II.[25] Not until 1960 did Contra Costa's Chinese population regain its 1880 level.

Oakland City Ordinance 1104, passed in 1889, prohibited the establishment of laundries within the "fire limits" of Oakland.[26] All of the 16 Chinese laundries which had concentrated in this area prior to the ordinance had moved or gone out of business by 1909 (see Map 4). City Ordinance 1298, passed in 1891, banned the vending of meats, fruits, vegetables, berries, or any other produce in the streets of Oakland.[27] Organized in 1878 against the "Basket Brigade," the Merchants Exchange and Free Market of Oakland succeeded in eliminating most of its Chinese competition by the turn of the century.[28] The Laundry Worker's Union of Alameda County (No. 55) continued to press for anti-Chinese legislation and was one of the most vocal labor organizations at the Chinese Exclusion Convention held in San Francisco in 1901. Oakland's delegation of labor organizations to the convention was exceeded in number only by that of San Francisco.[29] Periodic unemployment became a way of life for most of the Chinese laborers in Oakland during this period.

Racism and the Growth of Oakland Chinatown

Conditions in early Oakland were exacerbated by racial violence and organized resistance. Chinese settlement in Oakland was beset by political as well as economic uncertainties. According to Edward W. Chew, the city kept relocating Chinatown Oakland until the 1880's. Initially situated on the east side of Telegraph Avenue between 16th and 17th Streets, it burned down in 1867. Oakland's second Chinatown was located on the east side of San Pablo Avenue between 19th and 20th Streets, but was soon displaced even farther out to San Pablo and 22nd Street.[30] City Hall, which had been located on Broadway between Third and Fourth Streets since 1852, was moved north to 14th and Washington in 1869. The new site reflected the northward expansion of the central Business District during the 1860's. Chinatown, which consisted of one-story shacks, apparently stood in the way of this "progress" (see Map 5).

Chinatown Number Four, reassigned to the western edge of town on First Street between Castro and Bush, was selected because it was owned by one of the city fathers.[31] The fifth and present site, centered at 8th and Webster, was not established until the late 1870's. Situated in the heart of the "Old City," Chinatown was surrounded by warehouses, factories, rooming houses, and junk yards.[32] Having little choice, the Chinese remained nestled in Oakland's "zone of discard" for the next fifty years. Chinatown Oakland, after such a tumultuous beginning, never really became the kind of symbolic place to which the Chinese in San Francisco were so emotionally attached. Adaptation to systematic displacement had become a way of life in a "climate" of racial hostility.

The threat of displacement did not fade. The Constitution of California, passed in 1879, authorized cities and towns to remove the Chinese from municipal limits or to segregate them within municipalities. Although ruled unconstitutional by a Federal Court in 1890, a state-sanctioned policy of racial segregation in housing prevailed throughout most of the 19th century period.[33] Boarding houses in Chinatown catered to the housing

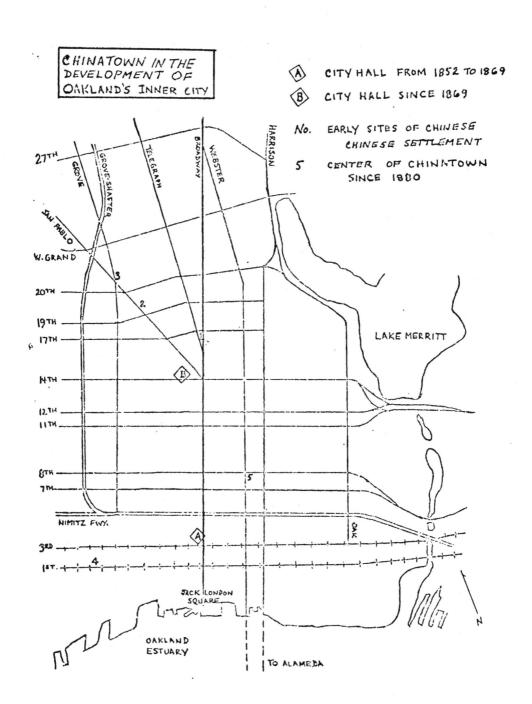

CHINATOWN IN THE
DEVELOPMENT OF
OAKLAND'S INNER CITY

Ⓐ CITY HALL FROM 1852 TO 1869
Ⓑ CITY HALL SINCE 1869

No. EARLY SITES OF CHINESE
       CHINESE SETTLEMENT

5 CENTER OF CHINATOWN
    SINCE 1880

27TH

GROVE
GROVE-SHAFTER
TELEGRAPH
BROADWAY
WEBSTER
HARRISON

SAN PABLO

W. GRAND

3

20TH

2

19TH

17TH

1

LAKE MERRITT

Ⓑ

14TH

12TH

11TH

8TH

7TH

5

NIMITZ FWY.

OAK

Ⓐ

3RD

1ST

4

JACK LONDON
SQUARE

N

OAKLAND
ESTUARY

TO ALAMEDA

needs of "transient" Chinese laborers. Commercial establishments serving the needs of Chinese workers were concentrated in the quarter, bounded by roughly Broadway and Harrison and by 6th and 10th Streets. In 1882, Chinatown included one doctor, one tailor, two barbers, two restaurants, one retail opium dealer, one butcher/druggist, two pork/grocery stores, one dry goods/grocery store, one fruit and cake retailer, one general merchandise store, and four employment offices.[34] Labor contractors became essential as employment became less secure.

In contrast, Chinese laundries were widely dispersed, because they served a growing non-Chinese market. Although seven were located in Chinatown, 27 were located elsewhere in Oakland (three in East Oakland, six in West Oakland, and 18 in the rest of the Inner City). The Christian missions which served the Chinese were likewise located outside of Chinatown in 1882. The Baptist Chinese YMCA, the Chinese Presbyterian Church and Christian Association, the Chinese Mission of the Methodist Church, and the Congregational Association of Christian Chinese nevertheless played a vital role in the community.[35] They taught the Chinese English, acted as their spokesmen, protected them against violence, and established "rescue homes" for women in concubinage and prostitution.[36] Oakland, the "City of Spires," boasted about 40 churches by 1880.[37] Churches provided an early avenue for acculturation.

By the 1890's, however, economic opportunities had become so restricted that many Chinese left the East Bay. The Chinese population of Alameda County plummeted from 4386 in 1880 to 3311 in 1890, while that of Contra Costa dropped from 732 to 465 during the same period. Both the number and variety of commercial establishments in Chinatown diminished. Only four general merchandise stores, a butcher/druggist, and a general merchandise/butcher were listed in 1892.[38] A small two-story building on Washington between 7th and 8th Streets, a Chinese-Japanese Bazaar on Washington between 13th and 14th Streets, were the only Chinese establishments to be listed in the Central Business District in 1896.[39] In the wake of community fragmentation, the tongs gained strength. Gambling dens had become common in Oakland before the turn of the century.[40] The Chinese population of the city sagged to 950 by 1900 as exploitation from without gave rise to exploitation from within the Chinese community.

Chinese laundries, ousted from downtown Oakland, emerged in Berkeley to the west of Stanford, Adeline, and Shattuck Avenues.[41] According to Rev. Edward Lee, the Chinese who settled in the East Bay after the Railroad Era were mostly houseboys.[42] The Chinese populations of Alameda and Berkeley reached 255 and 154, respectively, by 1900. The shaky foundations of Chinatown Oakland wavered in a period of intense agitation. Opposition to Chinese labor in Oakland was voiced by labor organizations in the industrial and building trades as well as in the retail service sector.[43] The growth of manufacturing in Alameda County, well under way by 1904, offered the Chinese little prospect of employment.[44] Not until 1906 did the Chinese population in the East Bay begin to revive.

Adjusting to Rapid Growth

The San Francisco earthquake and conflagration of April 18, 1906, left the East Bay cities relatively unscathed. Boatloads of refugees from San Francisco arrived at the Oakland Pier, at the Estuary, or wherever they could get a landing. An estimated 100,000 to 150,000 refugees were sheltered in Oakland during that week.[45] Relief camps were set up throughout the city, including a large camp for Chinese refugees between 8th and 9th Streets near Lake Merritt.[46] Thousands of Chinese from San Francisco Chinatown, which lay in ruins, sought shelter in Oakland Chinatown. According to the Oakland Tribune:

> San Francisco's hoards (sic) of Chinese is fleeing in terror from the stricken city and Chinatown there. . . . These Chinese are coming to Oakland in vast throngs and the local Chinatown is being flooded with their numbers. That section will probably be overrun with Mongolians before night.[47]

Driven to the brink of economic collapse by over three decades of racial

DOWNTOWN OAKLAND IN 1882

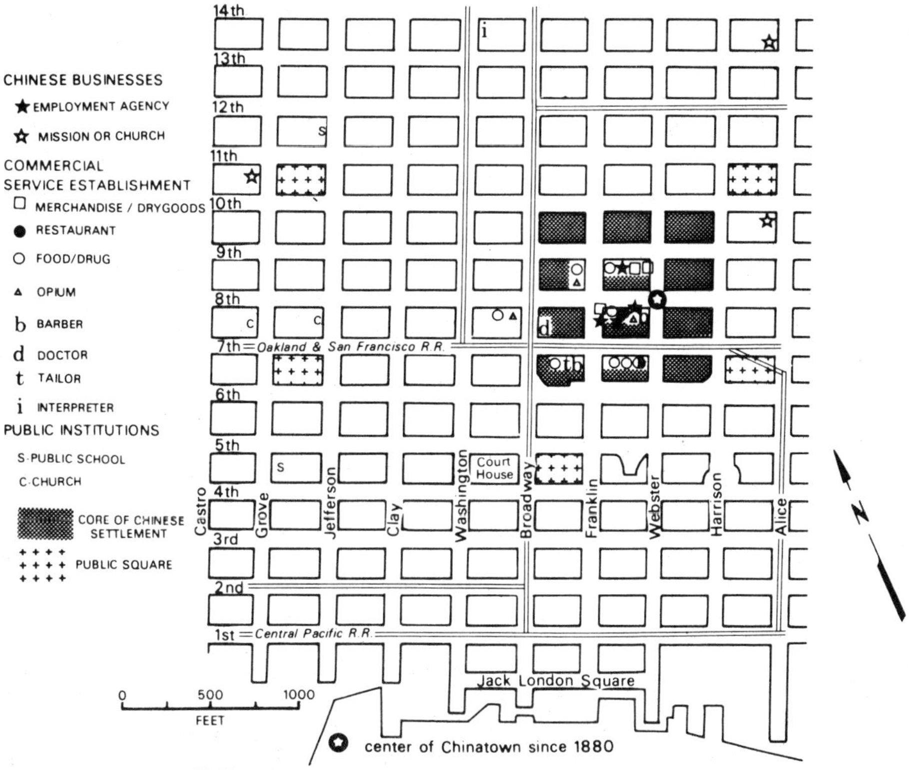

CHINESE BUSINESSES
★ EMPLOYMENT AGENCY
☆ MISSION OR CHURCH

COMMERCIAL
SERVICE ESTABLISHMENT
□ MERCHANDISE / DRYGOODS
● RESTAURANT
○ FOOD/DRUG
▲ OPIUM
b BARBER
d DOCTOR
t TAILOR
i INTERPRETER

PUBLIC INSTITUTIONS
S·PUBLIC SCHOOL
C·CHURCH

▓ CORE OF CHINESE SETTLEMENT
+ + + + PUBLIC SQUARE

14th
13th
12th
11th
10th
9th
8th
7th = Oakland & San Francisco R.R.
6th
5th
4th
3rd
2nd
1st = Central Pacific R.R.

Castro
Grove
Jefferson
Clay
Washington
Court House
Broadway
Franklin
Webster
Harrison
Alice

N

0   500   1000
FEET

Jack London Square

⊙ center of Chinatown since 1880

SOURCE WELLS FARGO DIRECTORY OF PRINCIPAL CHINESE BUSINESS HOUSES

53

agitation and systematic restriction, Chinatown rallied to meet the disaster. Clan leaders helped to coordinate assistance and assure city officials that new capital investments would be forthcoming from San Francisco's Chinese merchants.[48] Temporary shelter was made available in the Chinese quarter, where familiar surroundings, customs, dialects, and institutions eased the suffering of thousands of Chinese refugees. Oakland's Chinese population tripled between 1900 and 1910. Lack of employment and housing, however, caused most to return to San Francisco Chinatown, where efforts to oust the Chinese were revived.[49] Attempts to move the Chinese to Hunter's Point failed and symbolic San Francisco Chinatown was rebuilt.

Still bursting at the seams in 1909, Chinatown Oakland supported 3 boarding houses, which emerged to accommodate the city's Chinese newcomers.[50] The Suey Sing Tong, situated in the heart of Chinatown Oakland, also capitalized on the resurgence of the quarter. The earthquake and fires of 1906, which wiped out the brothels, gambling dens, and tong headquarters of San Francisco, prompted many of the hatchetmen to relocate in Oakland, as well as in other cities with large Chinese populations.[51] Gambling houses lined a whole block along Webster Street and tong wars would break every so often.[52] Clan associations (the Lims, Gees, Chans, and Lows, for example), mainly headquartered on Eighth Street, looked after members' needs.[53] Cigar, cigar box, and ladies underwear factories were established by 1909 to provide Chinese laborers with menial jobs; labor contractors furnished them with employment information and contracts.[54] Chinatown Oakland, a city for refugees, was becoming a city within a city.

The tong and clan associations, which acquired increasing control over the Chinese in Oakland after the earthquake of 1906, encountered more resistance in the East Bay than they had in San Francisco. Christian missions, founded in the 19th century, were joined by the Episcopal "True Sunshine" missions. The Presbyterian, Baptist, Methodist and Episcopal missions, initially located in temporary accommodations outside the Chinese quarter, expanded their programs into new and larger accommodations within Chinatown.[55] Open to all, without regard to district, clan, or tong affiliation, they provided continuing alternatives to the traditional mutual aid associations which had heightened social dependence in San Francisco.

The Oakland chapter of the Native Sons of the Golden State, which later became the Chinese American Citizen's Alliance, was established in 1912 as a champion of Chinese assimilation and an advocate of Chinese civil rights.[56] Comprised mainly of businessmen, the C.A.C.A. has been the foremost organization in the Oakland Chinese community since its inception and growth after the earthquake.[57] Chinatown commercial establishments, diversifying with the increase in the East Bay Chinese population from 2838 in 1900 to 5138 in 1910, provided the basis for C.A.C.A. strength. The Chinese Six Companies, headquartered in San Francisco, were never able to penetrate into Oakland. In the face of continuing anti-Chinese discrimination, the Chinese in the East Bay nevertheless were able to rely on alternative avenues of mutual assistance and social mobility.

Early Patterns of Residential Confinement

Although Chinese laundry men, quartered in the rear or above their establishments, and domestic servants housed where they worked, had dispersed outside of Chinatown long before the turn of the century, few Chinese residents managed to acquire property in the residential areas of the East Bay before 1920. Restrictive covenants, legally enforceable until 1848, were made to contain the spread of non-white minorities during the 1920's into the newly built working-class homes in East Oakland as well as into the newer upper-class districts in the hills.

Not until 1906, however, were legal restrictions even necessary. Residential segregation had been a way of life. The Chinese had neither the income or the power to challenge the system in a period of sporadic racial violence. A wealthy landowner in East Oakland, for example, was publicly chastised for leasing a house to Chinese victims of the earthquake of 1906. Chinese merchants from San Francisco, routed from their homes in Chinatown, were so desperate in 1906 that they dressed like whites and wore their hair cropped in hopes of finding housing in East Oakland.[58]   Chinese refugees in Oakland were assigned to Chinatown, where they would be less of a threat.[59]

Overcrowded housing and rising rents forced many Chinese to seek accommodations outside of Chinatown. Although excluded from the better residential areas, many dispersed into the northwestern sector of the Inner City. By 1920, the Chinese were about equally distributed among Chinatown, the rest of the Inner City, and the North Oakland-South Berkeley sector of the city. However, covenants kept about three-fourths of the Chinese in the East Bay in Oakland until the 1950's (see Table 5).

Economic opportunities in Berkeley, which sheltered hundreds of Chinese refugees, remained too limited to maintain a large Chinese community. Although its Chinese population jumped from 154 in 1900 to 451 in 1910, it fell to 337 by 1920. Established Chinese families with businesses in San Francisco or in the East Bay were attracted to the flats of south Berkeley. The city gradually became a "professional" town for non-whites as well as whites.[60]   Occupational barriers nevertheless kept the town out of reach for most until World War II.

One of the major stumbling blocks to the dispersal of the Chinese was the limited number of families in the East Bay. Thwarted by anti-miscegenation laws and immigration restrictions, family households remained the exception and not the rule until the end of World War II. Females comprised only 13.5 and 14.5 percent of the Chinese populations in San Francisco and Oakland, respectively, in 1910. Oakland Chinatown, like its neighbor across the bay, remained a bachelor society until 1950. The American dream of a single-family detached house in the suburbs was beyond the reach of most Chinese. Some bribed merchants to list them as business partners in order to exempt their wives from the Exclusion Act of 1882.[61]   The overwhelming majority of Chinese immigrants entering between 1882 and 1924, when a new law prohibited this practice, were classified as members of merchants' families.[62]   Laundrymen, restaurant operators, and even laborers who accumulated enough wealth were among the few Chinese who could bring in their wives and raise families.

Although most Chinese settled in or near Oakland Chinatown, where their special social, recreational, and personal needs could most conveniently be met, it was not solely by choice. Discriminatory housing practices excluded them from the better residential districts of the city.

The Mechanics of Residential Segregation

Legitimized by the Age of Regulation following World War I, the rise of city planning in the United States from 1910 to 1930 paved the way for residential zoning.[63]   The adoption of New York City's first zoning ordinance in 1916 set the precedent for cities across the country. In California, the State Supreme Court declared in 1925:

> In addition to all that has been said in support of the constitutionality of residential zoning as part of a comprehensive plan, we think it may be safely and sensibly said that justification for residential zoning may, in the final analysis, be rested upon the protection of the civic and social values of the American home.[64]

The United States Supreme Court, after upholding broad zoning authority for localities in 1926, still honors the decisions of local boards. Racially restrictive covenants, drawn to insure the development of white residential communities, became the major device used by the National Association of Real Estate Boards to create segregated districts.[65]

Gresham's Law of Neighborhoods was adopted by real estate theoreticians and engraved in textbooks. This law read that just as bad dollars drive out good dollars, so people of the wrong race, complexion, or status will drive out good people and drive down property values. This restatement of racism's pivotal principle formed the basis for the discriminatory code of ethics governing members of the NAREB and openly underlay the thinking of F.H.A. officials, lenders, and other housing agencies until 1965.[66]   Rooted in the

TABLE 5

PERCENTAGE OF EAST BAY CHINESE IN OAKLAND

	Chinese Population	Percentage Chinese	Percentage of Chinese in the East Bay Residing in Oakland
1860			
Alameda	193	2.2	
Contra Costa	2	0.4	
East Bay	195	1.4	
1870			
Alameda	1939	8.0	
Contra Costa	160	1.9	
East Bay	2099	6.4	43.1
1880			
Alameda	4386	7.0	
Contra Costa	732	5.8	
East Bay	5118	6.8	38.6
1890			
Alameda	3311	3.5	
Contra Costa	465	3.4	
East Bay	3776	3.5	29.9
1900			
Alameda	2211	1.7	
Contra Costa	627	3.5	
East Bay	2838	1.9	33.4
1910			
Alameda	4588	1.9	
Contra Costa	550	1.7	
East Bay	5138	1.8	70.3
1920			
Alameda	4505	1.3	
Contra Costa	343	0.6	
East Bay	4848	1.2	79.0
1930			
Alameda	3700	0.8	
Contra Costa	330	0.4	
East Bay	4030	0.7	74.88
1940			
Alameda	3947	0.8	
Contra Costa	219	0.2	
East Bay	4166	0.7	76.9
1950			
Alameda	7760	1.0	
Contra Costa	438	0.1	
East Bay	8198	0.8	69.8

TABLE 5

(Continued)

	Chinese Population	Percentage Chinese	Percentage of Chinese in the East Bay Residing in Oakland
1960			
Alameda	11913	1.3	
Contra Costa	1006	0.2	
East Bay	12919	1.0	40.7
1970			
Alameda	20072	1.9	
Contra Costa	3086	0.6	
East Bay	23158	1.4	49.0

ecological models of the Chicago School of Urban Sociology in the 1920's, the threat of "invasion and succession" became a self-fulfilling prophecy under the direction of realtors and neighborhood associations.

Fears of declining property values, although thoroughly undercut by studies during the late 1950's at the University of California at Berkeley, were nevertheless elevated to credibility by those who had the most to gain by segregation.[67] Bigotry by individuals, which persists, could not have created or maintained the segregated pattern of housing that crystallized in the East Bay after 1920. The institutionalization of prejudice required the concerted efforts of many parties, who were able to scare and pressure unbiased individuals to cooperate as a means of protecting communal or property values. The old notions about neighborhood homogeneity, the property maintenance habits of non-white families, and impact of race on property values continued to influence the decisions of lenders during the 1960's. After so many decades without challenge, they had become sacred.

Developers in the East Bay seized the idea of racial exclusiveness as a promotional tool. In actuality, it was the search for a distinctive lifestyle in a sequestered residential area, not the demand for racial homogeneity, that launched the growth of suburbs.[68] Middle-class households, which differentiated more sharply between private and public space than working-class households, tend to be more concerned about the physical character and property value of their surroundings than about its social composition.[69] Every neighborhood has a few "bad apples." The fear that a few "bad apples" would necessarily lead to racial swamping and to physical and symbotic degradation was created by block-busting real estate practices and by organized groups of property owners.

Few sellers suffered financial losses by dealing with minority buyers unless they panicked. Most profited or at least broke even from the dual housing market. Artificial shortages in housing for upward bound minority families bid up the price and rent in "unrestricted" areas. Many sellers, who profited handsomely from selling their property in "unrestricted" areas, moved to better accommodations in "restricted" districts, where the demand for housing was relatively low and prices were much more reasonable. Acting through local real estate boards and financial intermediaries, realtors were able to divide the market along racial lines and thus distort the process of filtering.

Panic selling meant higher turnover, which resulted in more commissions and more opportunities to profit from personal investments. Although the separation of the two housing markets was legally enforceable and widely observed, the inevitable uncertainties, ambiguities, and obsolescence of the system enabled realtors to create new "unrestricted" areas in response to increases in minority demands. Racially restricted areas, although perceived as real places, were inherently impossible to delineate and maintain. Minority households, unable to distinguish between "restricted" and "unrestricted" residential

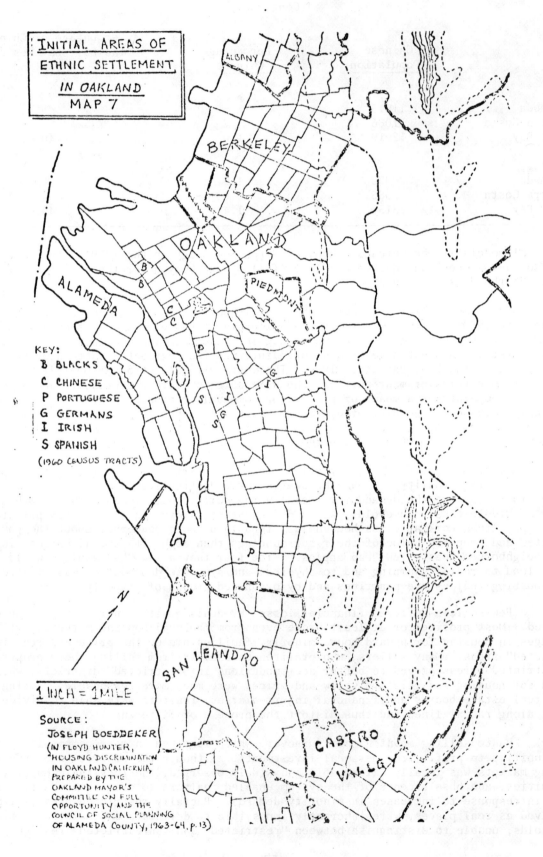

INITIAL AREAS OF
ETHNIC SETTLEMENT
IN OAKLAND
MAP 7

ALBANY

BERKELEY

OAKLAND

PIEDMONT

ALAMEDA

KEY:
B BLACKS
C CHINESE
P PORTUGUESE
G GERMANS
I IRISH
S SPANISH
(1960 CENSUS TRACTS)

N

SAN LEANDRO

CASTRO VALLEY

1 INCH = 1 MILE

SOURCE:
JOSEPH BOEDDEKER
(IN FLOYD HUNTER,
"HOUSING DISCRIMINATION
IN OAKLAND CALIFORNIA"
PREPARED BY THE
OAKLAND MAYOR'S
COMMITTEE ON FULL
OPPORTUNITY AND THE
COUNCIL OF SOCIAL PLANNING
OF ALAMEDA COUNTY, 1963-64, p.13)

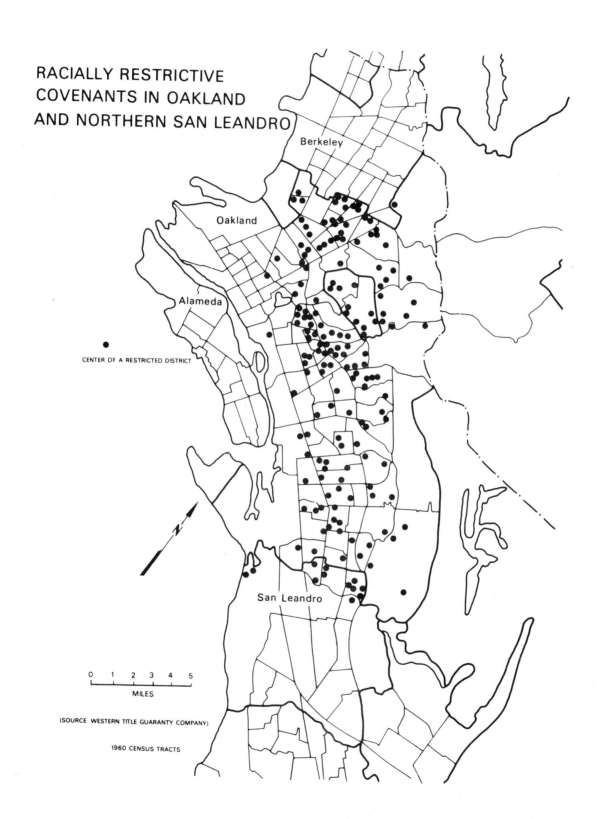

RACIALLY RESTRICTIVE
COVENANTS IN OAKLAND
AND NORTHERN SAN LEANDRO

Berkeley

Oakland

Alameda

● CENTER OF A RESTRICTED DISTRICT

N

San Leandro

0 1 2 3 4 5
MILES

(SOURCE: WESTERN TITLE GUARANTY COMPANY)

1960 CENSUS TRACTS

property, were forced to rely on realtors. Sellers who were not opposed to non-white buyers were forced to seek the assistance of sympathetic and knowledgeable realtors and lenders who were able to deal with the problems of racial barriers.

Associations of homeowners rose to the forefront of civic life and community esteem. Although many association leaders believed that property values would decline, most also shared racist beliefs. Concealed in liberty and dedicated to the proposition that non-white neighbors would be less than equal, their convictions made the system work. Without organized pressure groups to prod the unwilling, "restricted" areas would have been little more than a realtor's ideal. The prospect of non-white neighbors, which gradually became viable after 1920, summoned them to defend their communities against the threat of "invasion and succession."

Segregation of the Chinese in the East Bay

The practice of housing discrimination in the East Bay reflects patterns exhibited by other areas in the country. Made possible by legal sanctions and racist attitudes, discrimination in housing has always existed in this region. The impact of racial discrimination on the evolution of Chinese settlement in the East Bay may be divided for analytical purposes into four periods, each with its own bearings.

The first 70 years of Chinese settlement in the region may be characterized by intense anti-Chinese agitation, few Chinese families, marginal employment opportunities, and restricted legal rights. Chinese demand for single-family housing remained negligible, except after 1906 when Chinese merchants from San Francisco tried to acquire property. During the second period from 1920 to 1940, slowly improving opportunities and attitudes resulted in selective dispersal and sporadic barriers to settlement. The third phase, 1940-1960, witnessed dramatic improvements in opportunities and accelerated household formation. Not until World War II. however, was the demand for housing large enough to warrant concerted and systematic discrimination by realtors and homeowners' associations. The final period since 1960 has been marked by fair housing legislation, occupational mobility, and escalated dispersal.

The shortage of housing in Oakland during the postwar period worsened as minority populations soared and purchasing power advanced.[70] The momentum of rising land prices and even tighter supplies, implicit in the workings of the urban land ratchet, continues to mount in the absence of large scale increases in housing construction.[71] Dispersal by minority households into the newer residential areas of the East Bay have only been possible within the last decade.

The experience of the Chinese has been shared by other minority groups in the region, to varying degrees depending on the circumstances of their own situation. Those with dark complexions have been more subject to racist attitudes. Those with strong family foundations have tended to disperse more readily. Those with bi-lingual backgrounds have been less prone to disperse. The case of the Chinese may be applied to other non-white groups in the East Bay with the above considerations.

De Facto Confinement: 1920-1940.

Although excluded from the better residential districts, the Chinese were never completely restricted to Chinatown Oakland. After the earthquake, many settled at the outskirts of the Central Business District. Four clusters of Chinese residents emerged outside the quarter by 1930.[72] Two nuclei appeared along Peralta at 7th Street and at San Pablo Avenue, both in West Oakland. A third cluster developed between "Pill Hill" and Mosswood Park in North Oakland. The fourth center formed along the eastern half of Park Street in Alameda (see Map 9). Chinese settlement in South Berkeley and in East Oakland was even more scattered with no distinct clusters. The pressure of individual bigotry apparently did not constitute an effective barrier to limited Chinese dispersal into the working-class neighborhoods on the East Bay flatlands.

60

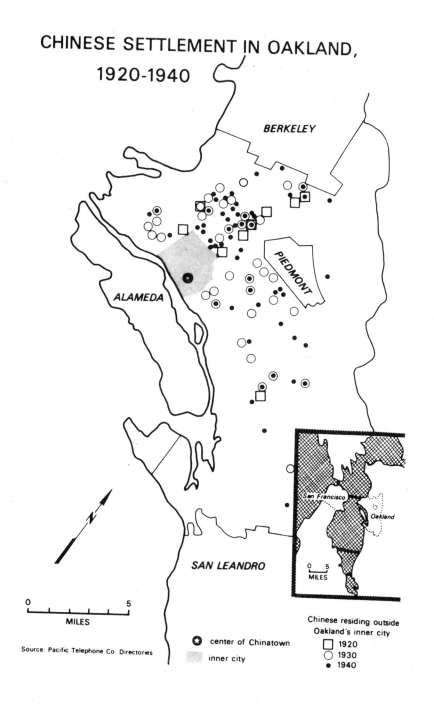

CHINESE SETTLEMENT IN OAKLAND, 1920-1940

BERKELEY

PIEDMONT

ALAMEDA

SAN LEANDRO

San Francisco

Oakland

0   5
MILES

0   5
MILES

Source: Pacific Telephone Co. Directories

⊛ center of Chinatown

inner city

Chinese residing outside
Oakland's inner city

☐ 1920
○ 1930
● 1940

As a whole, however, the Chinese were too poor and too limited in number to generate an organized backlash. The Chinese population of Oakland and Berkeley dropped from 1920 to 1930. Oakland decreased from 3821 to 3048, while Berkeley declined from 337 to 333. Immigration restrictions kept the Chinese populations of Oakland, Berkeley, and Alameda 83, 79, and 86 percent male, respectively, in 1920. Nuclear family households were the exception and not the rule. The birth rate remained low until after World War II.

Fears that the nation would be overrun after World War I led to passage of the Immigration Act of 1924. The law established a quota for each nationality group based on the number of persons of that national origin in the country in 1920. Only 105 Chinese immigrants were allowed under the quota system each year. The wives of Chinese merchants and American-born Chinese were no longer exempt from regulation, as permitted by the Exclusion Act of 1882. The Act was revised in 1930 to allow the Chinese wives of American citizens who were married before May 26, 1924, to immigrate.[73] Fears of Chinese swamping could not be kindled under such conditions.

Employment restrictions kept the Chinese out of manufacturing, construction, civil service, and the professions. Garment factories, laundries, restaurants, groceries, and general merchandise establishments provided limited markets for Chinese workers and marginal opportunities for entrepreneurs. Intense competition within these markets bid both wages and prices down, which in turn made capital accumulation difficult. Without capital, small-scale competition became a vicious circle. Chinese workers, unwelcome in the mainstream of the economy, had to accept low wages, long hours, and poor working conditions. Housing in Chinatown, with relatively low rents and minimal transport costs, enabled them to survive.

A study of labor conditions in factories employing women or minors in the Chinese quarters of San Francisco and Oakland was made in 1922 by the Industrial Welfare Commission. The following is from this study:

> Both men and women operators were employed in the factories. In some cases there were retail stores manufacturing their own products. . . . Garment making was the principal kind of work performed. In addition, there was the picking or shelling of shrimps and a small amount of miscellaneous occupations, such as basket triming, tobacco-stripping, hem stitching and embroidery, and the placing of small photographs in cardboard frames for advertising matter. . . . All work places were congregating points for youngsters who had no place to stay and would not be left at home or on the street by the working mother or grand-mother.[74]

Merchandise companies, concentrated within or on the fringe of Chinatown, were the most common form of Chinese commercial establishment in Oakland in 1920, when economic opportunities began to stagnate.[75] Opium, gambling, and prostitution were permitted to flourish in Chinatown Oakland before the Depression at a cost of $500 a day in "protection money," with city officials getting their cut.[76] The frustrations of systematic exploitation had again begun to surface. Not until the early 1930's were the underworld activities of the tongs brought to a close.

Economic opportunities during the Depression years of the 1930's continued to be limited but began to diversify as Oakland's Chinese population grew to 3201 by 1940. Lotteries became a popular source of income in Oakland until forced out by the need for Federal certification in 1943.[77] Herb retailers, meat and fish markets, doctors offices, and employment offices, all of which had emerged by 1930, were joined by a host of new Chinese restaurants. The number of Chinese restaurants in both Chinatown and the East Bay as a whole doubled between 1930 and 1940.[78] "Chop Suey Houses" and "Cafes" were opened in Berkeley and East Oakland as well as in the Central Business District of Oakland to serve Caucasian demands.

The Oakland Chinese Center was founded by Chinese business and professional men in 1935 as a community service club. Although the number of Chinese professionals had been rising since 1920, many Chinese doctors, dentists, and pharmacists had trouble getting established during this period and had to accept temporary employment outside their field.[79] Educational opportunities at the University of California paved the way for increasing Chinese settlement in Berkeley during the 1930's. Many students from China were quartered near the University by the Chinese Community Church of Berkeley which was formerly a mission of the United Church of Christ. The Chinese Students Club, headquartered at Etna and Parker Streets on the south side of campus by 1930, played a key role in the Chinese student community of the city. By 1940, 397 Chinese had settled in Berkeley.

Alameda County's Chinese population, which rose to 3927 in 1940, managed to grow as Chinese business establishments sought to meet the needs of Caucasian clientele and as San Francisco became more crowded. The Chinese population of San Francisco, after more than doubling from 7744 in 1920 to 16,330 in 1930, increased by only 9 percent to 17.782 in 1940. Construction of the San Francisco-Oakland Bay Bridge in the early 1930's made commuting more attractive to Chinese businessmen who worked in San Francisco. The Chinese population of Oakland, whose crude birth rate declined from 24.20 per thousand in 1930 to 10.65 per thousand in 1940, gained little by natural increase.[80] Not until after the war did the Chinese population of the East Bay revive.

Although commonly practiced by individuals, racial discrimination was neither profitable enough nor crucial enough to be systematically enforced by realtors or neighborhood associations. The Chinese, like Oakland's Portuguese, Italians, and Mexicans, were scattered throughout the city rather than being settled in well-defined foreign quarters.[81] Although most of the Chinese remained in the Inner City, posing no threat to the middle-class residential areas in the East Bay, Chinatown did not become a city of refuge. Dispersal into working-class neighborhoods was feasible for established Chinese families with well-paying jobs, even though discriminatory behavior by individuals was a common practice.

Occupational Dispersal: 1940-1960

World War II marked the "take-off" stage of economic growth in the San Francisco Bay Area.[82] The demand for labor multiplied so rapidly that large numbers of immigrants had to be recruited from the South to man defense plants, factories, and construction crews in the region. The population of the Bay Area increased by almost 600,000 between 1940 and 1960--the largest increase of any metropolitan area in the nation.[83] According to the California State Planning Board in 1942:

> Huge war contracts have in one year transformed the Bay Area economy
> from one of moderate peacetime activity to one of intense effort con-
> centrated in a few greatly enlarged industries. Shipbuilding, a
> near idle industry for more than twenty years, is now the Area's lar-
> gest and most important industry, employing about half as many workers
> as all other manufacturers combined.[84]

The growth of shipbuilding in the East Bay was most spectacular in Richmond, whose population swelled from 23,642 in 1940 to 110,000 in 1943. War-time activities at the Oakland Naval Depot, the Oakland Army Supply Base, and the Alameda Naval Air Station expanded greatly to meet the needs in the Pacific. The production of iron and steel, heavy machinery, and food products for the war effort brought billions of dollars in defense contracts into the East Bay cities.

Local labor shortages permitted the employment of minority workers, such as the Chinese, in the region's traditionally "restricted" industrial and construction trades. The heroic Chinese resistance against the Japanese, beginning in 1931, allayed racial fears in the interest of patriotism. Job security, vulnerable during Depression years, was no longer an issue. Thousands of Blacks were recruited by government agencies and industrial organizations. Oakland and Richmond, which housed most of these newcomers during the war, were only 2.8 and 1.1 percent Black in 1940. The Chinese remained the largest

63

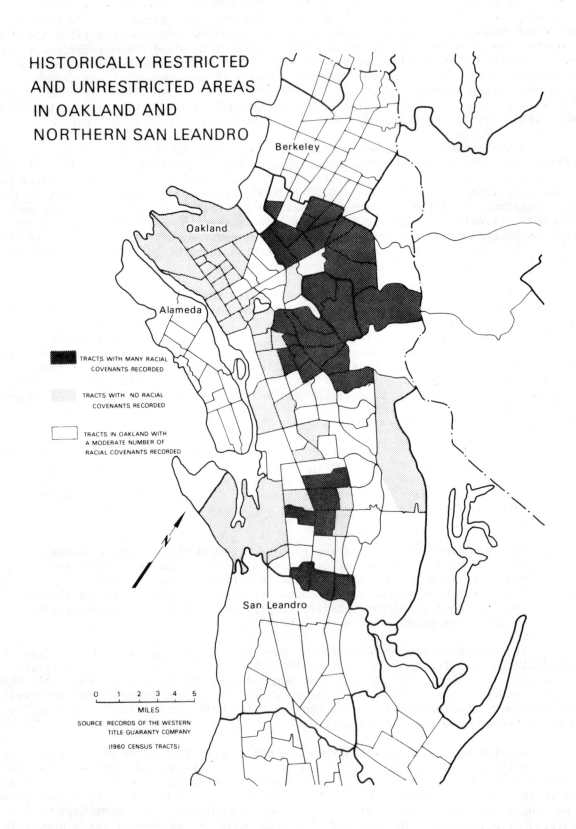

HISTORICALLY RESTRICTED
AND UNRESTRICTED AREAS
IN OAKLAND AND
NORTHERN SAN LEANDRO

Berkeley

Oakland

Alameda

TRACTS WITH MANY RACIAL
COVENANTS RECORDED

TRACTS WITH NO RACIAL
COVENANTS RECORDED

TRACTS IN OAKLAND WITH
A MODERATE NUMBER OF
RACIAL COVENANTS RECORDED

San Leandro

N

0 1 2 3 4 5
MILES

SOURCE: RECORDS OF THE WESTERN
TITLE GUARANTY COMPANY

(1960 CENSUS TRACTS)

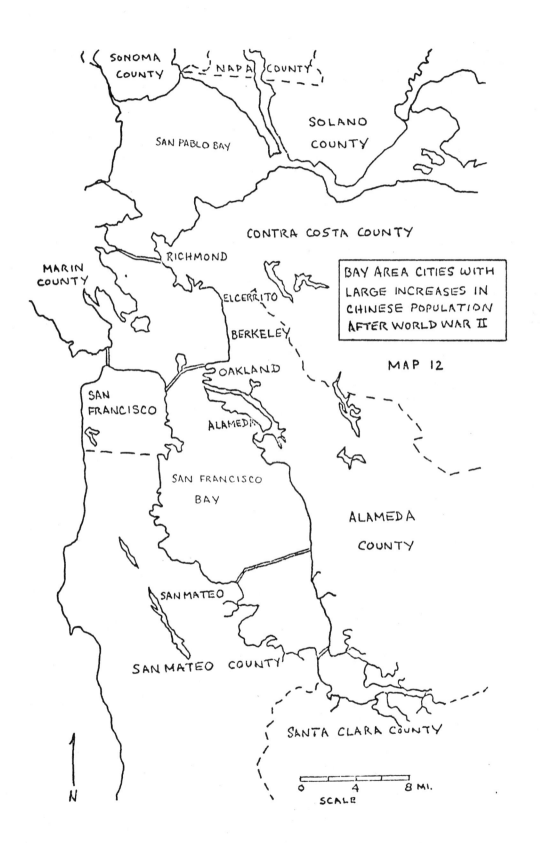

SONOMA COUNTY

NAPA COUNTY

SOLANO COUNTY

SAN PABLO BAY

CONTRA COSTA COUNTY

RICHMOND

MARIN COUNTY

ELCERRITO

BERKELEY

OAKLAND

SAN FRANCISCO

ALAMEDA

SAN FRANCISCO BAY

ALAMEDA COUNTY

BAY AREA CITIES WITH LARGE INCREASES IN CHINESE POPULATION AFTER WORLD WAR II

MAP 12

SAN MATEO

SAN MATEO COUNTY

SANTA CLARA COUNTY

0   4   8 MI.
SCALE

N

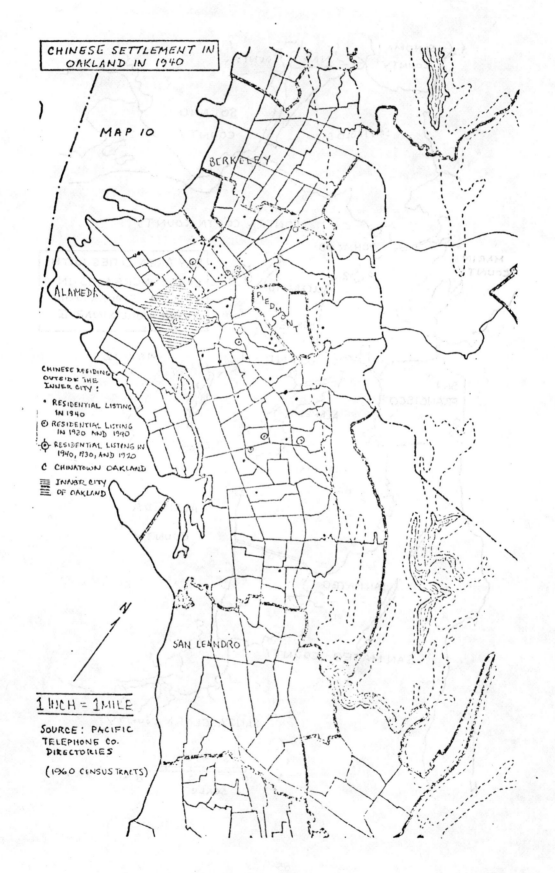

CHINESE SETTLEMENT IN OAKLAND IN 1940

MAP 10

BERKELEY

ALAMEDA

PIEDMONT

CHINESE RESIDING OUTSIDE THE INNER CITY:

· RESIDENTIAL LISTING IN 1940
⊙ RESIDENTIAL LISTING IN 1920 AND 1940
⊕ RESIDENTIAL LISTING IN 1940, 1930, AND 1920
C CHINATOWN OAKLAND
☰ INNER CITY OF OAKLAND

N

SAN LEANDRO

1 INCH = 1 MILE

SOURCE: PACIFIC TELEPHONE CO. DIRECTORIES

(1960 CENSUS TRACTS)

ethnic minority in Oakland during the 1930's.

For the Chinese in the country as a whole, however, who did not share as heavily in the war-time industrial expansion, occupational gains were not as immediate. Employment in the most marginal occupations (operatives and private household servants), in which 28.5 percent of the Chinese were employed in 1940, dropped to 20.0 percent by 1950. Employment in other traditionally Chinese occupations (service workers and managers, proprietors, and officials), in which 50.5 percent of the Chinese were concentrated in 1940, still constituted 49.3 percent of the labor force in 1950 and did not drop to 30.7 percent until 1960.[85] Those confined to menial occupations before the war were able to move to better paying jobs as discriminatory hiring practices were abandoned in the 1940's. The Chinese populations of Alameda, Berkeley, Oakland, and Richmond soared in response to new employment opportunities between 1940 and 1950 (see Table 6).

But after 5 years of war-time occupational mobility, the halcyon days were over. Chinese gains in the manufacturing sector of the East Bay region were quickly curtailed by rising unemployment rates in the lackluster shipbuilding, munitions, and food processing sectors after the war.[86] A survey by the San Francisco Regional Office of the Equal Rights Commission indicated that only 1.9 percent of the construction workers in San Francisco-Oakland SMSA were Asian in 1970. Discrimination was most prevalent in the mechanical trades (boiler makers, electrical workers, elevator constructors, iron workers, plumbers, and sheet metal workers).[87] Under such conditions, progress could only be made when unemployment was negligible. Not until legal pressures changed this "climate" did most craft unions finally permit a few token minorities during the 1950's.[88]

Although most Chinese couples who ran laundries, groceries, restaurants, or general merchandise stores were either too old or not educated enough to improve their occupational status during the war, their children benefitted immensely from changing attitudes. Chinese employment in the professional and technical occupations rose from 2.9 percent in 1940, to 7.2 percent in 1950, to 17.9 percent of the Chinese labor force throughout the country in 1960.[89] In the San Francisco Bay Area, opportunities for the college educated children of established Chinese families blossomed after the war. Opportunities for engineers, technicians, and scientists in the region's expanding electronics, missiles, and research and development sector opened the gates to Chinese occupational mobility. Many, who were educated in Bay Area universities, sought employment and housing in the "peripheral" areas of the region, to which most of the new defense-oriented industries had moved.[90] Bay Area employment in these industries climbed from 1400 in 1950 to 27,100 in 1957 to 68,100 in 1964.[91]

Chinese engineers, architects, social workers, chemists, pharmacists, physicists, educators, opticians, doctors, and dentists sought new and better housing in the suburbs. By 1960, substantial Chinese populations had emerged in the booming cities of San Mateo (926 Chinese at San Mateo, 104 at Menlo Park, 89 at Belmont, 71 at Redwood City) and Santa Clara (55 Chinese at Palo Alto, 232 at Mountain View, 235 at Sunnyvale, 121 at Santa Clara) Counties. Chinese business and professional people were likewise moving into the growing East Bay suburbs of El Cerrito (276), San Leandro (146), Hayward (339), Castro Valley (124), and Fremont (115) by 1960. Increasing occupational mobility and the decentralization of East Bay manufacturing and retailing witnessed the beginnings of large-scale Chinese dispersal by the late 1950's. The Chinese population of Alameda and Contra Costa Counties jumped from 7760 and 438 in 1940 to 11,913 and 1006 in 1950, respectively.

Demographic Dispersal: 1940-1960

World War II also marked the onset of a new era in American immigration policies toward the Chinese. The postwar years saw a gradual turnabout in the laws which had made so many Chinese subject to exploitation by Chinese as well as white employers, landlords, and officials for nearly a century. Restoration of the Chinese family in the United States removed another disqualification which tended to maintain residence in a Chinatown.

Repeal of the Chinese Exclusion Act in 1943 gave Chinese aliens the right to

	1970	1960	1950	1940	1930	1920	1910	1900	1890	1880	1870
Oakland	11335	7658	5531	3201	3048	3821	3069	950	1128	1974	906
Berkeley	4035	2678	703	397	333	337	451	154			
Alameda	1021	293	267	88	103	94	217	255			142
Richmond	635	285	169	32	28						
San Leandro	464	146	25	33	10						
El Cerrito	761	276	103								
Albany	305	92	47								
Hayward	790	339	14								
Piedmont	208	86	30								
Pittsburg	75	77	56								
San Pablo	111	70	31								
Fremont	569	115									
Castro Valley	319	124									
Concord	281	44									
Livermore	151	35									
Antioch	98	12									
San Lorenzo	82	11									
Newark	249										
Walnut Creek	232										
Pinole	142										
Union City	105										

Source: U.S. Census Data

TABLE 6

EAST BAY CITIES WITH 10 OR MORE CHINESE IN 1970

naturalization for the first time. California Land Laws, which had forbidden those ineligible for citizenship from owning agricultural land, were no longer a barrier to Chinese
settlement. Political power through the ballot, which had been impossible for the Chinese
up to this point, was now an alternative where they were numerous. The legal profession,
open only to citizens, was finally within the grasp of the Chinese. Assimilation was at
last possible for many Chinese-Americans.

The War Brides Act of December, 1945, which facilitated the immigration of the
wives of American servicemen, was extended to Chinese wives in July of 1947. In August of
1946, the alien wives of American citizens were finally exempted from the quota and the
families of resident aliens were assigned preference for admission under the quota.[92]
Thousands of Chinese were reunited in the Bay Area. Thousands of new Chinese brides were
brought to the region. Of the 12,151 Chinese immigrants admitted to the country from 1945
to 1953, 89 percent were female.[93] In addition, the anti-miscegenation law in California,
which prohibited Chinese-Caucasian marriages, was finally ruled unconstitutional in 1948.

The female component of Oakland's Chinese population rose by 82.4 percent between
1940 and 1960, while the male portion increased by only 60.7 percent. Overcrowding in
Chinatown became acute as many families were forced to live in one hotel room or hastily
converted bachelor's quarters with limited kitchen and bath facilities.[94] The concentration of new immigrant families in San Francisco and Oakland Chinatowns after World War II
bid up the price of housing and strained community facilities.[95] The sudden influx of
immigrants had social as well as economic implications. Many of the established families
in the Chinese community who had lived near or within Chinatown for decades did not wish to
be associated with the new arrivals and moved into outlying areas of the two cities. The
Richmond and Sunset Districts in San Francisco and the foothills of Berkeley and East
Oakland experienced the postwar growth of large Chinese communities. By 1960 only 40.7

percent of the Chinese in the East Bay resided in Oakland, compared with 69.8 percent in 1950.

The dispersal of hundreds of Chinese families into Berkeley and East Oakland was often the subject of bitter controversy. The following exerpt from the Oakland Tribune is an example of housing discrimination in East Oakland in 1946:

> The Oaknoll Improvement Club, Inc., voted last night to take legal action to oust Horace Y. M. Fong, 32, Chinese-American cafe owner and navy veteran, from his East Oakland home for alleged violation of non-Caucasian occupancy restrictions after he ignored an "invitation to leave." . . . Benjamin I. Clark explained the club's stand in the matter: "We have no quarrel with any race, religion, or color. This is purely business with us. Contractual covenants - I don't like to use the word restrictions - as to the occupancy of property in the district were placed in force in 1927 to preserve and enhance it.". . . . Clark conceded that the club was incorporated in December, 1944 for the express purpose of achieving Fong's ouster from the district.[96]

Similar incidents occurred in many parts of the Bay Area. Attempts to bar Chinese residents from the Silver Terrace district by the Portala Heights Boosters' Club and from the Kensington-North Berkeley area by the Berkeley Hills Property Owners, Inc., in 1946 were also widely publicized.[97]

Although the Supreme Court of the United States, Shelly vs. Kramer, 334 U.S. 1 (1948), finally decided in 1948 that racially restrictive covenants were no longer legally enforceable, housing discrimination remained legal. Discriminatory practices and policies continued to hinder the dispersal of Chinese families into "restricted" neighborhoods. The residents of Southwood, a suburban tract in South San Francisco, for example, voted to reject the family of Sing Sheng, an intelligence captain in World War II and airline mechanic, as a prospective neighbor. The seller was subjected to pressure and Sheng was threatened, leaving him little recourse but to accept the vote and move out in 1952.[98] Non-white families were also excluded in subtle ways which violated no law. Prospective buyers, often required first to be members of the homeowners association, could be easily screened out by the membership committee of the association; according to one salesman, "no Negro, Jap, or Chinaman can ever get in here--the association sees to that."[99]

Despite these tactics, the Chinese and other minority groups managed to disperse during the 1950's. They had at least become a major threat to the racial homogeneity of numerous residential districts and consequently a prime target of abuse. The alternative of retroactive legal enforcement was no longer available after 1948. Resistance to Chinese infiltration was only tempered by even greater fears of settlement by Blacks, who outnumbered all other minorities by a 3:1 ratio in Alameda County and by a 4:1 ratio in Contra Costa County in 1960. The Chinese, less vocal in their protests and less imposing in their numbers, were regarded as less of a threat than the Blacks. The non-Negro minority groups in the Bay Area met discrimination with polite silence and, wherever possible, with accommodation during this period.[100]

Pushed and pulled out of the inner city after World War II, the Chinese were harrassed but not contained by the practice of systematic racial discrimination in housing. Choices were narrower and more difficult to locate. With the help of realtors and in some cases community contacts, the Chinese were able to find more suitable accommodations in less crowded areas. The experience of discrimination nevertheless remains indelibly ingrained in their memories. Even after Fair Housing in the 1960's, the shackles of restriction have not been completely broken.

Real Estate Practices: 1940-1960:

Systematic discrimination within the real estate industry flourished during this

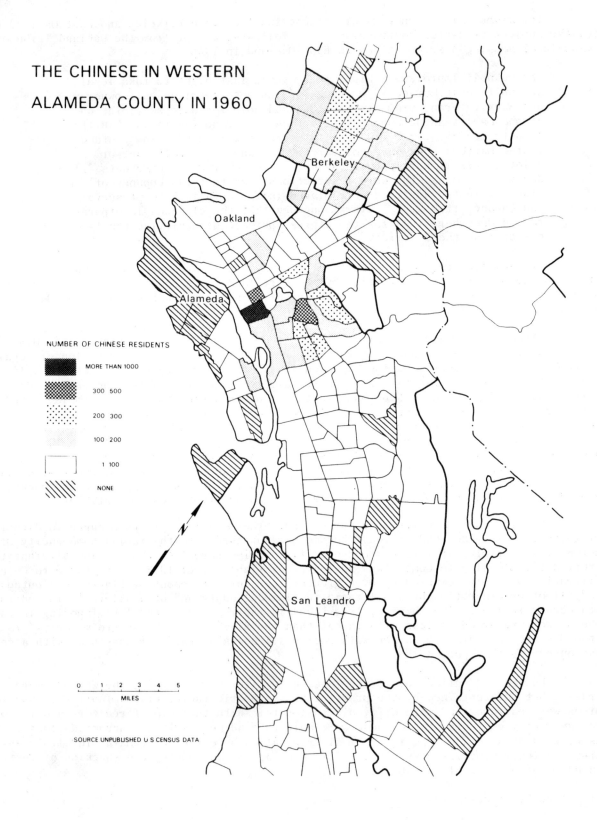

THE CHINESE IN WESTERN

ALAMEDA COUNTY IN 1960

Berkeley

Oakland

Alameda

San Leandro

NUMBER OF CHINESE RESIDENTS

MORE THAN 1000

300 500

200 300

100 200

1 100

NONE

N

0 1 2 3 4 5
MILES

SOURCE UNPUBLISHED U S CENSUS DATA

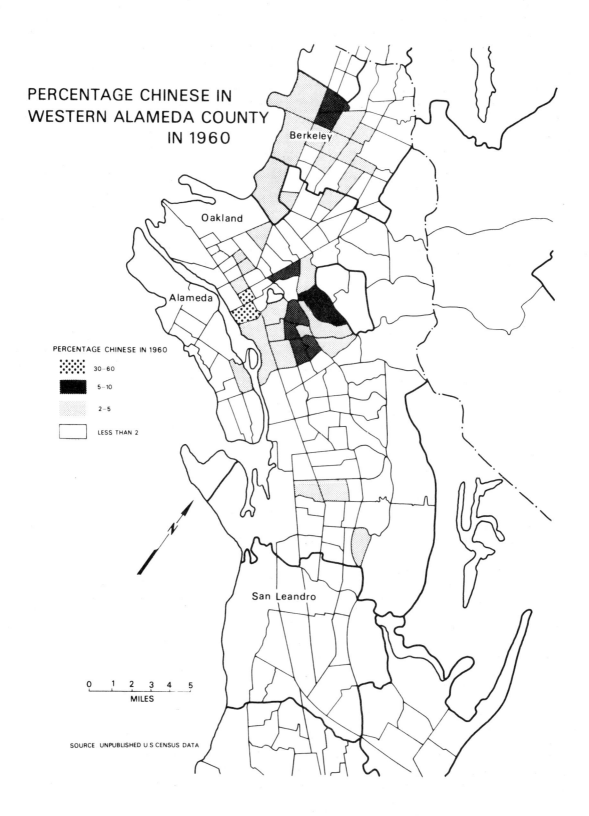

PERCENTAGE CHINESE IN
WESTERN ALAMEDA COUNTY
IN 1960

Berkeley

Oakland

Alameda

PERCENTAGE CHINESE IN 1960

30-60

5-10

2-5

LESS THAN 2

San Leandro

0 1 2 3 4 5
MILES

SOURCE UNPUBLISHED U S CENSUS DATA

period because it was profitable and legal. Now, neither legal nor profitable, it is no longer commonly practiced. The creation of dual "racial" housing markets (white versus non-white) at the end of World War II was a response to the rising demand for single-family housing by minority groups. More profitable where minority demands exceeded existing supplies, the dual housing concept was most commonly accepted in the older parts of the East Bay, where new housing was relatively scarce and where minority needs could most easily be met in terms of purchasing power and accessibility to work.

The ordinary process of filtering was distorted by "block busting" designed to drive prices down and profits up. The notion of a "tipping point" acquired widespread acceptance without a shred of scientific support. Newspapers, like the Oakland Tribune, helped to legitimize and institutionalize the restrictive practices of realtors by separating housing advertisements into "restricted" and "unrestricted" categories.

A rough sampling of Tribune issues indicated that "restricted" residential areas had crystallized by the early 1950's. Restricted listings applied mainly to apartments in Berkeley, Oakland, and Alameda. Districts designated in the ads as "unrestricted" included those areas in East Oakland "south of East 14th Street" and "from Park Boulevard to 73rd Avenue."[101] Most listings made no specific mention of being either "restricted" or "unrestricted." The boundaries of the dual-housing market could not be ascertained without the assistance of realtors, who not only observed but also helped to effect the transition.

Oriental districts were poorly defined and did not really materialize, even though homes for sale were sometimes prefaced with "Attention Chinese" and apartments for rent were sometimes labeled "Orientals Welcome." Clouded with innuendo and inference, the housing market in the East Bay was in theory fragmented but in fact steeped in ambiguity. The dual-housing market was not really a clear cut black or white phenomenon. Sellers rarely panicked at the sight of a few Chinese neighbors, which meant that turnover and profits for brokers would be relatively low. The threat of Black infiltration was much more awesome and could be exploited more readily. Rarely were there one or two isolated Negro families, a pattern common to Chinese and Japanese households. Block-busting in the case of the Chinese did not work. Realtors used the Chinese in other ways.

Realtors and neighborhood associations tried to persuade the public that the Chinese would bring in a wave of other minorities. With the arrival of Negroes, sometimes with the aid of a Caucasian "front," efforts were made by various real estate dealers, Caucasian and minority, to get options on other homes in the area to offer to minority buyers. According to Floyd Hunter, these dealers were not above telephoning and attempting to panic Caucasians into selling at bargain prices. Fear of swamping made the Chinese, as a harbinger of other minorities, a leading target for homeowners associations and pivot for realtor operations.

A study of changing neighborhoods in the East Bay by researchers from the University of California at Berkeley's School of Social Welfare in the 1950's found that of the neighbors surveyed 70 percent felt that non-whites had made no difference (12 percent negative effect and 8 percent positive effect). The study revealed that only 4 percent planned to move because of non-white arrivals and concluded that there was no longer any sign of panic.[104] Without organized and systematic resistance by homeowners associations and segregation by realtors, the dual-housing market would not have become such a widespread phenomenon in the Bay Area.

If Hunter's estimates are correct that 60 percent of the Caucasians in Oakland harbored prejudice and that one-third of them would act upon their feelings in a discriminatory manner, then only about 20 percent of the residential property in Oakland would have been restricted.[105] With the help of brokers and neighborhood groups, however, others could be pressured into compliance. According to Hunter, 80 percent of these two groups harbored racial prejudice.[106] More disposed to discrimination and more likely to benefit from discrimination either financially or politically, both brokers and neighborhood associations were at the helm of segregated housing.

Interviews with 64 white brokers in 1960 by the San Francisco Council for Civic Unity disclosed that the main reasons for not selling to non-whites in a white neighborhood were "fear of losing business" and "bad for business reputation."[107]   A study of housing discrimination in Berkeley found that the apartment manager or owner feared reaction from his tenants, the homeowner feared his neighbors' reaction, the real estate broker feared the effect on his business and felt constrained to accede to his seller's wishes.[108]   The basis for this fear was not individual but rather concerted retribution. Fear brought neighbors associations powers and local real estate boards prosperity. Racism kept the vicious circle turning. Although unfounded, fears of swamping and financial loss were perpetuated at the expense of those who panicked and those who took their place.

A survey of Chinese families in the East Bay suburbs revealed that only 12 of the 75 households responding had moved into their homes before 1960. Of these 12 "pioneer" families, 8 relied on realtors to help them find homes. Of those who moved after 1959, when the Fair Housing Era began, only about one-third depended on realtors for help.[109] Friends have since become the primary means by which the Chinese have been able to find houses in the suburbs. Of the nine families which were aware of anti-Chinese discrimination in their areas, only one said it occurred during the past decade, when discriminatory practices have been outlawed. Of these nine families, six settled in El Cerrito and three moved to Hayward, two early districts of Chinese suburban dispersal. Residents of El Cerrito, which blossomed after World War II, were less vulnerable to realtors and homeowners associations. The Chung Mei Home for Chinese boys was an accepted part of the community since it was built in 1935.[110]

The Prospect of Fair Housing

Passage of two state housing laws in 1959 heralded the dawn of a new era in East Bay housing practices. The Civil Rights of 1959 (Unruh Act), an extension of the Public Accommodations Law of 1866, made discrimination illegal for all business establishments in California, including real estate brokers and housing developers, and increased penalties to cover actual damages plus $250. The Fair Housing Act of 1959 (Hawkins Act) prohibited discriminatory renting or selling practices in publicly assisted dwellings of three or more families, to include housing exempted from taxes or financed by government insurance and guarantee programs. It provided for enforcement by injunction and for civil damages of not less than $500.[111]

Passage of the Rumford Act in California in 1963 made discrimination also illegal in conventionally financed housing and on land acquired by public condemnation. Most importantly, it assigned enforcement responsibilities to the Fair Employment Practices Commission. Although the FEPC has proven to be an effective agency for handling complaints, for making people aware of their housing and employment rights, and for taking action, disenchantment with the Rumford Act was based on much more than objections to the new FEPC role. According to Denton, Proposition 14--the initiative sponsored by the California Real Estate Association--was not aimed merely at repealing the Rumford Act but rather was directed at eliminating all anti-discrimination laws in housing.[112]   Passed in November of 1964, Proposition 14 was the climax of a well engineered "white backlash," which had begun in Berkeley with the defeat of a fair housing ordinance in April of 1963.[113]   After years of legal maneuvering, Proposition 14 was finally held to be unconstitutional under the equal protection clause of the 14th Amendment to the Constitution of the United States by the California Supreme Court in May of 1966.

The legal barriers enshrined in the "right of any person who is willing or desires to sell, lease, or rent any part or all of his real property, to decline to sell, lease or rent such property to such person or persons as he in his absolute discretion chooses" were at last broken in California.[114]   The Chinese, as well as any minority, could now disperse with the law behind instead of against them. After decades of exploitation at the hands of the "dual" housing market, the Chinese were finally free, at least in theory, to live where they preferred.

Hundreds of acculturated, college educated, professionally employed, middle-class

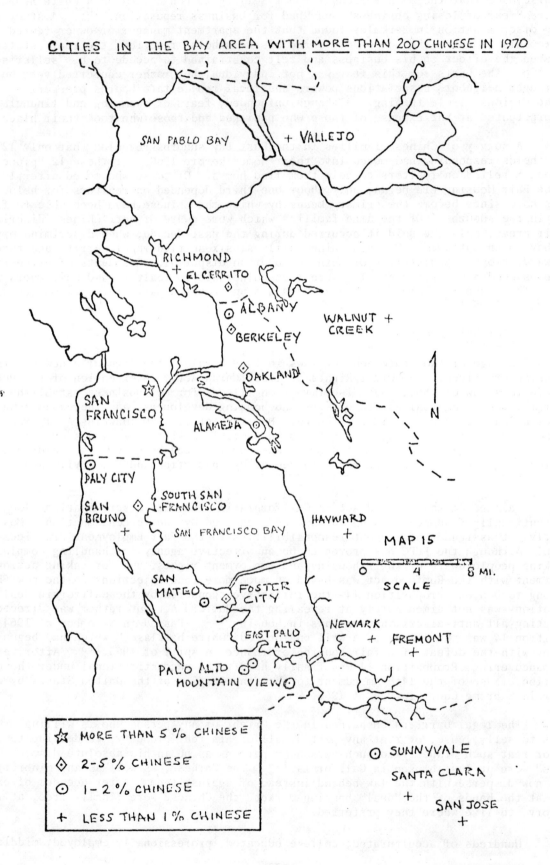

CITIES IN THE BAY AREA WITH MORE THAN 200 CHINESE IN 1970

SAN PABLO BAY

+ VALLEJO

RICHMOND
+ EL CERRITO

ALBANY

BERKELEY

WALNUT +
CREEK

OAKLAND

SAN
FRANCISCO

ALAMEDA

DALY CITY

SAN
BRUNO
+

SOUTH SAN
FRANCISCO

SAN FRANCISCO BAY

HAYWARD
+

MAP 15

0   4   8 MI.

SCALE

SAN
MATEO

FOSTER
CITY

NEWARK
+   FREMONT
+

EAST PALO
ALTO

PALO ALTO
MOUNTAIN VIEW

N

☆ MORE THAN 5% CHINESE
◇ 2-5% CHINESE
⊙ 1-2% CHINESE
+ LESS THAN 1% CHINESE

⊙ SUNNYVALE

SANTA CLARA
+

SAN JOSE
+

Hundreds of acculturated, college educated, professionally employed, middle-class Chinese families acquired homes in the East Bay suburbs as the barriers of discrimination were gradually lowered during the 1960's. A survey of families in these suburbs indicated that the Chinese had arrived in El Cerrito by 1945, in Hayward by 1957, in Concord by 1961, in Walnut Creek by 1965, in Kensington by 1967, in Orinda by 1968, and in Moraga by 1969.[115] Most moved for the "standard" reasons: better schools, more stable neighborhood, and more relaxing surroundings were the most frequently mentioned reasons for choosing their area over others. Proximity to relatives and to other Chinese were both mentioned relatively few times, in each of the suburbs surveyed. Among those surveyed, 61 percent arrived after 1963 during the decade of fair housing.

Young Chinese families living in San Francisco, Oakland, and Berkeley seized the opportunity to move to better housing. Those from Berkeley tended to settle in El Cerrito. Those from Oakland chose either Hayward or El Cerrito, while those from San Francisco picked either Walnut Creek or El Cerrito. Aesthetic concerns were significant in El Cerrito, Kensington, Walnut Creek, and Moraga. More reasonably priced homes were a key factor in Hayward.

The pattern of Chinese settlement in the East Bay had recrystallized by 1970. Berkeley's Chinese population, which tripled from 703 in 1950 to 2678 in 1960, grew more slowly as other residential areas opened during the 1960's (see Table 7). Hayward, El Cerrito, and Castro Valley, which housed increasing numbers of Chinese during the 1950's, continued to be attractive, doubling between 1960 and 1970. Other suburbs, opened after fair housing, witnessed more rapid rates of growth. The Chinese populations of Fremont multiplied by five-fold, while those of San Leandro and Albany tripled from 1960 to 1970. Other suburbs, opened after fair housing, witnessed more rapid rates of growth. The Chinese populations of Fremont multiplied by five-fold, while those of San Leandro and Albany tripled from 1960 to 1970. Concord, Newark, and Walnut Creek have likewise soared in Chinese population in the wake of the Rumford Act, having less than 50 Chinese in 1960. Alameda's Chinese population, which barely increased during the 1950's, tripled between 1960 and 1970 as barriers were lowered and new apartments were built.

The impact of fair housing laws, and the Rumford Act in particular, on central city housing was just as dramatic. As enforcement by the Fair Employment Practices Commission became more vigilant, brokers and neighborhood associations became more wary. Of 162 cases received by the FEPC from September 20, 1963 to December 31, 1968 within Alameda County, two-thirds involved apartments and only one-fifth involved brokers. The 21 cases within Contra Costa County indicated a weaker pattern, with about half of the complaints dealing with apartments and one-third implicating brokers.[116] Minority groups, previously confined to apartments in crowded districts, were finally able to disperse.

Of all the FEPC housing cases in Alameda County, 36.4 percent came from Oakland, 13.0 percent were in Berkeley, 11.7 percent came from Hayward, but 30.8 percent were in Alameda. The Rumford Act made dispersal in the central city feasible for thousands of Chinese. Hundreds moved out of West Oakland and the Inner City, where they had been forced to tolerate rundown quarters, blighted surroundings, and high rents for so many decades (see Map 16). East Oakland and Alameda furnished the Chinese with alternatives which had been closed in the past. Low-income minority households could no longer be exploited by artificially created demands for rental housing in "unrestricted" areas. Although discriminatory practices by individual apartment managers, sellers, realtors, and lenders persist, the practice of systematic segregation is no longer feasible in the East Bay, except to the extent that minorities tend to have lower incomes. The Civil Rights Act of 1968 made it unmistakably clear that discrimination due to race, color, religion, or national origin by anyone was illegal.

The Chinese had by 1970 spread east of Chinatown Oakland into what had been "forbidden" territory. Instead of swamping or concentrating in certain tracts, as realtors and property owners' associations had predicted, Chinese families dispersed. Only in Chinatown did the Chinese tend to concentrate. Most tracts in the East Bay with numerous Chinese residents ranged from 2 percent to 20 percent Chinese in 1970 (see Map 16). The dispersal

TABLE 7

CITIES IN THE BAY AREA WITH MORE THAN 800 CHINESE IN 1970

City	Chinese Population	Total Population	Percent Chinese
San Francisco (SF)	56,696	715,674	7.9
Oakland (A)	11,335	361,561	3.1
Berkeley (A)	4,035	116,716	3.5
San Jose (SC)	2,583	443,950	0.6
Sunnyvale (SC)	1,273	95,408	1.3
San Mateo (SM)	1,143	78,991	1.4
Daly City (SM)	1,108	66,922	1.7
Alameda (A)	1,021	70,968	1.4
Palo Alto (SC)	1,001	55,768	1.8
Hayward (A)	790	93,004	.8
El Cerrito (CC)	761	25,190	3.0
Richmond (CC)	635	79,043	.8
Fremont (A)	555	99,665	.6
S. San Francisco (SM)	548	12,606	4.3
Mountain View	541	51,092	1.1
Santa Clara (SC)	479	225,833	0.2
Foster City (SM)	467	9,327	5.0
E. Palo Alto (SC)	347	17,837	1.9
Albany (A)	305	14,674	2.0
Newark (A)	249	27,153	0.9
Walnut Creek (CC)	232	39,844	0.6
San Bruno (SM)	210	36,254	0.6
Vallejo (S)	323	66,733	0.5

A = Alameda County
CC = Contra Costa County
S = Sonoma County
SC = Santa Clara County
SM = San Mateo County

---

of working class as well as professionally employed Chinese families into the hills and flat-lands of East Oakland reflected the rebirth of the filtering process which had been so severely distorted by over a century of racial discrimination in housing. Working-class immigrant families were no longer confined to the Inner City, which still functioned as their social and commercial center. Housing in mixed ethnic neighborhoods at lower rents, but near friends and relatives, finally became available during the late 1960's. Chinatown had begun to loose its function as the reception area for Chinese immigrant families by 1970, as the walls of de jure segregation ceased to function as a reservoir for power and profits.

Working-class Chinese families were finally able to settle beyond the San Antonio Park, Clinton Park, and Highland districts of East Oakland and the Chinatown-Lower Broadway area of Central Oakland. By 1970, the Glenview, Dimond, 23rd Avenue, Allendale, Maxwell Park, and Kennedy districts of Oakland housed growing numbers of Chinese working-class families. Middle-class Chinese families, confined and concentrated in West Berkeley and the Peralta Heights and Trestle Glen districts of East Oakland diffused into the Broadway Heights, Grand Lake, Laurel, and Redwood Heights areas of the lower hills. Upper middle-class Chinese families dispersed into the Leona Heights, Crestmont, and Skyline districts of the Oakland Hills under the umbrella of Fair Housing. The Southshore district of Alameda, the Mulford Gardens area of San Leandro, the Berkeley Hills, the Arlington area of El Cerrito, and the Fairmede district of San Pablo likewise became open to Chinese families

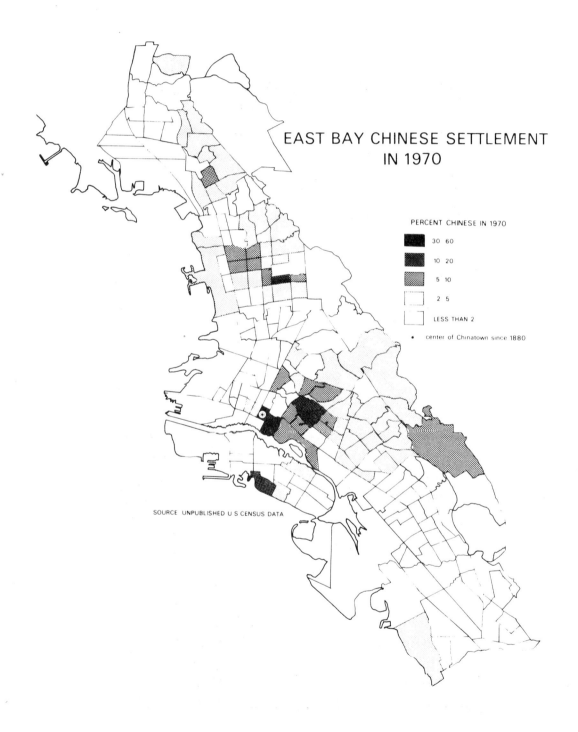

EAST BAY CHINESE SETTLEMENT
IN 1970

PERCENT CHINESE IN 1970

30 60

10 20

5 10

2 5

LESS THAN 2

● center of Chinatown since 1880

SOURCE UNPUBLISHED U S CENSUS DATA

CHINESE MIDDLE AND WORKING CLASS
RESIDENTIAL DISTRICTS

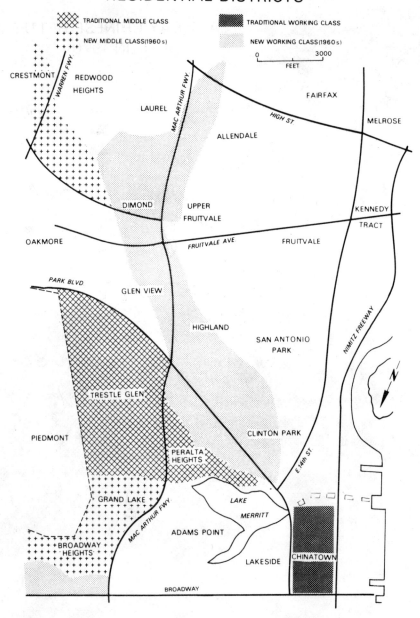

THE CHINESE POPULATION OF BERKELEY
AND ALBANY

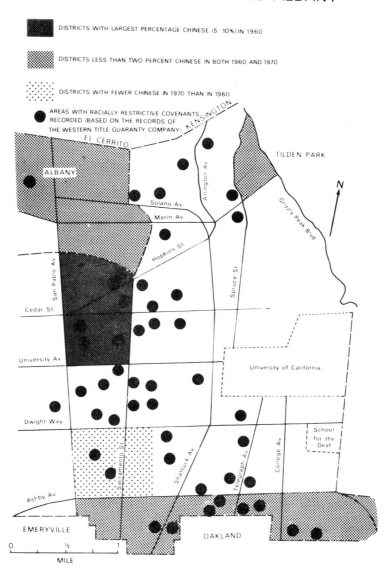

DISTRICTS WITH LARGEST PERCENTAGE CHINESE (5 10%) IN 1960

DISTRICTS LESS THAN TWO PERCENT CHINESE IN BOTH 1960 AND 1970

DISTRICTS WITH FEWER CHINESE IN 1970 THAN IN 1960

AREAS WITH RACIALLY RESTRICTIVE COVENANTS RECORDED (BASED ON THE RECORDS OF THE WESTERN TITLE GUARANTY COMPANY)

KENSINGTON

EL CERRITO

TILDEN PARK

ALBANY

Solano Av

Arington Av

Grizzly Peak Blvd

Marin Av

Hopkins St

San Pablo Av

Spruce St

Cedar St

University Av

University of California

Dwight Way

School for the Deaf

Sacramento St

Shattuck Av

Telegraph Av

College Av

Ashby Av

EMERYVILLE

OAKLAND

0   ½   1

MILE

only after discriminatory practices by realtors and homeowners associations were finally made illegal during the 1960's (see Map 17).

Conclusion

As demonstrated in the foregoing analysis, the impact of housing discrimination on Chinese settlement perpetuated their confinement in a period of mellowing racial attitudes. Early racial tension and harassment kept the Chinese out of the general housing market until bigotry began to subside by 1920. Lack of Chinese purchasing power due to job discrimination and the lack of Chinese women kept most of the East Bay Chinese in Oakland until World War II. De facto segregation governed the process of Chinese settlement until the war.

Reliance upon de jure controls, although not particularly effective against the Chinese in the absence of de facto constraints, was nevertheless the only means by which individuals were able to exclude minorities from their neighborhoods. After racially restrictive covenants were ruled legally unenforceable in 1948, the only alternative was group action. Paradoxically, as individual antagonism toward the Chinese waned, racist practices by realtors and homeowners' associations had finally become apparent. The importance of exploitation for profit and power should not be underestimated. Although institutionalized racism made segregation possible, collusion made it happen.

At the metropolitan level, Chinese families who could afford to acquire better housing after World War II were channeled and contained in cities like Alameda, Berkeley, and Richmond. El Cerrito and Hayward were opened to serve as "zones of assimilation" for acculturated Chinese families in the 1950's. Not until the discriminatory practices of realtors and homeowners' associations were made illegal did previously "restricted" towns like Albany, Fremont, Newark, and Walnut Creek open to substantial numbers of Chinese. Towns in the East Bay which failed to attract Chinese families by 1970 were avoided either because of the prohibitive prices of their houses or the unrelenting racist attitudes of their residents. Realtors and homeowners' associations made less of a difference in these areas.

At the local level, realtors and homeowners' associations tried to channel and restrict Chinese working-class families to Chinatown Oakland, West Oakland, East Oakland, and South Berkeley. Overcrowding and undermaintenance in these areas have led to blighted conditions. The dispersal of working-class families into formerly "restricted" districts in the wake of Fair Housing reflects a revival of the market process of filtering, which for the first time became operative for working-class as well as upper-middle-class Chinese families. The diffusion of middle-class Chinese families into the Oakland and Berkeley Hills during the 1960's paved the way for the spread of working-class Chinese households into the previously "restricted" districts of the lower slopes.

The experience of the Chinese in the East Bay dramatized the extent to which realtors and homeowners' associations perpetuated discrimination in housing long after it had become outmoded in terms of de jure and de facto constraints. The decade of the 1960's witnessed the emergence of a new pattern of Chinese settlement, one which reflected neither a sharp increase in occupational mobility nor a sharp decrease in racist sentiments, as had been experienced by Blacks during this period. Discriminatory practices against the Chinese were simply a manifestation of the systematic nature of residential segregation and the degree to which it had become institutionalized in local real estate practices and ideals. The impact of collusive factors on the dynamics as well as the pattern of minority settlement has yet to be fully recognized, despite their persistence in central cities across the country.

Footnotes to Chapter Four:

1. Roy C. Beckman, The Romance of Oakland, Landis & Kelsey (Oakland, 1932) p. 8.

2. Historical Atlas of Alameda County, Thompson & West (Oakland, 1878) p. 163.

3. The Montclairon, Oakland, Nov. 21, 1973.

4. G. A. Cummings and E. S. Pladwell, Oakland. . . . A History (Oakland, 1942) p. 57.

5. The Bay of San Francisco, Its History (1892) p. 319.

6. George Pettitt, Berkeley, The Town and Gown of It (Berkeley, 1973) p. 152.

7. Directory of Principal Chinese Business Houses, Wells Fargo & Co., 1882.

8. Ping Chiu, Chinese Labor in California, 1850-1880 (Ann Arbor, 1963) pp. 74, 76, 82.

9. Historical Atlas of Alameda County, op. cit., p. 163.

10. George Pettitt, Clayton: Not Quite Shangrila (Martinez, 1969) p. 60.

11. Contra Costa County, California, W. B. Bancroft & Co. (San Francisco, 1887) p. 8.

12. Ping Chiu, op. cit., pp. 74, 76, 82.

13. Lee D. Fridell, The Story of Richmond (Richmond, 1954) pp. 40-41.

14. Calvin Lee, Chinatown U.S.A. (Garden City, 1965) p. 8.

15. Oakland Tribune (May 13, 1952).

16. Calvin Lee, op. cit., p. 62.

17. Cummings and Pladwell, op. cit., p. 60.

18. Ibid., p. 61.

19. Ibid., p. 63.

20. Alexander Saxton, The Indispensable Enemy, Labor and the Anti-Chinese Movement in California (Berkeley: 1971) p. 147.

21. Ibid., pp. 121-213.

22. Cummings and Pladwell, op. cit., p. 68.

23. Stanford Lyman, "Strangers in the Cities: the Chinese on the Urban Frontier," in Wollenberg, Ethnic Conflict in California History (Los Angeles, 1970) p. 94.

24. Contra Costa Gazette (April 29, 1882).

25. Thomas Chinn, ed., A History of the Chinese in California (San Francisco, 1969), p. 40.

26. Fred Button, General Municipal Ordinances of the City of Oakland, California, Tribune Publishing Co. (Oakland, 1892) pp. 151-152.

27. Ibid.

28. Oakland Daily Times (July 14, 1878) p. 3.

29. Proceedings and List of Delegates - Chinese Exclusion Convention, San Francisco, Nov. 21-22, 1901, the Star Press (San Francisco, 190) pp. 17-18.

30. Oakland Tribune (May 13, 1952) p. 10.

31. Ibid.

32. Sanborn Insurance Maps of Oakland, California, Vol. 2 (New York, 1889).

33. Loren Miller, "Government's Responsibility for Racial Segregation," in Denton, Race and Property (Berkeley, 1964), p. 60.

34. Directory of Principal Chinese Business Houses, op. cit.

35. Ibid.

36. Ann Kellam Manuel, "Chinese in Oakland," unpublished manuscript, Sociology 191 Project, University of California, Berkeley, 1965, p. 4.

37. Peter Thomas Conway, The Beginnings of Oakland, California (Oakland, 1961), p. 46.

38. A. R. Dunbar's Chinese Directory of the U.S., British Columbia, and Honolulu, A. Anderson & Co. (Portland, 1892).

39. The History of Alameda County, M. W. Wood (Oakland, 1883) pp. 248, 252.

40. Richard H. Dillon, The Hatchet Men (New York, 1962) p. 321.

41. Sanborn Insurance Maps of Oakland, California, Vol. 3 (New York, 1903).

42. Oakland Tribune (June 12, 1966).

43. Proceedings and List of Delegates - Chinese Exclusion Convention, op. cit.

44. For growth of manufacturing, see Mel Scott, The San Francisco Bay Area (Berkeley, 1959), p. 137.

45. Cummings and Pladwell, op. cit., pp. 83-84.

46. William Bronson, The Earth Shook, The Sky Burned (Garden City, 1959) p. 136.

47. Oakland Tribune, Extra Edition (April 19, 1906).

48. Oakland Tribune, Regular Edition (April 19, 1906).

49. Bessie May Ferina, "The Politics of San Francisco Chinatown," unpublished M.A. thesis, University of California, Berkeley, 1949, p. 1.

50. Pacific Telephone Directory, Oakland, October 1, 1909.

51. Dillon, op. cit., pp. 356, 360.

52. Oakland Tribune (Jan. 23, 1955).

53. Oakland Tribune (Jan. 2, 1955).

54. Pacific Telephone Directory, Oakland, Oct. 1, 1909.

55. Oakland Tribune (May 13, 1952).

56. The Chinese Family in San Francisco, op. cit., pp. 120-123.

57. Ann Kellam Manuel, op. cit., p. 4.

58. Oakland Tribune (April 4, 1906).

59. William Bronson, op. cit., p. 136.

60. Thomas W. Casstevens, Politics, Housing, and Race Relations, Institute for Governmental Studies (Berkeley, 1965) p. 5.

61. Victor and Brett de Bary Nee, op. cit., p. 148.

62. S. W. Kung, Chinese in American Life (Seattle, 1962) p. 101.

63. Christopher Tunnard, The Modern American City (Princeton, 1968) pp. 67-68.

64. "Declaration of Restrictions," Oakmore Highlands, Oakland, California, Walter H. Leimert Company (May 15, 1926), introduction.

65. John H. Denton, Apartheid American Style (Berkeley, 1967) p. 1.

66. Charles Abrams, The Language of Cities (New York, 1971) p. 126.

67. Race and Housing Series, University of California Press (Berkeley, 1960).

68. James E. Vance, Jr., "California and the Search for the Ideal," Annals, Assn. of Amer. Geog. (June, 1972) p. 186.

69. Suzanne Keller, The Urban Neighborhood: A Sociological Perspective (New York, 1968) (New York, 1968) p. 109.

70. Edward C. Hayes, Power Structure and Urban Policy: Who Rules Oakland? (New York, 1972) pp. 55-69.

71. Wallace Smith, Housing: The Social and Economic Elements (Berkeley, 1970.)

72. Pacific Telephone Directory, Oakland, Alameda, Berkeley and San Leandro, 1930.

73. "The Immigrant and the Law," working paper, Bay Area Social Planning Council, San Francisco, 1970.

74. Eliot Grinnell Mears, Resident Orientals on the American Pacific Coast, (Palo Alto, 1927) pp. 263-264.

75. Pacific Telephone Directory, Oakland, Alameda, and Berkeley, 1920.

76. Victor and Brett de Bary Nee, op. cit., p. 95.

77. Ann Kellam Manuel, op. cit., p. 2.

78. Pacific Telephone Directory, Oakland, Berkeley, Alameda, and San Leandro, 1940.

79. Beulah Kwoh, "The Occupational Status of American-born Chinese Male College Graduates," Amer. Journ. of Soc. (1947) pp. 192-200.

80. Rose Hum Lee, The Chinese in the U.S.A. (Hong Kong, 1960), p. 30.

81. San Francisco: the Bay and Its Cities, Work Projects Administration, Writers' Program (New York, 1940) p. 377.

82. James E. Vance, Jr. Geography and Urban Evolution in the San Francisco Bay Area, Institute for Governmental Studies (Berkeley, 1964) p. 66.

83. William L. Nicholls II and Earl R. Babbie, "Oakland in Transition: A Summary of the 701 Household Survey," Survey Research Center, University of California, Berkeley, June, 1969, p. 4.

84. Jobs, People and Land, Bay Area Simulation Study, Center for Real Estate and Urban Economics, University of California (Berkeley, 1968) p. 129.

85. Figures based on Betty Lee Sung, Mountain of Gold (New York, 1967) p. 189.

86. Jobs, People and Land, op. cit., p. 132.

87. "Chinese in San Francisco," Testimony of Jimmy Ong, California Fair Employment Practice Commission, December, 1970, pp. 32-33.

88. "Chinese in San Francisco," Testimony of Mark Lai, California Fair Employment Practice Commission, December, 1970, pp. 6-7.

89. Betty Lee Sung, op. cit., p. 189.

90. Vance (1964), op. cit., p. 66.

91. Jobs, People and Land, op. cit., p. 133.

92. Rose Hum Lee, "The Recent Immigrant Chinese Families of the San Francisco Bay Area," Marriage and Family Living (Feb., 1956) p. 14.

93. Ibid., p. 16.

94. Rose Hum Lee, "The Established Chinese Families of the San Francisco Bay Area," Midwest Sociologist (December, 1967) p. 20.

95. Ibid.

96. Oakland Tribune (March 19, 1946) p. 13.

97. San Francisco Chronicle (Feb. 26, 1946).

98. "Among These Rights," Council for Civic Unity of San Francisco Newsletter (March-April, 1952).

99. "San Francisco's Housing Market - Open or Closed?" Civil Rights Inventory of San Francisco, Council for Civic Unity of San Francisco, 1960, p. 17.

100. Floyd Hunter, "Housing Discrimination in Oakland, California," A Study Prepared for the Mayor's Committee on Full Opportunity and the Council of Social Planning of Alameda County, 1963-64.

101. Based on a sampling of Classified Ads section of the Oakland Tribune, January 1 issues from 1951-1955.

102. Hunter, op. cit., p. 42.

103. Ibid., p. 43.

104. "Changing Neighborhoods: A Follow-Up Study of Community Stability in 35 Racially Changing Neighborhoods in San Francisco and the East Bay," Group Research Project, School of Social Welfare, University of California, Berkeley, June, 1957, pp. 73-74.

105. Hunter, op. cit., p. 72.

106. Ibid.

107. "San Francisco's Housing Market - Open or Closed?" Ibid.

108. "Housing Discrimination in Berkeley," A Report by a Citizen's Committee to the Community Welfare Commission, 1962, p. 5.

109. See Appendix.

110. Fridell, op. cit., pp. 115-117.

111. "San Francisco's Housing Market - Open or Closed?" op. cit., p. 43.

112. Denton (1967) op. cit., pp. 1-8.

113. Casstevens, op. cit., pp. 1-2.

114. From Proposition 14 in Denton (1967), op. cit., p. 1.

115. See Appendix.

116. "Case Experience in Northern California Under Rumford Fair Housing Act," Fair Employment Practice Commission, San Francisco Regional Office.

CHAPTER FIVE

LAND USE POLICIES IN THE REEMERGENCE OF THE INNER CITY

Introduction

Chinese settlement in the East Bay Region emerged as an offspring of both racial constraints and public land-use policies. Not until the 1960's, however, was the seminal role of public policies clear. The Inner City of Oakland, which had housed the city's non-white minorities for over a century, began to show signs of new life by the early 1970's. Capital improvements poured into the long neglected heart of the city in an effort to re-build its deteriorated commercial structures and restore its tarnished image. New trans-port facilities were constructed to make the Central Business District more accessible by auto as well as by mass transit. The evolution of the Chinese quarter of Oakland, situa-ted at the edge of the Central Business District, reflects its changing functions during different periods of the city's development. Chinatown's recent transformation has been molded to suit the Inner City's rapidly crystallizing new structure. This chapter will deal with the impact of public land-use policies on the physical form of the Chinatown com-munity since its inception.

The effects of racial confinement and displacement by redevelopment are not unique to Oakland Chinatown. Chinatown communities in Sacramento, San Jose, Boston, Philadelphia, and Pittsburgh have also been disrupted by public improvements designed to further the pub-lic interest.[1] The case of Oakland illustrates a general pattern, followed in many central cities across the country. The failures of the city planning process have been no more sen-sational in Oakland than in other American cities with large Chinatown populations. Plan-ning in Oakland has in actuality gone to great lengths to be "community-oriented." The problem with city planning in Oakland is conceptual. The costs of reviving the Central Business District have been much greater than anticipated.

The benefits of higher property taxes and federal subsidies to the city, more jobs for workers, and higher property values and rents for landowners are undeniable. As critics have pointed out, however, the social opportunity costs of displacement and reloca-tion tend to be underestimated.[2] For Oakland's Chinatown residents, the lag between plan-ning and fruition has already exceeded a decade. Not a single housing unit has yet to be built for the community under urban renewal. Meanwhile, rents continue to rise as the quarter is transformed from a light-industrial zone into a middle-income residential dis-trict, as envisioned under redevelopment. Lower-income residents have been forced to re-side in the older residential districts of East Oakland where neither specialized commun-ity institutions nor nearby jobs are available. The problems of low-income Chinese families have simply been diverted to other areas of the city, where they do not threaten the viabil-ity of the Central Business District. Conflicts among displaced ethnic groups in these outlying neighborhoods have been common not only in Oakland but throughout the country.

The development of land-use policies in Oakland may be divided into five phases: Athenian, Progressive, Industrial, Metropolitan, and Redeveloping Oakland. Land-use pat-terns during each of these phases were shaped by prevailing policies, formed for the most part by the city's most influential businessmen. What was good for business was good for Oakland. Private investments became identifiable with the public good almost from the city's speculative beginnings. City planning in Oakland continues to be guided by the views and interests of powerful commercial and industrial leaders in the community.[3] Re-development may be regarded as one more effort by private interest to work through the political process. Although unprecedented in scope, its benefits likewise have never before appeared to be so broad or so open to public scrutiny.

The reluctance of national policy makers to recognize the inherently politicized nature of the city planning process has frustrated efforts to redeem the American city for nearly two decades. Preoccupied with transforming the Central Business District, national

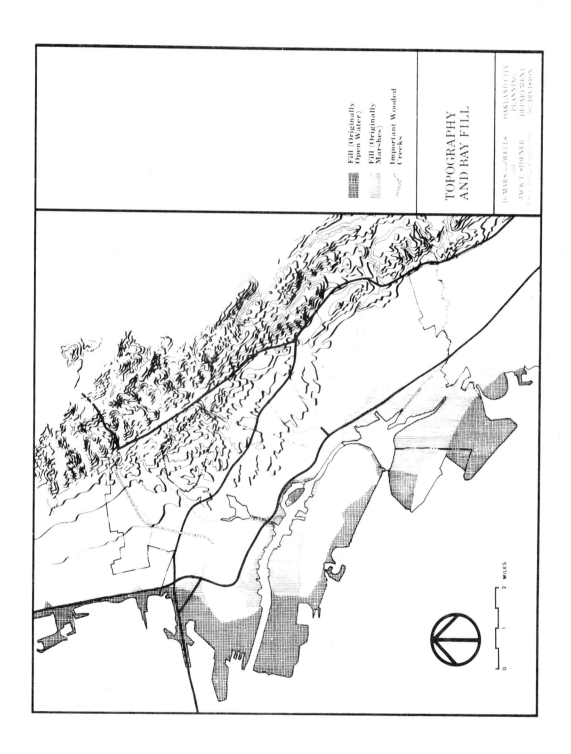

TOPOGRAPHY
AND BAY FILL

Fill (Originally
Open Water)

Fill (Originally
Marshes)

Important Wooded
Creeks

2 MILES

0   1   2

policies did not show much concern for the dislocation of inner city communities until 1970.[4] In the absence of community involvement and comprehensive guidelines in planning, the plight of inner city residents worsened as Federal commitments to urban housing seemed to intensify during the 1960's. Even stable communities, like Chinatown Oakland, which had endured and even flourished within a zone of discard for decades, struggled for survival under urban renewal. Land-use policies in Oakland, still formulated by single function public agencies in a milieu of political games, continue to thwart efforts by ethnic communities to shape their destiny in inner city.

"Athens of the Pacific"

Town planning in Oakland commenced with its founding in the early 1850's. The site of Oakland originally belonged to Don Luis Maria Peralta, who received his land as a grant from Spain in recognition of his service to the Crown as an explorer and soldier in 1842. Peralta divided his vast holdings in the East Bay among his four sons, who raised cattle in the rolling hills. The site was not settled until 1849, when Moses Chase leased some land from Peralta and built a house in a luxuriant grove of oaks. The site was called Encinal (oak grove) since Spanish times. Its present name was chosen in 1850.[5] Horace W. Carpentier, Edson Moon, and Andrew J. Adams arrived in 1850, leased 480 acres from Vicente Peralta between Lake Merritt and Market Street and then proceeded to sell purportedly fee simple land to buyers from San Francisco.[6] Having acquired the ferry franchise to Oakland from the Alameda County Supervisors, Carpentier & Co. had a vested interest in the growth of the town.

Conflicts between Peralta and the "squatters," who had bought land from the three speculators, were temporarily resolved in 1851. The "squatters" were allowed to remain on the condition that they lay out a townsite. Julius Kellersberger, a Swiss surveyor, was hired to lay out the town. Lots were sold by reference to Kellersberger's Map of Oakland which was filed with the County Recorder in 1853.[7] The town rose quickly as the demand for lumber in San Francisco stimulated the growth of logging and sawmills in the East Bay. Speculation in real estate expedited the city's expansion. Kellersberger's grid pattern town, oriented toward the busy waterfront, facilitated the sale of real property. Easy to survey and subdivide, the right-angled plan has been a favorite among real estate speculators.[8] Rapid settlement enhanced the squatters' political leverage over Peralta's legal claims. Growth had become so important that Carpentier deeded the waterfront (except for Lake Merritt and the landing) to Leland Stanford's Western Pacific Railroad in 1869 in return for a transcontinental terminus in Oakland.[9]

In view of the town's shady beginnings, it is not surprising that early land-use restrictions were used as a protective device and not as a planning tool. Restrictions do not appear until the 1870's when the most pressing threat to property owners emanated from the Chinese "menace." As stated in Chapter Four, the Chinese were not allowed to settle permanently in Oakland until 1880. Prior to this period, they were periodically relocated to make room for the city's bustling Central Business District. The principal Chinese settlement in 1876 consisted of 17 buildings, including stores, four gambling dens, and a joss house (temple) between Grove and Jefferson Streets near the railroad tracks (First Street). Another Chinese section was situated near San Pablo Avenue and 22nd Street.[10]

Mayor Andrus commented at length on February 3, 1879, upon the unsanitary conditions of the Chinese quarter and deplored the infiltration of the Chinese into residential sections, where their presence caused a depreciation in property values. Andrus insisted that the City Council had complete authority to regulate trades and occupations that might become nuisances and recommended that licenses for Chinese laundries be granted only when a majority of property owners on the block consented.[11] City Ordinance 1104, passed in 1889, banned laundries from locating within the fire limits of the city under pressure from organized laundrymen (see Chapter Four).

The most valuable business property in Oakland in 1876 was along Broadway, between 7th and 14th Streets.[12] The construction of a wharf at the foot of Broadway and the expansion of regular ferry service to San Francisco during the 1860s made it the town's most

CHINATOWN OAKLAND IN 1889

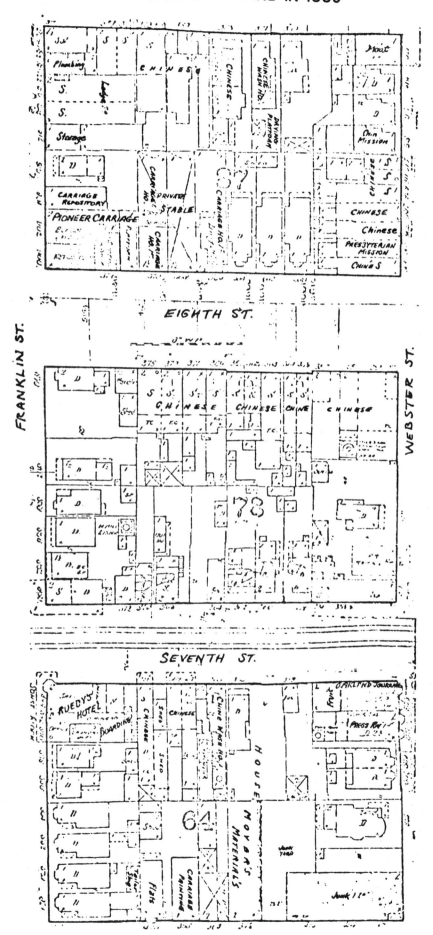

important thoroughfare. Local transport funneled traffic into Broadway at 7th and at 14th Streets. San Francisco ferry connections for those living in East and West Oakland were made along 7th Street, where the San Francisco and Oakland Railway had operated since 1863. Oakland's first street railway ran along First Street, up Broadway, and north along Telegraph Avenue (connecting with Broadway near 14th Street). Initiated as a horse car line in 1869, it was replaced by a steam powered engine in 1875. Crowds of people going to and from local trains from early morning until late in the evening made Broadway "the paradise of retailers."[13] Washington Street, adjacent to Broadway, ranked next in terms of commercial property value.

Heavy industrial growth did not occur until after 1900.[14] Oakland functioned as a commercial center and suburb of San Francisco until the close of the century. Early residents preferred to live near the center of town where transportation was most accessible and manufacturing was still rare. The Victorian dwellings of 19th century Oakland were built at the edge of the Central Business District, testifying to its early attractiveness. First class residential land in 1876 was sold for $75 per front foot in the most central locations and from $20 to $75 in other parts of Oakland.[15] Not until the expansion of local mass-transit lines after 1875 were outlying residential districts made accessible even on a limited basis. The early street railways were built to develop and exploit real estate holdings.[16] Horsecar lines linking downtown Oakland with the Dimond District, Fruitvale, East Oakland, and Mills Seminary opened in 1875-1876.

Intensive Chinese settlement was ideologically inconceivable within the precious "Old City" section of town until 1880. The arrival of Oakland's first carriage factories in 1873 began to change the complexion of the section along Franklin Street. Sohst Brothers at the northeast corner of Eighth and Franklin and the Oakland Carriage Factory at 10th and Franklin paved the way for the establishment of warehouses and other light manufacturing in the Old City east of Franklin.[17] The Chinese managed to settle near Eighth and Webster, which had been transformed into a commercial-industrial area during the 1870's. Situated in Oakland's zone of discard, Chinatown flourished in the midst of blight. Excluded from the city's central residential districts and fashionable retail streets, the Chinese crowded into lodging houses and modified existing structures to suit their needs until the turn of the century.

Progressive Oakland

Formation of the Realty Syndicate in 1895 marked the beginning of a new period in Oakland's development. The Syndicate, directed by F. C. Havens & F. M. "Borax" Smith, consolidated 27 miles of narrow guage railway and several ferries into the Key System, which started to serve the East Bay in 1903. Having acquired some 13,000 acres of residential land in the hills between Mills College and North Berkeley, the Syndicate turned its subdivided lots into residential sites with the help of the Key System and other public utilities.[18] As the largest private owner of real estate in Alameda County, it reportedly did more for Oakland during this period than any other organization.[19] Modern street work and other public improvements facilitated the development of the foothill districts between 1906 and 1911. Brought within a few minutes ride of downtown Oakland by street car, Piedmont, Claremont, Broadway Heights, and Rockridge experienced one of the most consistent and rapid increases in land values to be found in any city in the United States at this time.[20]

By 1912, residential growth had fanned out across the North Oakland plain to link with Berkeley and the University of California. Industry had begun to extend north and south along the waterfront into Emeryville, Berkeley, and San Leandro, and tall buildings had begun to rise in downtown Oakland.[21] Factories and commercial establishments tended to cluster along trolley lines, permitting their workers to commute.[22] Gregarious inner city living in the Victorian districts of Oakland was undermined by industrial expansion. The well-to-do, who had made Madison Square their home for a half-century, moved toward the hills. The hills that extend down from Piedmont to Lake Merritt were developed after 1900 as the city's best area of homes--shingle and stucco villas surrounded by gardens.[23]

OAKLAND'S CENTRAL BUSINESS DISTRICT, 1850 -1959

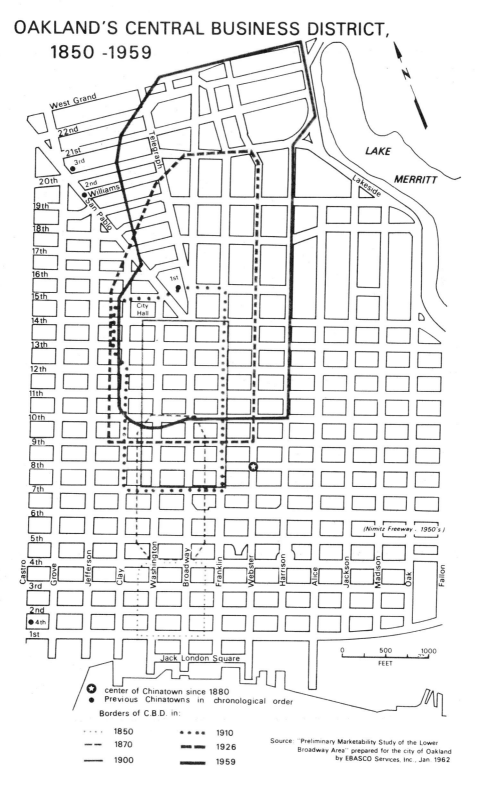

LAKE MERRITT

West Grand
22nd
21st
3rd
20th
2nd
Williams
19th
18th
17th
16th
15th
14th
13th
12th
11th
10th
9th
8th
7th
6th
5th
4th
3rd
2nd
4th
1st

Telegraph
San Pablo
Lakeside
1st
City Hall

(Nimitz Freeway, 1950's)

Castro
Grove
Jefferson
Clay
Washington
Broadway
Franklin
Webster
Harrison
Alice
Jackson
Madison
Oak
Fallon

Jack London Square

0   500   1000
FEET

⊛ center of Chinatown since 1880
● Previous Chinatowns in chronological order

Borders of C.B.D. in:

· · · ·	1850	● ● ● ●	1910
– – –	1870	▬ ▬ ▬	1926
——	1900	▬▬▬	1959

Source: "Preliminary Marketability Study of the Lower
Broadway Area" prepared for the city of Oakland
by EBASCO Services, Inc., Jan. 1962

FORSYTH LIBRARY
FORT HAYS STATE UNIVERSITY

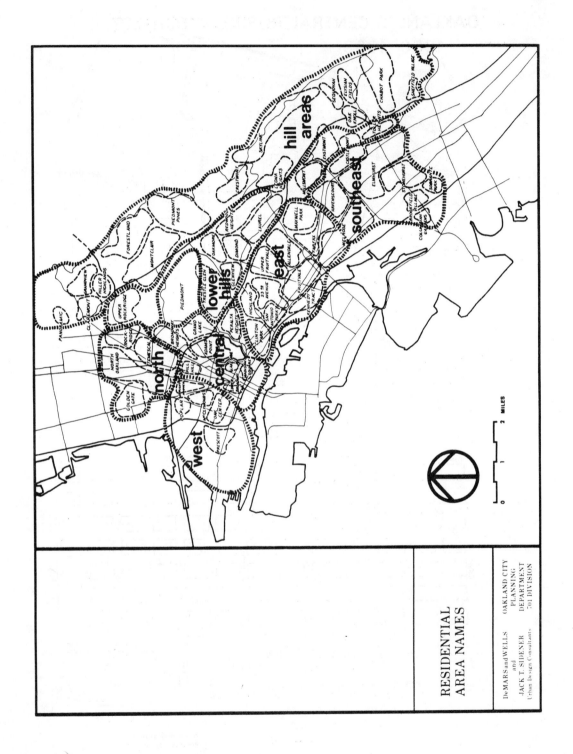

RESIDENTIAL
AREA NAMES

DeMARS and WELLS
and
JACK T. SIDENER
Urban Design Consultants

OAKLAND CITY
PLANNING
DEPARTMENT
701 DIVISION

The city's most famous citizen, Jack London, was raised in the working-class neighborhoods of Brooklyn and West Oakland during the 1890's. His book People of the Abyss, was based on his early experience with the Oakland waterfront boys and girls.[24] London observed that public improvements were channeled by real estate developers toward the newer residential districts. Profits from the sale of Realty Syndicate lands helped to finance the growth of a new aristocracy. "Financing is not only an art," London insisted, "it is a social force; once established, however frenzied its inception, it challenges whatever social structure it encounters."[25] Land-use policies favored the beautification of new housing areas and the industrialization of flatlands, where many of the city fathers as well as the Southern Pacific Railroad held vested interests. Even Charles Mulford Robinson, a pioneer in the beautification of cities, found that waterfront land in Oakland was too expensive to make practical the relinquishment of any part of it for aesthetic purposes.[26]

Planning in Oakland before 1914 was at best an ad hoc response to the exigencies of rapid economic growth. Public land-use decisions were guided by the needs of the business community. The Oakland Real Estate and Merchants Exchange, established in 1877, was the first real estate exchange on the Pacific Coast and the city's first civic organization. Formation of the Oakland Board of Trade in 1886, the Merchants Exchange of Oakland in 1895, the Oakland Chamber of Commerce in 1905, and the Oakland Real Estate Association (which became the Oakland Real Estate Board in 1915) in 1906 insured that the interests of various business groups would be well represented in City Hall.[27] Oakland thrived as new industries were attracted into the city, whose laissez-faire political climate was conducive to progress through industrial growth.

Not until after the first decade of the 20th century did Oakland, like other American cities, begin to accept land-use planning as a legitimate function of local government.[28] The Age of Regulation had not yet begun. Oakland's Board of Public Works, created in 1889 to control the city's capital improvements, remained the principal vehicle for implementing public land-use policies for two decades.[29] Land-use restrictions were intended to promote the city's growth. In the absence of a city planning department until 1911, no city agency could rival the power of the private sector over land-use planning.[30] Regarded as a threat to the city's residential image and commercial prosperity, the Chinese were tolerated only where they could do no harm to property values.

By 1912, housing conditions in the Inner City had deteriorated to such an extent that the Chinese were able to acquire properties within Chinatown and scattered parcels in the industrial section to the south.[31] The Madison Square District, however, continued to remain "off limits." Although victimized by racism, the Chinese adapted to prevailing conditions in the quarter. Employment, not housing, was their most pressing problem. Most of the Chinese could not afford better housing. Many of those who had the money did not have families to house. The County Rollbook for 1912 reveals that 21 parcels were owned by 12 Chinese, five of which were Chinese women. Although the bachelor society could readily adjust, Chinese families could not be accommodated in Chinatown lodging houses. Many dispersed in search of more suitable structures.

"Industrial Capital of the West"

Oakland's pro-industrial policies began to pay off after the Earthquake of 1906, which left San Francisco in ruins and the East Bay relatively undamaged. Alameda County, with only 8002 employed in manufacturing and 12.8 percent of the Bay Area's manufacturing jobs in 1899, supported 35,909 manufacturing employees and 30.7 percent of the Bay Area's manufacturing jobs in 1919.[32] Oakland had become the industrial, warehousing, and transport center of the San Francisco Bay Area by the close of World War I.[33] Shipbuilding, food processing, iron works and mills, and automobile production spread into the older neighborhoods of the city, where access to rail and water transport was available. "California bungalows" were built in the expanses of southeast and east Oakland between 1910 and 1940 for working-class families.[34]

By 1914, Athenian Oakland had begun to suffocate under the ill effects of its

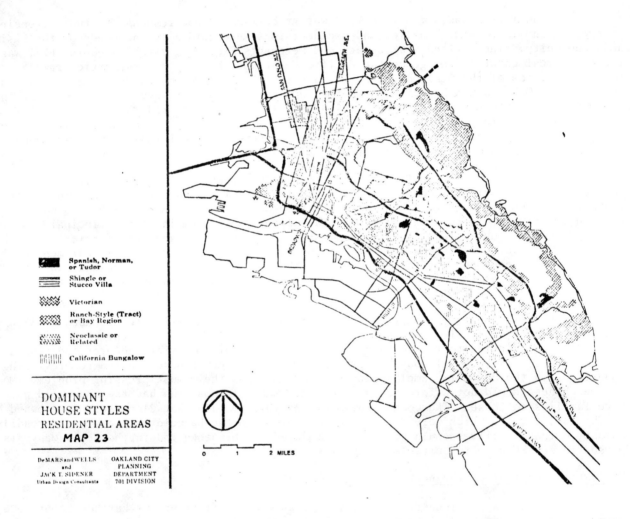

Spanish, Norman, or Tudor

Shingle or Stucco Villa

Victorian

Ranch-Style (Tract) or Bay Region

Neoclassic or Related

California Bungalow

DOMINANT
HOUSE STYLES
RESIDENTIAL AREAS
MAP 23

DeMARS and WELLS
and
JACK T. SIDENER
Urban Design Consultants

OAKLAND CITY
PLANNING
DEPARTMENT
701 DIVISION

0   1   2 MILES

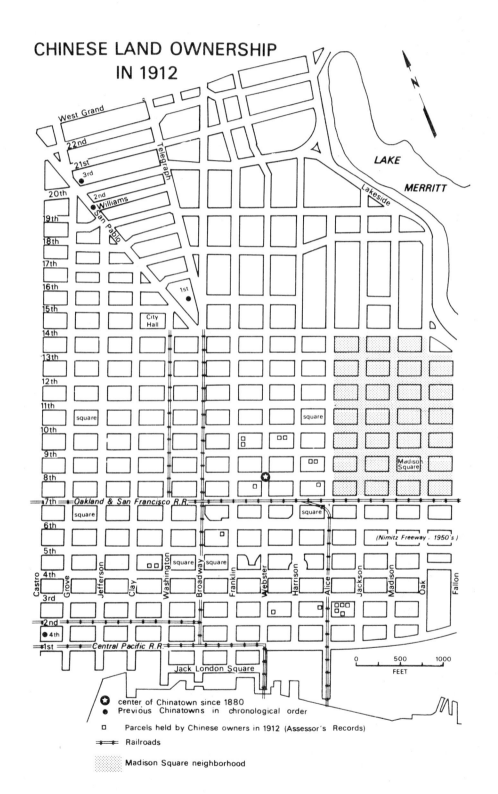

CHINESE LAND OWNERSHIP
IN 1912

West Grand

22nd

21st
3rd

20th   2nd
Williams

19th

18th

17th

16th   1st

15th

City Hall

14th

13th

12th

11th   square   square

10th

9th   Madison Square

8th

7th Oakland & San Francisco R.R.

square   square

6th
                                    (Nimitz Freeway . 1950's)

5th

4th   square   square

3rd

2nd

4th

1st   Central Pacific R.R.

Jack London Square

LAKE

MERRITT

Lakeside

Castro   Grove   Jefferson   Clay   Washington   Broadway   Franklin   Webster   Harrison   Alice   Jackson   Madison   Oak   Fallon

Telegraph   San Pablo

N

0   500   1000
FEET

⊛ center of Chinatown since 1880
● Previous Chinatowns in chronological order

▫ Parcels held by Chinese owners in 1912 (Assessor's Records)

╫╫╫ Railroads

Madison Square neighborhood

industrial growth. Land-use policies finally emerged to exclude the most repugnant activities from the residential areas of the city. Ordinance 700 N.S. in 1914 assigned the following activities to the non-residential section of town which paralleled the railroad tracks: quarrying, stone crushing, rolling mills, machine shops, slaughter houses, reduction works, vinegar works, pickle works, hospitals, asylums, stables, wood and lumber yards, undertakers and funeral parlors, and all factories using any source of power except animals.[35] Zoning controls were finally introduced as a systematic instrument of public policy. Although weakened nine months later at the urging of businessmen, the precedent was established.

As in many American cities, zoning was adopted in Oakland during the 1920's as a means of strengthening the institution of private property in the face of rapid and unsettling changes.[36] The tremendous growth of manufacturing was accompanied by negative externalities like air and water pollution. The intrusion of industrial operations into newly built housing tracts made protective zoning politically imperative. Zoning was needed to encourage the city's real estate boom and to protect homeowners and developers desirous of maintaining the residential character of their investments.[37] Every square foot of land in the city was included in some district or zone by 1921. Not yet conceived of as a tool for guiding the development of the entire city, zoning was applied during this period as a safeguard available for the protection of areas which cared enough to request such protection.[38]

Originally used to protect property values, zoning did not appear to be a means of social segregation or a method of minimizing property taxes until much later.[39] Racially restrictive covenants were legally enforceable and property taxes were borne by industry during this period. The Garden City ideals of developers and planners could no longer be realized without zoning regulations in a period of unprecedented industrial growth. At stake was the essential character of Oakland, its spacious unpretentious residential heritage.

Chinatown, nestled in the "non-residential" district of Oakland, did not "deserve" such protection. Ordinance 700 N.S. was not designed to insulate the quarter from industrial blight. Of the 30 Inner City Chinese listings in the Pacific Telephone Directory in 1909, none lived in the central residential districts. Most of them (18) lived in the Chinatown core, eight resided in the industrial section to the south, two lived in the area west of Broadway, and two were situated in the Central Business District.[40] Oakland's Inner City, the oldest section of town, is bounded by the Oakland Estuary, Lake Merritt, Grand Avenue, and Market Street.

Manufacturing continued to push north into the quarter in the absence of zoning restrictions. The impact of Ordinance 700 N.S., passed in 1914, was observable by 1920. Of the 27 Inner City Chinese listings in the 1920 Pacific Telephone Directory, only 12 were located in the Chinatown core and only five were situated in the industrial area to the south. Other areas continued to harbor Chinese residents. The Central Business District had two Chinese residential listings and the area to the west of Broadway listed three Chinese. The Madison Square District, however, which deteriorated rapidly during this period, included five listings.[41] The blighting effects of industrial land use opened the way for Chinese settlement in the Madison Square neighborhood.

Unregulated manufacturing and wholesaling activities in the Inner City likewise dictated the fate of the Central Business District. The growth of the "Uptown" retail core in the 1920's accelerated as conditions in the older "Downtown" section of the city turned from bad to worse. The Downtown section, running along Broadway and Washington between 11th and 14th Streets, replaced the Old City commercial area as the leading retail center in Oakland during the first decade of the 20th century. By 1920, however, it also began to deteriorate and was succeeded by the Uptown Business District, north of 14th Street, by 1930.[42] The movement of Kahn's Department Store from 12th and Washington Streets to 15th and Broadway in 1913 was a harbinger of retail trends. The move by Capwell's Department Store from 14th and Clay to 20th and Broadway in 1929 provided the coup de grace. Breuners, I. Magnin, and several major theaters located in the Uptown core by the early

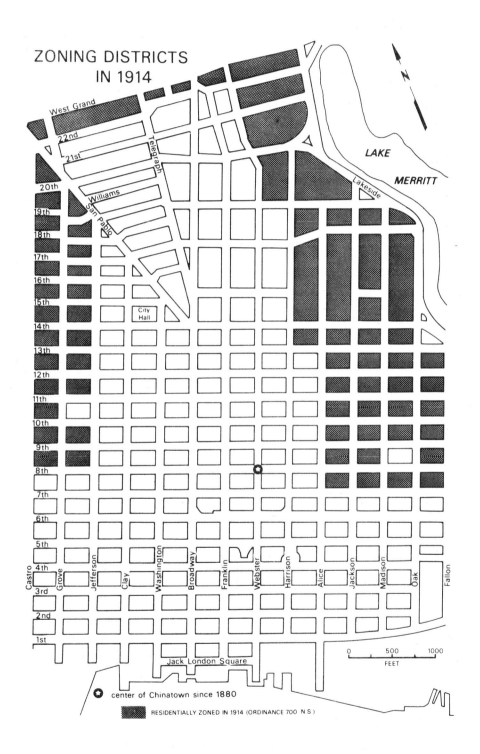

ZONING DISTRICTS
IN 1914

West Grand
22nd
21st
Telegraph
20th
Williams
19th
San Pablo
18th
17th
16th
15th
City Hall
14th
13th
12th
11th
10th
9th
8th
7th
6th
5th
Castro
4th
Grove
Jefferson
Clay
Washington
Broadway
Franklin
Webster
Harrison
Alice
Jackson
Madison
Oak
Fallon
3rd
2nd
1st

LAKE
MERRITT
Lakeside

Jack London Square

0   500   1000
FEET

⊛ center of Chinatown since 1880

▨ RESIDENTIALLY ZONED IN 1914 (ORDINANCE 700 N S)

97

OAKLAND'S CENTRAL BUSINESS DISTRICT SINCE 1900

MAP 26

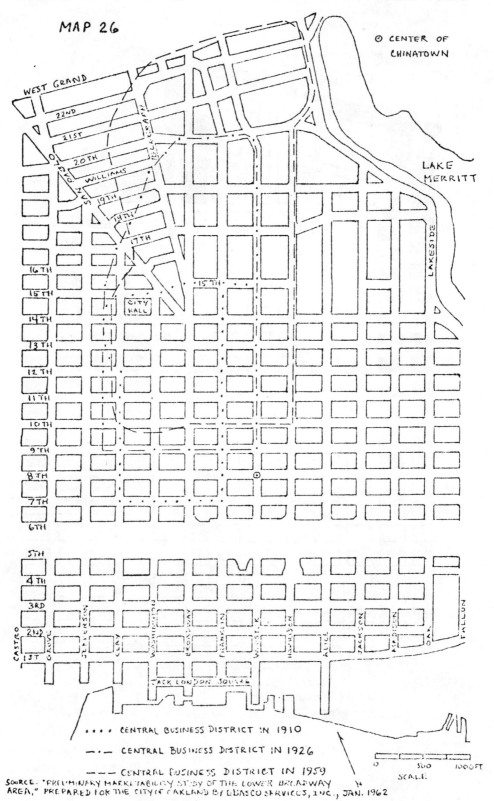

⊙ CENTER OF CHINATOWN

LAKE MERRITT

•••• CENTRAL BUSINESS DISTRICT IN 1910

—•—• CENTRAL BUSINESS DISTRICT IN 1926

——— CENTRAL BUSINESS DISTRICT IN 1959

SOURCE: "PRELIMINARY MARKETABILITY STUDY OF THE LOWER BROADWAY AREA," PREPARED FOR THE CITY OF OAKLAND BY EBASCO SERVICES, INC., JAN. 1962

0   500   1000 FT
SCALE

1930's.[43] The Uptown Association, organized in 1919 to develop the business district of the city lying north of 14th Street, played a pivotal role in facilitating this shift.[44]

Flanked by residentially zoned districts to the east and west until 1935, the Central Business District expanded north in response to industrial expansion along its southern margins. Oakland had become the greatest freight terminal west of Chicago by 1921.[45] As the terminus for three transcontinental railroads and many shipping lines, Oakland attracted hundreds of new manufacturing and wholesaling firms during the 1920's. Most gravitated to the southern edge of town, which had been zoned for this purpose. Although the Central Business District was included in the non-residential zone in 1914, rents in the retail quarter were too prohibitive for manufacturing operations.[46] The decline in land values in the Old City section of the Central Business District, which accompanied the movement of retail establishments up Broadway, made it possible for light manufacturing and wholesaling operations to take their place.[47]

Although attempts were made in the early 1920's to reclassify the city into general (unrestricted), mixed residential, and exclusive single-family housing zones, they were designed to protect the city's outlying residential areas from invasive forces.[48] The city fathers did not assign noxious industrial activities to specific areas until 1930. The regulation of industry became acceptable only after growth had threatened to drive down residential and then commercial property values. The urge to grow bigger and faster, which had dominated the course of land-use policies in Oakland since its founding, finally began to lose its aura. The concept of regulated growth, untenable for The City Practical, was finally institutionalized during the 1930's in the name of Civic Progress. The effects of its industrial revolution, which had permeated the Chinese quarter for decades, finally began to be felt Downtown and in the single-family detached dwellings that supported its retail establishments. Regulations were needed to uphold Oakland's Garden City ideals in the face of industrialization.

Metropolitan Oakland

Heralded in 1933 as one of the five most progressive cities in terms of industrial and commercial development in the nation, Oakland had become a dynamic central city. Its early preoccupation with industrial growth appeared to be bearing fruit. At the same time, however, it also shared in the pessimism of the Great Depression. Unanticipated decentralization, a cause for alarm in most central cities in the United States, had also become a problem in Oakland. The city's eminence as a rail, shipping, and streetcar hub was jeopardized by increasing reliance on truck and automobile transportation. Wholesaling and retailing dispersed into suburban and outlying commercial centers in quest of lower rents, taxes, and labor demands.

Conflicts among business groups heightened as Oakland's share of Alameda County retail sales dropped from 76.2 percent in 1929 to 72.2 percent in 1939. This trend eventually reduced the city's share to 53.6 percent by 1958.[49] The Downtown Property Owners Association, formed in 1931 to attract patrons from other sections of town into the district, emerged as an effort to stem the centrifugal forces of outmigration and the invasive consequences of industrial blight. Rivalry between the two merchant associations persisted until 1961, when the Uptown and Downtown groups merged in the interest of developing the Central Business District as a whole.[50]

What was good for industry was no longer good for retailing in the Central Business District. More jobs meant more business, but not necessarily for Oakland in general or for the Downtown merchants in particular. The rise of outlying residential districts like Montclair, Forestland, and Piedmont Pines during the 1930's and 1940's was made possible by the automobile. Served by commercial strips and neighborhood shopping areas, new houses were built in the hills of East Oakland to accommodate the city's burgeoning population. The "Bay Region" style of their architecture, an open-plan, post-and-beam house opening into carefully landscaped patios or to view decks, reflected their hillside setting.[51] World War II witnessed the construction of Ranch Style or "tract" houses in the Lower Hills and Southeast Oakland, designed to meet the needs of Oakland's growing

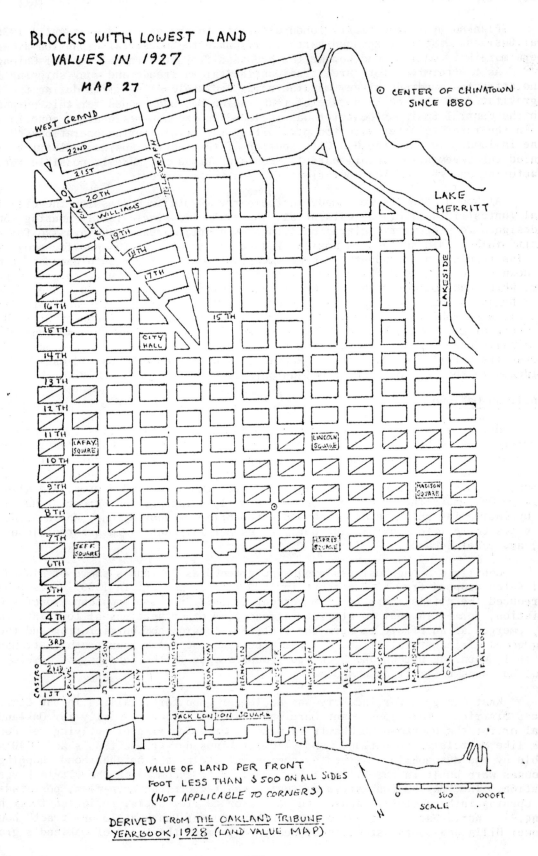

BLOCKS WITH LOWEST LAND
VALUES IN 1927

MAP 27

WEST GRAND

22ND

21ST

20TH

WILLIAMS

19TH

18TH

17TH

TELEGRAPH

⊙ CENTER OF CHINATOWN
SINCE 1880

LAKE
MERRITT

LAKESIDE

16TH

15TH

14TH

CITY
HALL

15TH

13TH

12TH

11TH

LAFAY.
SQUARE

LINCOLN
SQUARE

10TH

9TH

MADISON
SQUARE

8TH

7TH

JEFF.
SQUARE

HARRIS
SQUARE

6TH

5TH

4TH

3RD

2ND

1ST

CASTRO

GROVE

JEFFERSON

CLAY

WASHINGTON

BROADWAY

FRANKLIN

WEBSTER

HARRISON

ALICE

JACKSON

MADISON

OAK

FALLON

JACK LONDON SQUARE

N

VALUE OF LAND PER FRONT
FOOT LESS THAN $500 ON ALL SIDES
(NOT APPLICABLE TO CORNERS)

0   500   1000 FT.
SCALE

DERIVED FROM THE OAKLAND TRIBUNE
YEARBOOK, 1928 (LAND VALUE MAP)

100

labor force. Commercial development along Grand Avenue, Park Boulevard, MacArthur Boulevard, Lakeshore Avenue, and East 14th Street accelerated to capitalize upon their increasing traffic.[52]

Problems with traffic congestion not only posed a threat to retail merchants in the Central Business District, they also constrained the city's industrial growth. The Port Commission, established in 1927 as an independent city agency to manage and promote the Port of Oakland, lost little time in pressing for highway development. Plans for an industrial highway skirting the East Bay waterfront from San Leandro to Richmond were already under way by 1928. Originally designed to run along Wood and 3rd and 4th Streets, the Major Street Plan urged the acquisition of rights of way and the control of industrial building well in advance of its eventual construction.[53] Faith in the promise of technological efficiency, advanced by Frank Lloyd Wright and Le Borbusier in the 1930's, presumed that problems of cities were rooted in their physical structure.[54] Redesigning the city along rational architectural principles was the object of city planning in Oakland during this period.

The adoption of the city manager system of government in Oakland in 1930 was welcomed as a step toward more efficient decision making. As part of this concern for municipal reform, the city fathers established a Board of Zoning Appeals and administrative procedures for rezoning in 1931.[55] Ordinance 4775 N.S. (1931) restricted the location of industries, businesses, trades, and apartment buildings. It limited the height and size of new buildings and specified the space which was required for yards. Moreover, the ordinance divided the city into five zoning areas: single-family dwellings, general residential, light manufacturing and commercial, unrestricted (industrial), and mixed non-industrial. Although by no means revolutionary in concept, this ordinance at last recognized the incompatibility between industrial and other non-residential land uses. Ordinance 4775 N.S. was replaced by Ordinance 4789 N.S. on March 20, 1931, two months after its passage. The new ordinance further refined the restrictions advanced in the previous ordinance.

Planning in Oakland during the early 1930's was clearly in a state of flux. One of the first tasks of the City Planning Commission, created in 1932, was to overhaul the city's outmoded zoning regulations in a more thoughtful manner than had been demonstrated in 1931. Ordinance 474-475 C.M.S., passed in 1935, embodied the commission's recommendations and laid the groundwork for zoning until the early 1960's.[56] It established nine zones: single-family residential, 2-4 family residential structures, multiple-dwelling units, mixed residential, central business, general business, commercial (with obnoxious but not necessarily blighting effects), mixed business, light industrial, and heavy industrial. The ordinance restricted activities, limited the height of buildings, and set open space requirements in each of these zones. District boundaries were designed to preserve existing land uses, especially commercial areas, which had been neglected before in the interest of promoting industrial development.

The Chinese quarter, designated as part of the light industrial district, was still regarded as an area with limited commercial or residential value to the city. It served as a buffer between the Central Business District and the heavy industrial zone along the waterfront. Although protected from "obnoxious, offensive, or hazardous" industrial activities, Chinatown nevertheless did not warrant further protection. Yards were not required. Buildings could not exceed 100 feet in height, which might detract from the Central Business District skyline. Completion of the Posey Tube in 1927, connecting Alameda Island with the Central Business District, more firmly established the function of the quarter as a major traffic corridor. The growth of Alameda during World War II accentuated Chinatown's function as automotive service center and thoroughfare. Chinatown's location along 7th Street, the major auto route through Oakland before the Nimitz Freeway, and along Webster, linking Alameda and Downtown Oakland made it ideal for wholesaling and auto repair.

Zoning regulations made no provision for single-family or 2-4 family housing areas in the Inner City, even along Lake Merritt, which had been one of the most fashionable residential areas in town during the 19th century. Even multiple-family zoning

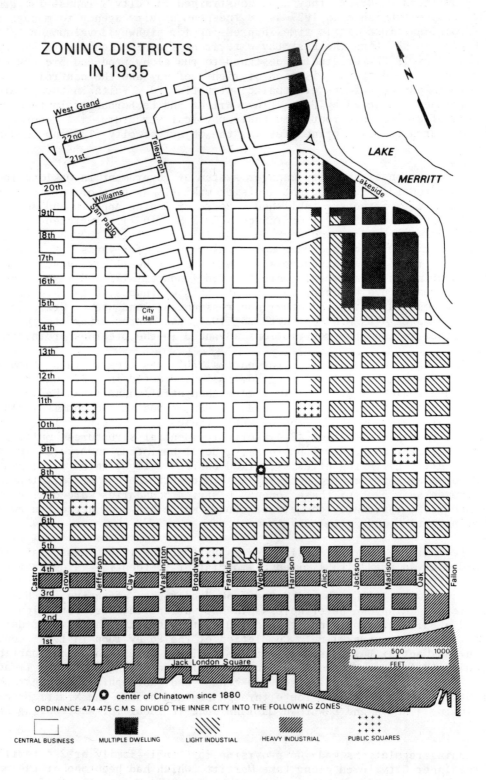

ZONING DISTRICTS
IN 1935

LAKE
MERRITT

center of Chinatown since 1880

ORDINANCE 474-475 C M S DIVIDED THE INNER CITY INTO THE FOLLOWING ZONES

CENTRAL BUSINESS   MULTIPLE DWELLING   LIGHT INDUSTIAL   HEAVY INDUSTRIAL   PUBLIC SQUARES

districts, however, were confined to the northern and western fringe of the Central Business District. The Madison Square section was included in the light industrial zone, despite its history as a residential district. As older residents passed away or moved into less blighted neighborhoods, Chinese residents moved in to take their place. Excluded from the more attractive areas of Oakland by legally enforceable racially restrictive covenants, Chinese families had no choice. Before rezoning in 1930, about 42 percent of the Chinese residential listings in the Inner City were concentrated in the Chinatown core. After rezoning in 1940, only 29 percent remained in the core. The number of Chinese residential listings in the core dropped during this period from 63 to 48.[57]Chinatown, bounded in 1939 by Broadway on the west, 10th Street on the north, Fallon on the east and 5th Street on the south, expanded in the aftermath of rezoning.[58]

Completion of the San Francisco-Oakland Bay Bridge in 1936 turned Oakland into an even more dynamic wholesale distribution center. The city's share of wholesale sales in the San Francisco Metropolitan Area climbed from 6.5 percent in 1929, to 8.5 percent in 1939, to 12.8 percent in 1948, to 16.2 percent in 1958.[59] Wholesale hardware, beverage, and grocery establishments tended to concentrate at the lower end of the city. Rezoning in 1935 facilitated their expansion into nearby areas. The boom in wartime shipbuilding and defense related manufacturing bid up the demand for space in the industrial section of Oakland and provided more impetus to the deterioration of housing. In anticipation of land-use conversion, landlords were reluctant to maintain and improve older structures.

Lack of housing alternatives for lower-income minority residents enabled landlords to undermaintain structures without risk of losing their tenants. Housing starts in Oakland plummeted from 1926 to 1935, as small builders were eliminated during the Depression.[60] The drop in new housing dampened the rate of filtering, turning Inner City housing into a seller's market. The shortage reached crisis proportions by March, 1938, when the rental vacancy rate shrank to 2.3 percent after soaring to 8.5 percent just six years earlier.[61] The Oakland Housing Authority was established in 1938 to meet the crisis. Its first two public housing projects, Campbell Village and Peralta Villa, were situated in West Oakland, where deterioration was most acute.

Property acquisition, clearance, and construction of the Nimitz Freeway during the 1940's and early 1950's worsened the plight of Inner City residents. The State Division of Highways project destroyed nearly 2000 dwelling units along 6th and Castro Streets, further reducing the supply of low-rent housing in Oakland.[62] Undermaintenance in expectation of clearance likewise allowed the supply to dwindle, which increased crowding in nearby areas. Building codes were loosely enforced until 1960, when Operation Padlock was finally launched by the City Building and Housing Department.

Despite these forces, housing in Chinatown remained in relatively good condition. Appraisal records of real property in Chinatown reveal the relatively stable physical condition of the quarter during the late 1940's and early 1950's. Of the 246 parcels in the quarter appraised in 1953, only one was considered in "poor" condition. About 12 percent were rated as "fair" and 70 percent as being in "average" shape. Although 17 percent of the parcels supported structures in "good" condition, only two parcels were classified as "excellent."[63] By no means physically blighted, the quarter was bolstered by sentiment and symbolism.[64] Community ties and pride insulated the community from degradation. The Chinese Community Center, which opened at 9th and Harrison in 1953, symbolized the vitality and cohesion of the community in the early days before the Nimitz Freeway. In the words of Dr. Raymond Eng, "the purpose of the center was to unite Western and oriental culture and to fight communism."[65] Assessor's records suggest that Chinese acquisition of real property in the quarter spiraled after World War II. Liberalized immigration laws helped to revive the community as refugees and war brides arrived from China.

Redevelopment as the Panacea

Unruffled by the onslaught of Oakland's transition from a center of employment to a center of unemployment, Chinatown forged ahead as a flourishing residential district.

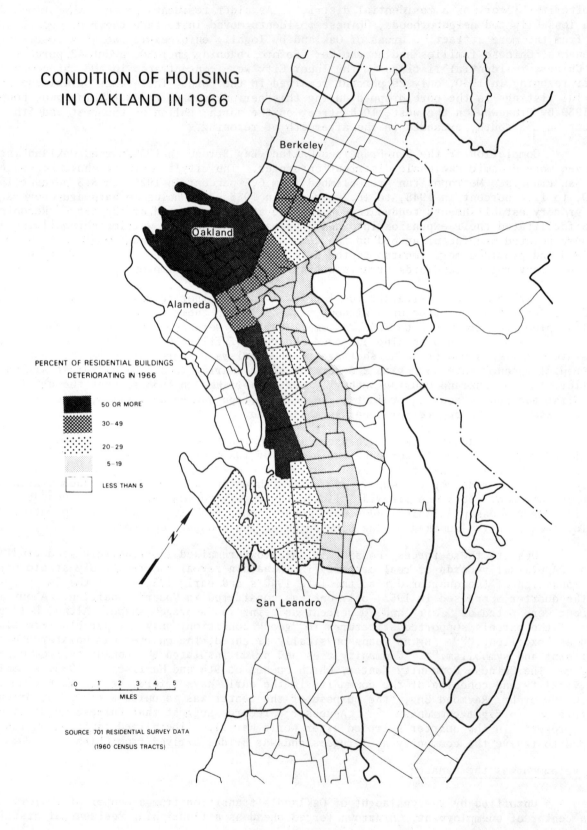

CONDITION OF HOUSING
IN OAKLAND IN 1966

Berkeley

Oakland

Alameda

PERCENT OF RESIDENTIAL BUILDINGS
DETERIORATING IN 1966

	50 OR MORE
	30–49
	20–29
	5–19
	LESS THAN 5

N

San Leandro

0 1 2 3 4 5
MILES

SOURCE 701 RESIDENTIAL SURVEY DATA

(1960 CENSUS TRACTS)

104

Of the 148 commercial properties in Chinatown to be appraised in 1953 and then again in 1958, 85 percent remained in the same condition. Although nine percent deteriorated during this period, five percent of the properties were upgraded. A much smaller sample of 21 residential properties in Chinatown indicates a little better trend. Only one parcel declined, 14 remained in the same condition, and six improved in rating during this period.[66]

Chinese acquisition of property in the quarter helped to insulate its structures from rapid turnover and speculation. Of the 231 Inner City properties held by Chinese owners in 1973, 46 percent were purchased before 1960. Only 14 percent were acquired between 1970 and 1973.[67] Widening employment opportunities for the Chinese after World War II and the Communist victory in China induced many Chinese to invest their savings in land. Scattered properties throughout the Old City section of Oakland were acquired by Chinese by 1960 as the area west of Broadway became increasingly blighted during the 1950's in the absence of new investment.

The Housing Act of 1949, which made Federal assistance available for housing construction and slum clearance for the first time, paved the way for major shifts in local policies. The exodus to the suburbs, kindled by Federal subsidies for freeways, single-family housing loans, and home ownership, accelerated during the 1950's. Suburban residential development following World War II made it possible for many of Oakland's more prosperous residents to move out, leaving behind less well-off residents, many of whom were unable to find employment in the post-war Bay Area economy.[68] Although initially unpalatable to the city fathers, urban renewal grew in esteem as Oakland's white population decreased by one-sixth between 1950 and 1960. The impending prospect of a non-white city was compounded by a 13.8 percent unemployment rate among non-white males in 1960.[69] In June of 1964, Oakland was cited as a depressed area by the U.S. Department of Commerce. Rising taxes and crime rates heightened the exodus. Oakland, like so many other central cities, was caught in the transition.

Oakland's share of retail sales in Alameda County declined from 59 percent in 1954 to 51 percent in 1961 to 46 percent in 1966.[70] Vacancies in the downtown area rose to a phenomenal 21 percent between 1959 and 1965.[71] Not until 1954, when John Houlihan was elected Mayor, did redevelopment really begin to be embraced as a vehicle for slum clearance. The concept of eminent domain and public resale, after all, went against the grain of American capitalism. Not until the city fathers perceived that the Central Business District was in jeopardy did they relinquish their belief in the efficacy of private enterprise. Under pressure from the Oakland Citizens Committee for Urban Renewal (OCCUR), the Oakland Redevelopment Agency was finally created in 1956. Composed of businessmen, property owners, and local government officials, OCCUR began a massive campaign between 1954 and 1957 to popularize redevelopment and to put the City Council on the defensive.[72]

The ballad of urban renewal in Oakland may be sung in different keys. It is clear, however, that the Redevelopment Agency's early penchant for slum clearance was rooted in its concern for the welfare of the city as a whole and not for the needs of disadvantaged people. Early redevelopment plans embodied the grandiose designs of city planners as well as their beliefs that bad housing was the cause of ill health, criminality, illegitimacy, and other social evils.[73] As William Alonso has observed:

> We have learned, for instance, that a slum is often a tightly knit
> social fabric that provides security and gradual acculturation to
> urban life, and that moving its inhabitants to antiseptic piles of
> brick can be cruel. We have learned that slums are often manifes-
> tations of racial as well as class inequality, but we have not
> learned much about solving this thornier problem. This does not
> mean that nothing need to be done about slums, but that the brave
> solutions that had seemed so evident have proved inadequate, and
> that learning advances slowly and painfully.[74]

TABLE 8

NEW BUILDING CONSTRUCTION-LOWER BROADWAY AREA
1945-1961

Year	Use	Location	Height Above Grade	Size Sq. Ft.
1946	Service Station	S.W. corner of 9th and Webster	-	-
1951	Sausage Factory	S.E. corner of 9th and Clay	one	5,600
1951	Community Center	9th between Franklin and Webster	two	6,000
1953	Housewives Market	S.E. corner of 9th and Jefferson	one	33,000
1958	Motel	N.E. corner of 6th and Broadway	two	30,000
1959	Service Station	S.E. corner of 7th and Broadway	-	-
1959[1]	Hall of Justice	Broadway, 6th, Jefferson and 7th	eight	256,000
1960	Simon's Garage	8th, 9th, and Franklin	two	80,000

[1]Construction initiated in 1959.

Source: "Preliminary Marketability Study of the Lower Broadway Area," Prepared by EBASCO Services, Inc., January, 1962.

TABLE 9

SUMMARY OF DOWNTOWN OAKLAND BUSINESS LOCATION SURVEY
April 1950, January 1954, and January 1961

	Total	Downtown[1]	Uptown[2]	Number of Vacant Stores Vacant More Than 1 Year
Total Locations Surveyed	1,364	941	423	
Number of Locations Vacant:				
April, 1960	41	32	9	0
January 6, 1954	61	35	24	16
January 5, 1961	93	49	44	33
Percent of Locations Vacant:				
April, 1960	3.0	3.4	2.2	
January 6, 1954	4.5	3.7	6.1	
January 5, 1961	6.8	5.2	10.4	

[1]Downtown: 10th Street to 15th Street between Webster and Clay Streets

[2]Uptown: 16th Street to Grand Avenue between Webster and Clay Streets

Source: Paul Wendt, "The Dynamics of Central City Land Value in San Francisco and Oakland, 1950-60," Institute for Business and Economic Research, University of California, Berkeley, 1961.

PROJECTS TO REVIVE OAKLAND'S INNER CITY

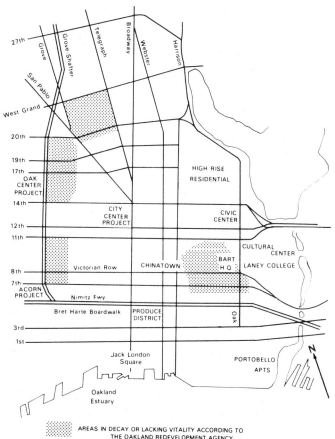

AREAS IN DECAY OR LACKING VITALITY ACCORDING TO
THE OAKLAND REDEVELOPMENT AGENCY

(BROCHURE ENTITLED 'CITY CENTER A QUALITY URBAN ENVIRONMENT FOR OAKLAND')

Chinatown, a product of social cohesion and racism, survived the crusade against blight only because it remained in relatively sound condition during the 1950's. Clinton Park Project, southeast of Lake Merritt, was Oakland's first urban renewal project. Carried out between 1958 and 1961, in involved housing inspection, compliance or demolition, tree planting, traffic modifications, the rebuilding of an elementary school, and other public improvements. The experience of residents with the Acorn Project, begun in 1962, dramatized the anguish and drawbacks inherent in demolition and relocation. Oak Center, which was also part of the General Neighborhood Renewal Plan for the area west of Market Street, emphasized rehabilitation in the aftermath of community bitterness over the Acorn Project.[75]

The Peralta College Redevelopment Area at the eastern edge of the Chinese quarter, the City Center Redevelopment Area northwest of the quarter, and the Chinatown Redevelopment Project between City Center and Chinatown all date back to the mid-1960's. The unfolding of these projects was an outgrowth of the Oakland Central District Plan, published in 1966. The thinking behind all three was guided by the Central Business District Association, which played an important role in formulating the plan, and the Oakland City Planning Commission, which sparked the idea. Urban renewal was conceived neither as a means of conserving nor as a means of expanding housing in the Inner City. It was regarded, at least by those in City Hall, as a vehicle for revitalizing the Central Business District through slum clearance.[76]

Rezoning of the Madison Square district from light industrial to multi-family residential in 1962, for example, was a protective measure. Redevelopment, however, required the transformation of the district into an attractive middle-income neighborhood. After functioning for decades as a buffer between the Central Business District and the industrial section of the city, the Madison Square district had again become valuable as a middle-income residential area, too valuable to be left to the Chinese. New housing would be needed if middle-income residents were to be lured back to the Inner City. As suggested by the Central District Plan:

> Expansion of employment in the Core and in the adjacent Civic Center
> will intensify the demand for close-in housing for single workers.
> The Nimitz Freeway, one block to the south, and a future rapid tran-
> sit station in the area should open the whole range of Bay Area
> activities to residents of this neighborhood. The future Junior
> College and Museum to the east and Chinatown on the west offer rich
> cultural, entertainment, and shopping opportunities.[77]

Suburbanization had not only drawn higher-income residents out of Oakland, it had also encouraged the decentralization of manufacturing, especially among defense-oriented firms, whose relatively well-paid employees were unaffected by the traditions of residence-workplace ties, which govern pre-war patterns of industrial location.[78] The shift out of San Francisco proper, which was in evidence prior to World War II, became more pronounced after it. Oakland experienced similar migrations of plants to a lesser degree, and the newer areas of southern Alameda and Santa Clara counties experienced significant gains. Warehousing and wholesaling functions have also been moving to open spaces where more land is available with less congestion.[79]

The growth of manufacturing and wholesaling at the Port of Oakland Industrial Park provided outlying alternatives even for those firms which preferred to remain in Oakland. The industrial district of the Inner City between the Nimitz Freeway and the waterfront, although no longer an ideal location for manufacturing or wholesale produce operations, was nevertheless anchored by existing investments in industrial property. Warehouses, meat processing plants, and the Grove Street Terminal west of Broadway and warehouses, factories, the Produce District, and the national headquarters of Safeway Stores east of Broadway could not be disloged, except at tremendous expense. Its value as an obstacle to the further dispersal of the Central Business Core made it worth saving.[80]

Housing would have to be built around the industrial district, along the water-

CHINATOWN REDEVELOPMENT IN OAKLAND'S INNER CITY

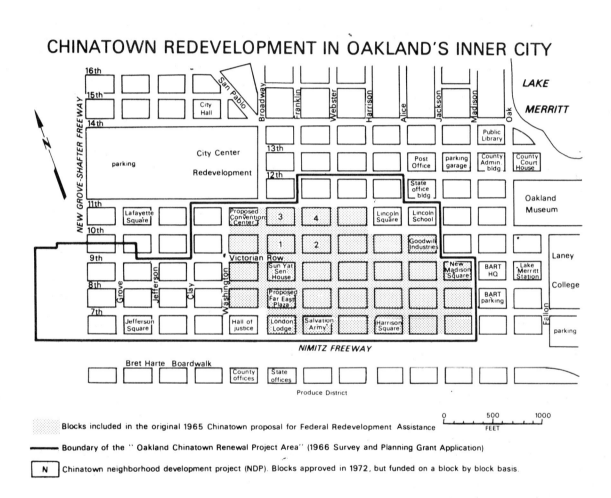

Blocks included in the original 1965 Chinatown proposal for Federal Redevelopment Assistance

Boundary of the "Oakland Chinatown Renewal Project Area" (1966 Survey and Planning Grant Application)

N Chinatown neighborhood development project (NDP). Blocks approved in 1972, but funded on a block by block basis.

front connecting Jack London Square with Laney College and Lake Merritt. The Portobello luxury apartment complex, a $25 million, 30 acre site on the Oakland-Alameda estuary, built on Santa Fe land in partnership with Grubb & Ellis, has spearheaded efforts to turn the waterfront from industrial into mixed land use. The emergence of Jack London Square, owned by the Port of Oakland, as a major restaurant, hotel, and entertainment center is part of the grand design.

Laney College, built to give Oakland an Inner City community college and a park along the slough draining Lake Merritt into the estuary, was made possible by urban renewal. Opened in 1969, Laney was expected to strengthen and upgrade property values in downtown Oakland.[81] Like Acorn and Oak Center, it was part of a General Neighborhood Renewal Plan. Peralta College Redevelopment Area was phase one of the plan. Chinatown was supposed to be phase two. The Redevelopment Agency purchased 40 percent of the campus land, which it sold to the Peralta Community College District at a subsidized price. The other 60 percent was bought from the City of Oakland, including Youell Field, the Exposition Building, and the City's corporation yard. Previously a "mixture of blighted industrial, commercial, and residential properties," Laney College was part of a blossoming institutional complex as well as an attempt to beautify the Inner City.[82] Its proximity to the Oakland Museum and Civic Center made Lake Merritt Station almost inevitable.

Under Housing and Urban Development formulas, the city must cover one-fourth of the net cost of urban renewal projects. The rest is picked up by the federal government. Locally funded public improvements may be credited to the city share to the extent that they benefit the project area. The Oakland Museum, financed by passage of a $6 million bond issue in 1959, and the Bay Area Rapid Transit District Headquarters and Lake Merritt Station helped Oakland finance its share of Peralta College redevelopment expenses. Madison Square, like Lakeside to the north and Portobello to the south, would accommodate College, Civic Center, and Central Business District employee demands for close-in housing.

BARTD facilities have already displaced 75 Chinese households, most of whom moved to East Oakland.[83] The impact of transport and institutional improvements extends far beyond their immediate relocation implications. The indirect effects of invasion and succession by other related activities have already been felt. Madison Square's days as a low-rent Chinese housing area are numbered. Many of the older buildings at its fringe are being either torn down or refurbished in anticipation of rising rents. The expansion of Oakland's Civic Center in the early 1960's has drawn financial establishments into what had been largely a wholesaling, auto repair, and low-rent housing area. The State Office Building was opened in 1960. The County Administration Building and Garage was completed in 1963. The quarter has been hemmed in from south, east, and north.

The vast $150 million City Center Project is situated to the northwest in the heart of the Central Business District. Covering 15 blocks between 11th and 14th Streets and Broadway and Castro, City Center is the quintessence of redevelopment in Oakland. Designed to make the Central Business District attractive to suburban shoppers and tourists, it includes office buildings, department stores, an enclosed multi-level mall, a 500-room luxury hotel, and parking facilites. Accessible by BART's City Center Station, the new Grove-Shafter Freeway, and the Nimitz Freeway, it has been applauded as the nation's most ambitious attempt to rebuild a major city from the ground up.[84] Plans for a Convention Center adjacent to City Center, Victorian Row, and the Chinatown Redevelopment Project have already been made. The beautification of Broadway, designed to connect Jack London Square with Uptown Oakland, has finally given Chinatown a new dimension.

Presently unfolding patterns in the Inner City have been shaped by the needs and ambitions of Oakland's business community. OCCUR and the Oakland Redevelopment Agency provided the means for revitalizing their investments, which had deteriorated for lack of past capital improvements. As stipulated in the Housing Act of 1949, the main motivation that prompted the new national involvement was not the creation of the city beautiful, the city efficient, or the city solvent. It was simply sought to expand slum clearance--already a national purpose--but now bolstered by yet another vehicle for private investment supported by new forms of federal assistance.[85] The zeal with which the redevelopment agency

CHINESE PROPERTY IN OAKLAND'S INNER CITY IN 1960

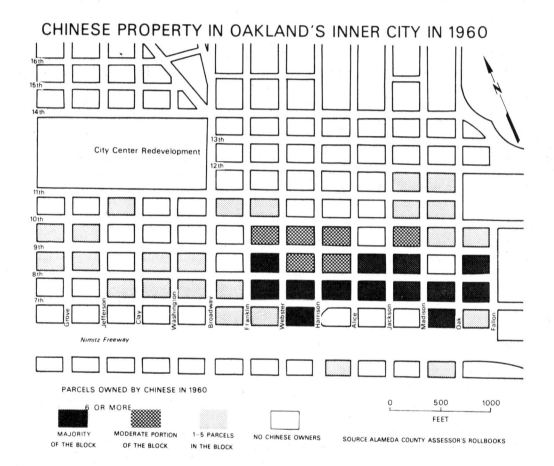

PARCELS OWNED BY CHINESE IN 1960

6 OR MORE

MAJORITY
OF THE BLOCK

MODERATE PORTION
OF THE BLOCK

1-5 PARCELS
IN THE BLOCK

NO CHINESE OWNERS

0   500   1000
FEET

SOURCE ALAMEDA COUNTY ASSESSOR'S ROLLBOOKS

attacked the Inner City was engraved in their plans, which sought to maximize the spoils of federal involvement.

> If the nation's inner cities are going to be rescued from the ravages
> of urban decay, neglect, and indifference, it's doubtful government
> will be the samaritan. Profit is still the great motivator. But
> Oakland is finding it also takes genuine concern and energetic commun-
> ity support before any visible progress can be made.[86]

Recognition that community as well as business involvement in the planning process emerges gradually and often at tremendous expense to local residents. The case of Chinatown redevelopment illustrates the trial and error nature of planning in Oakland.

The Saga of Chinatown Redevelopment

Conflicting views as to the function of Chinatown Oakland as an inner city in a rapidly changing East Bay Chinese community had taken root early in the redevelopment game. The reluctance of the Chinese community in Oakland to air its differences in public allowed city planners to avoid the issues of community function and community control. Not until state and Federal guidelines required increasing community participation in the early 1970's did feuds within the community finally surface. Not until faced with the prospect of community resistance did the Redevelopment Agency, acting in concert with Oakland's business leaders, begin to deal with fundamental questions of community definition and community representation. Oakland's relatively strong present concern for local residents in urban renewal areas rose out of necessity and not design.[87]

The idea of redevelopment for Chinatown germinated among Chinatown's business leaders during the early 1960's. Suburbanization in the wake of Fair Housing had escalated the movement of middle-income Chinese families out of Chinatown Oakland, which housed 70 percent of the East Bay's Chinese in 1950, included only 41 percent in 1960. The prospect of declining sales and land values and Black encroachment from West Oakland could not be ignored. As pillars in the Chinese community, Chinatown businessmen seized upon redevelopment as a means of preserving the identity of the quarter as well as enhancing their own private interests.

The ensuing battle to save Chinatown, like the battle to salvage the Central Business District did not receive the immediate endorsement of the city fathers. Although attempts by Chinatown "elders" to bring redevelopment to the quarter began by 1961, it was not until 1966 that the Redevelopment Agency submitted a proposal to the federal government for survey and planning assistance funds.[88] According to Mayor John Houlihan:

> The Chinese have gone out and raised $100,000 of their own money to
> get the show on the road, the most generous and enthusiastic effort
> by any citizen group to improve the city that I have ever seen. I
> don't see how we can do anything but stand in amazement and give you
> (the community) our cooperation and encouragement.[89]

Structural conditions in the Chinatown section of the Lower Broadway area had remained relatively stable. The City Building and Housing Department's program of concentrated code enforcement, begun in 1959, had arrested most of the deterioration in the area.[90] The threat to the Central Business District from more blighted areas west of Broadway deserved the city's immediate attention. Not until November, 1965, when a preliminary plan for the renewal of Chinatown was published, did the City Council pay much attention to Chinese demands. "Oakland Chinatown Redevelopment Project," prepared by consultants commissioned by Chinatown business leaders, made further delay politically inexpedient.

Covering 30 contiguous blocks from Washington to Madison and from 7th to 10th Streets, the objective of the project was to rebuild and rehabilitate the quarter into a distinctive Chinese cultural, commercial, and light industrial center. Housing would be provided for families, single persons, and the elderly, all related to the Chinese

CHINESE PROPERTY IN OAKLAND'S INNER CITY IN 1973

16th
15th
14th

City Center Redevelopment

13th
12th
11th
10th
9th
8th
7th

Grove
Jefferson
Clay
Washington
Broadway
Franklin
Webster
Harrison
Alice
Jackson
Madison
Oak
Fallon

NIMITZ FREEWAY

NUMBER OF PARCELS WITH CHINESE OWNERS IN EACH BLOCK IN 1973

6 OR MORE   1-5   NONE

0   500   1000
FEET

LONG RANGE PLAN FOR OAKLAND'S INNER CITY IN 1974

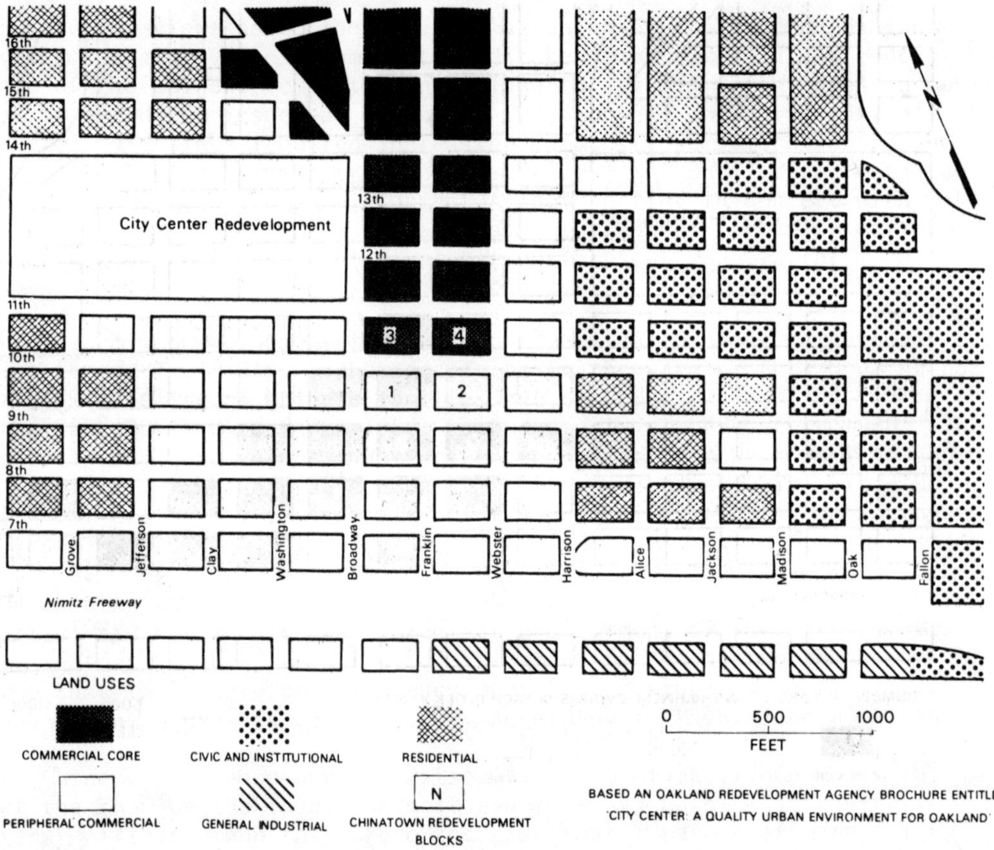

City Center Redevelopment

16th
15th
14th
13th
12th
11th
10th
9th
8th
7th

3   4

1   2

Grove
Jefferson
Clay
Washington
Broadway
Franklin
Webster
Harrison
Alice
Jackson
Madison
Oak
Fallon

Nimitz Freeway

N

LAND USES

COMMERCIAL CORE

CIVIC AND INSTITUTIONAL

RESIDENTIAL

PERIPHERAL COMMERCIAL

GENERAL INDUSTRIAL

CHINATOWN REDEVELOPMENT BLOCKS

0   500   1000
FEET

BASED AN OAKLAND REDEVELOPMENT AGENCY BROCHURE ENTITLED
'CITY CENTER A QUALITY URBAN ENVIRONMENT FOR OAKLAND'

114

Cultural Center, Peralta Junior College, and other elements of the Central Business District. Embodied in the plan was the belief that "dramatic changes will soon be required to attract people back to Chinatown and to make room for expanding business activities and new demands for residential space."[91] The impact of Bay Area Rapid Transit District facilities dramatized the community's need for tighter control over its own destiny. The plan provided a systematic means for saving Chinatown. Back in 1962, Edward B. Wong, a widely respected community leader, proclaimed that Chinese businessmen were willing to construct first class restaurants, a bowling alley, a small theater, and other attractions to get Chinese senior citizens and suburban residents back to Chinatown. Without redevelopment, he warned, the ailing district would die.[92]

The status of Chinatown's elders was at stake. Of the 12 census tracts with 6.2 percent or more Chinese in 1970, only tract 4030 (the Chinatown core) failed at least to double its median monthly contract rent from 1950 to 1970.[93] Their failure to arrest deterioration in the quarter and prevent the encroachment of BART, both outside their control, was nevertheless regarded as an indication by those who had placed so much trust in their elders. Resistance to redevelopment plans by non-Chinese firms (Bay Alarm Company, Supreme Parts Unlimited, and Oakland National Engraving and Gravure Company) was based on the unconstitutionality of condemnation and resale. Councilman John Reading told the objectors that the city, if it went ahead with any future redevelopment project, would "make every effort to keep businesses in Oakland." He said the council was "very sensitive" to the needs of businessmen.[94]

Submission of the Oakland Chinatown Renewal Project - Survey and Planning Application in October of 1966 may be considered a victory by Chinatown businessmen over non-Chinese businesses in the quarter. The Old City-Chinatown Project Area, covering 44 blocks on the southern margins of the Central Business District between Brush and Madison Streets, was designed to "fill the gap" between the Acorn Project to the west and Peralta College Project to the east. Although rooted in the wishes of Chinatown businessmen, the plan envisioned much more. The Redevelopment Agency proposal estimated that 75 percent of the single individuals, 75 percent of the families, and 68 percent of the businesses in the Project Area would be displaced.[95] Fortunately for Chinatown's residents, H.U.D. did not comply with the request.

In 1967, the same basic plan was resubmitted, this time as part of a General Neighborhood Renewal Plan. Phase one, Peralta College, was approved. Phase two, Chinatown-Old City, was scheduled for reconsideration after completion of phase one. A second Survey and Planning Application was submitted by the Redevelopment Agency for the Chinatown-Old City Urban Renewal Project in June, 1968. Although similar to previous plans in scope, more emphasis was focused on rehabilitation, reflecting new concerns about the disrupting effects on businesses in the area. Only 43 percent of the families in the area would be displaced according to plans.[96] Pandemic disgust with urban renewal programs following Martin Anderson's The Federal Bulldozer and other exposés forced Congress to revise its thinking. The Housing Act of 1968 marked the onset of heightened concern about housing for low to moderate residents as well as increasing distress about the soaring cost of housing in general.

The Redevelopment Agency submitted a Chinatown Neighborhood Development Project application in 1969 to conform to the new NDP approach enacted by Congress in 1968. Apparently convinced that large-scale redevelopment would not win H.U.D. funding, Chinatown business leaders opted for a four-block action area proposal. Much to their dismay, the NDP application also went unfunded. Chinatown meanwhile had turned into a reception area for thousands of immigrant Chinese, who arrived in Oakland after immigration laws loosened in 1965.

The intent of Chinatown business leaders has consistently been to transform Chinatown Oakland into a regional center, serving the entire East Bay Chinese population. Chinatown would serve as the nucleus for the East Bay Chinese community, as a tourist attraction, and as a financial center for trans-Pacific trade. In the absence of federal funding for Chinatown, the quarter continued to function as an area of low-rent housing. Instead of following in the steps of San Francisco Chinatown as a cultural, tourist, and trade center for a widely dispersed market, the quarter provided housing alternatives to the crowded accommodations of San Francisco Chinatown. The social and employment needs of foreign-born Chinese families far exceeded those of the sojourners who had settled in Oakland before World War II and those of the couples who arrived after the war.

Major community institutions in Oakland, churches and family associations, were unable to meet their needs. Newcomers, who had not experienced the racism and hardships of long-time Californians, showed little respect for community elders. Well-educated American-born Chinese professionals and students likewise began to question the legitimacy as well as the wisdom of established community leaders by the late 1960's. Not until 1970, however, did signs of community divisiveness become apparent, at least to Redevelopment Agency officials. Planners had assumed from the outset that Chinatown businessmen spoke for the Chinese community in the absence of formal challenge to their authority.

The Application for Loan and Grant for the Chinatown Project, submitted in June, 1970, reflected the Redevelopment Agency's continuing position that Chinatown businessmen were not only the most powerful but also the most representative force in the community. Attempts by the Asian Urban Renewal Association (AURA) to participate in the planning process in August, 1970, were crushed by Chinatown community leaders. Increasing disenchantment with the Redevelopment Agency's narrow approach to community involvement and failures to acquire federal funding surfaced in the summer of 1970. The Rev. Frank Mar, pastor of the Chinese Presbyterian Church, complained: "We don't want this advisory committee to be a rubber stamp. We want to do our homework and decide what we feel should be there." In the words of Dr. Kenneth Hoh, a co-chairman of the Oakland Citizens Committee for Urban Renewal, "I prefer no development at all rather than have development imposed upon us only for our ratification." Charles Chao, a pillar in the Four Families Association of Chinatown and in the Chinese American Citizens Alliance, endorsed the Redevelopment Agency plans for Chinatown in principle but warned that many Chinese organizations felt they had not been given either a say in the planning or an opportunity to participate in the eventual development.[97]

Submission of the third Chinatown Neighborhood Development Project application in May, 1972 finally bore fruit. An invitation for proposals from prospective developers was published in June, 1973, after H.U.D. approval in July, 1972. Lifting of the Nixon moratorium on H.U.D. funds unveiled the fragmented character of the Chinese community. Efforts by the Redevelopment Agency to resolve differences through representative organizations have been fraught with dissent and distrust. Creation of the Oakland Chinatown Redevelopment Advisory Committee (OCRAC) in March, 1972, was undermined by its limited membership. Establishment of a 15 member Project Area Committee in October, 1973 represented a broader cross-section of the community. Its 5/5/5 structure in which the Oakland Chinese Consolidated Association, Greater Oakland Chinatown Renewal Association, and property owners and businessmen within the four-block NDP area are each assigned five votes has clearly worked to the advantage of conservative business interests and community organizations.[98]

Oakland Chinatown Redevelopment, Inc., one of the three developers to bid on Block One of the Chinatown NDP, is backed by the Chinese Consolidated Association, Edward B. Wong, and Dr. Raymond Eng. Charged with conflict of interest in a suit filed by the Asian Law Caucus in November, 1973, under Section 33130 of the California Health and Safety Code, both City Planning Commissioner Wong and Vice-Mayor Eng have adjusted their positions. Wong chose to resign from the Planning Commission and Eng has pledged to give up his financial interests in OCDI if it is selected. Disqualification of the OCDI proposal by Wong in December, 1973, was followed by rejection of the Cal-East proposal for inadequate financial backing and the Sun Yat-sen House proposal for insufficient parking by the Redevelopment Agency. The deadline for new proposals were extended to April 3, 1973. OCDI, the only developer to submit a proposal, was awarded the right to develop Block One for its Hua Tsun (Chinese Village) project on May 5, 1974. Reactions to PAC and Redevelopment Agency procedures among younger, more liberal groups in the Chinese community have been bitter.

The battle for Chinatown continues to rage. At stake is not merely the function of the place but also political control over the community. Plans for Block One do not include housing for low to moderate income families but rather condominium units for the elderly. Although the OCDI plan met Agency requirements for commercial, community, office, open, and parking space, it fell short of residential housing unit stipulations by 34 percent.[99] Its office and condominium emphasis reflected the motives of businessmen who presented the original Chinatown redevelopment idea to the City Council in 1961. Their ambitions and interests have remained consistent, although dampened, since then. What have changed are the character and attitudes of the community they purport to represent and the demands which are made on city planners responsible for carrying out the public interest. From its inception, redevelopment in Oakland has been bent upon transforming the Central Business Districts into an attractive metropolitan core capable of serving at least the East Bay, if not the San Francisco Bay Area as a whole, as a major commercial and office concentration. Chinatown Oakland played a vital role in this transition, providing facilities for cultural, commercial, and middle-income housing activities.

The Chinese "community" in this sense embraced not only the Chinese in Oakland, but the Chinese population of the East Bay. The Chinatown population, which in 1970 constituted less than 14 percent of the East Bay Chinese population, would not be able to support the kinds of new activities which both Chinatown businessmen and the Redevelopment Agency had envisioned. Median family incomes in the two Chinatown tracts limited the purchasing power of residents. More than 40 percent of the families in the two tracts (4030 and 4033) had incomes less than $500 per year, compared with 21.5 percent in this income range for Oakland.[100] It is clear that both Chinatown businessmen and the Redevelopment Agency preferred to view the "community" as a regional, not as a local, entity. Not until 1970 was this regional concept of "community without propinquity" seriously challenged.[101] Attempts to address the needs of the local Asian (Chinese, Japanese, and Filipino) "community" by American-born, liberal college students and social agencies have not been well-received by those in power. Chinatown redevelopment represents the most visible and perhaps the most crucial point of conflict between the two "communities."

Redesign or Revitalization?

Urban renewal in Oakland, which was originally intended as a vehicle by which saving the Central Business District could be made profitable, has been attacked for its narrow ends. Plagued by changing federal policies, economic downswings, and community opposition, it has at the same time been criticized for failing to produce within a reasonable time. The physical redevelopment of Oakland's Inner City, like that of most large American cities, will not revitalize the Central Business District, no matter how profitable its rebuilding and how rapid the pace of its reconstruction, unless our attitudes toward the city change. In the words of William Alonso, "if there is to be any fundamental change, it will have to be by an extraordinary innovation in the field of taste, offering an alternative type of housing and manner of living which is as deeply rooted in the traditions and feelings of our society as is the present suburban house."[102] Although valiant in its attempts, redevelopment in Oakland shows few signs of making progress toward this end.

Aspiring historically to the Garden City ideal, Oakland continues to stand out as a "low key" city of homes in contrast to its exhilarating sister across the Bay.[103] Although Oakland would like to be "where the action is," plans for its physical rebuilding indicate little concern for the functional diversity and dependency which have made San Francisco such an exciting city. "The tendency to equate environmental change with social and intellectual improvement and to argue that we may live in an area in psychological health only if it is modern and well-planned" is particularly disturbing.[104] City Center, for example, was designed to provide a feeling of psychological comfort to the suburban housewife. Grubb & Ellis and Bay Shore Properties, one of the most successful shopping center developers in the country, claim that she will feel safer at City Center than at an outlying shopping area.[105] It is not surprising that critics argue that City Center, which has been made accessible by BART and two freeways, is a self-contained development which will not be functionally integrated with adjacent activities. According to William Alonso:

> Most downtowns have evolved with buildings standing side by side, filling up the blocks, with streets as channels between them. According to their economic strength and ability to pay rent, activities take locations on main streets, all close to each other and dependent on each other. Most of the new developments place their buildings standing free within the block, and little or no provision is made for those businesses that would go on side and back streets because they cannot pay prime rents. Yet many of these smaller businesses are the lubrication and the ball bearings needed for the smooth operation of the larger businesses, and many of them, such as restaurants, bars and book and specialty stores, make downtown interesting and human.[106]

City Center, a glorified pedestrian plaza, was designed to be safe, convenient, and clean, serving the middle-class tastes and values of Oakland and its suburbs. Yet instead of introducing new limited appeal functions to the beleaguered district, it will simply add more of the same. The Inner City's economic woes stem from its decline as a center of limited appeal retailing. Although specialty retail sales in Oakland as a whole increased by 43 percent between 1958 and 1971, the Central Business District's share dropped from 31.2 to 19.8 percent during this period.[107] Limited appeal establishments have flocked not to Oakland's Inner City but to San Francisco and to Berkeley, where tastes are more varied and extraordinary.

The fate of Oakland's Central Business District hinges on the magnetism of its limited appeal retail areas. Jack London Square and Chinatown are its two main sources of untapped limited appeal potential.[108] Designation of the four block Chinatown NDP between Broadway and Webster and 9th and 11th Streets extended Chinatown into the heart of the Central Business District, after over a century assignment along its back and side streets. Its position on the Stranger's Path between Jack London Square and the New Paramount Theater may have tremendous implications for the CBD. The Stranger's Path, described by J. B. Jackson as the part of the city devoted to the outsider, the transient, devoted to receiving him and satisfying his immediate needs, has been demolished by city planners in most cities.[109] The prime function of the path, according to Jackson, is to introduce new life to the city. Whether or not the streets of redeveloped Chinatown and Victorian Row, west of Broadway, become exciting places where a large cross-section of the city's population can mix with strangers may well decide the fate of Oakland's Inner City.

At this point, prospects do not look particularly promising. Offices and condominiums for the elderly are not likely to kindle the imagination, incite spontaneous exchange, or bring the city the kind of image it needs. The design of the Chinatown NDP was geared neither to the needs of low-income residents in the community nor to the needs of the Inner City in its entirety. Like City Center, it was supposed to maximize profits within the development area, itself. Although a hotel, exhibition space, and a small performing arts theater are planned for Block 3, its drawing power may be negligible. Chinatown's main attraction among its suburban Chinese "community" is its restaurants and groceries.

In a recent survey of suburban Chinese families, 95 percent went to Chinatown Oakland either once or twice a month, almost invariably to shop for groceries and to have lunch or dinner at a restaurant.[110] Most felt that San Francisco, not Oakland, Chinatown was the center of the Chinese community in the East Bay. Of the 79 households responding, 74 said they would not move to Chinatown even if it were improved by redevelopment. The five who indicated that they would stipulated that the following changes would have to be made: "modernization," "big kinds," "better environment," "more view apartments," or "social gathering." Although Oakland Chinatown would be hard pressed to compete with Chinatown San Francisco as a cultural center, its promise as dining and entertainment area has been underestimated, perhaps because it would mean competition for existing Chinese restaurants. Increasing opportunities for night life would fill the Central Business District's empty streets after dark, rectifying an untenable district dilemma.

Chinatown redevelopment may thus be challenged on two counts. First, it has failed to deal with its shattering impact on the local Chinatown residential community. If it is to be justified in the public interest, then it should be the responsibility of public agencies to anticipate and meet the needs of those who are displaced. Provisions for special educational and social assistance outside of Chinatown have been at best ineffective. The Redevelopment Agency ought to take the responsibility for coordinating assistance for resettlement, not just relocation. Second, Chinatown redevelopment has failed, at least in its design, to benefit surrounding activities which need to be on the Stranger's Path. Although new housing will expand the market for commercial services in the traditional Chinatown core, it is questionable that its new residents will contribute to either the sales or the evening pedestrian flow so desperately needed outside the quarter.

Conclusions

The evolution of Oakland Chinatown continues to be shaped by the quarter's changing function in terms of the city's growth and dynamic character. New aspirations and old ideals still play an instrumental role in Oakland's transition. Although the profit motive remains the major force behind the rebuilding process, the role of public institutions in mobilizing private investment and in land-use decisions has escalated. The re-emergence of the Inner City in Oakland has been an out-growth of new public policies designed to alter its physical form at the expense of its historic function as a place for acculturation.

Ecological forces have not been the sole factors to govern the course of inner city evolution. The case of Chinatown Oakland demonstrates the pivotal role which land-use policies played in deciding the fate of the Inner City. Perpetuated as a low-rent residential area by capital improvement programs which neglected its needs, by zoning ordinances which encouraged its development as an industrial and commercial district, and by code enforcement policies which allowed it to deteriorate, the quarter could not help but decay after functioning initially as one of the city's better Victorian neighborhoods. The "natural" competition which led to the growth of Chinatown in the Madison Square quarter of the city occurred within the constraints imposed by prevailing public policies. Not until challenged by the increasing popularity of suburbs and the prospect of Central Business District decline were these policies seriously questioned. The reversal in public policies toward Inner City land-use, facilitated by redevelopment, is transforming Chinatown into a middle-class residential and commercial area in spite of ecological pressures from increasing immigration. It is clear that the significance of ecological forces in Inner City evolution has been highly overstated.

Ethnic settlement in the Inner City is no longer feasible in many of the nation's cities. Problems in these cities do not disappear but reappear in the "next most vulnerable district."[111] Most cities hope that the next most vulnerable district will be outside their limits. In Oakland, as Chapter Six will demonstrate, this hope has yet to be fulfilled.

The lessons of urban renewal meanwhile have already erupted. According to Wallace Smith:

The brief era of urban renewal and model cities has also been the era of emergent militancy and community organization among urban minority and low-income groups. . . . Their aims with respect to housing, employment, education, and other matters are generally very clear. They are not immediately concerned with fixing up buildings or fixing up people. They want to fix up the system which crippled the people

and which let the buildings rot. This rather fundamental approach
has the ring of truth. It means revising the rules of the urban
game - the ownership of property and business, the governing of the
streets and schools and professions. It is not what the framers of
urban renewal legislation had in mind, but it is what they have
helped to evoke. That may finally turn out to be the best thing
said about urban renewal in the United States.[112]

Footnotes to Chapter Five:

1. See Calvin Lee, Chinatown U.S.A. (Garden City, 1965) p. 123.

2. See Jerome Rothenberg, Economic Evaluation of Urban Renewal (Washington, D.C., 1967) pp. 30-31.

3. Edward C. Hayes, Power Structure and Urban Policy: Who Rules in Oakland? (New York, 1972) pp. 27-42.

4. "The San Francisco Redevelopment Process," San Francisco Planning and Urban Renewal Association, Report No. 71 (April, 1972) p. 3.

5. Erwin G. Gudde, 1000 California Place Names (Berkeley, 1947) p. 57.

6. Peter Thomas Conmy, The Beginnings of Oakland, Oakland (1961) p. 16.

7. Ibid.

8. Christopher Tunnard, The Modern American City (Princeton, 1968) p. 19.

9. G. A. Cummings and E. S. Pladwell, Oakland. . .A History (Oakland, 1942) p. 49.

10. Edgar J. Hinkel and William E. McCann, eds., Oakland, 1852-1938, 2 volumes, Works Progress Administration, Oakland Public Library (Oakland, 1939) p. 744.

11. Ibid., p. 747.

12. Ibid., p. 129.

13. Ibid.

14. William L. Nicholls II and Earl R. Babbie, Oakland in Transition, Survey Research Center, University of California, Berkeley, 1969, p. 2.

15. Hinkel, op. cit., p. 129.

16. Ibid., p. 29.

17. The History of Alameda County, M. W. Wood (Oakland, 1883) p. 130.

18. Fred E. Reed, "What the Development of the Foothills Has Meant to Oakland's Growth," in J. L. Pederson, Greater Oakland, Pacific Press (Oakland, 1911) p. 261.

19. J. L. Pederson, Greater Oakland, Pacific Press (Oakland, 1911) p. 269.

20. Reed, op. cit., p. 263.

21. Oakland's Form and Appearance, Oakland City Planning Department, Report No. 177 (October, 1968) p. 261.

22. James E. Vance, Jr., Geography and Urban Evolution in the San Francisco Bay Area (Berkeley, 1964) p. 58.

23. Oakland's Form and Appearance, op. cit., p. 51.

24. Joseph Noel, Footloose in Arcadia (New York, 1940) p. 21.

25. Ibid., p. 123.

26. Tunnard, op. cit., p. 64.

27. Hinkel, op. cit., pp. 130-157.

28. Tunnard, op. cit., p. 67.

29. Hinkel, op. cit., p. 752.

30. Hayes, op. cit., pp. 10-11.

31. Alameda County Assessor's Rollbook for 1912 (in storage).

32. Jobs, People and Land, Bay Area Simulation Study (Berkeley, 1968) pp. 144-145.

33. Nicholls and Babbie, op. cit., p. 3.

34. Oakland's Form and Appearance, op. cit., p. 34.

35. Available at the office of the City Clerk of Oakland.

36. John Delafons, Land Use Controls in the U.S. (Cambridge, 1962) p. 23.

37. Carlos Cardona, Marcos Fulop, and Marilyn Pray, "Evolution and Evaluation of Zoning
     in Oakland," unpublished manuscript, Department of City and Regional Planning (Violich),
     University of California, Berkeley, Spring, 1959, p. 2.

38. Ibid., p. 3.

39. "Development Regulations and Housing Costs," Supplemental Report, Assn. of Bay Area
     Governments, Berkeley, July, 1970, pp. 10-13.

40. Pacific Telephone and Telegraph Directory, October, 1909.

41. Pacific Telephone Directory for Oakland, Alameda, and Berkeley, 1920.

42. Oakland Central District Plan, Oakland City Planning Commission, 1966, pp. 38, 45.

43. Ibid., p. 6.

44. Hinkel, op. cit., p. 100.

45. Cummings and Pladwell, op. cit., p. 100.

46. City Ordinance 700 N.S. (1914).

47. Paul Wendt, "The Dynamics of Central City Land Values in San Francisco and Oakland,
     1950-1960," Institute for Business and Economic Research, University of California,
     Berkeley, 1961, p. 5.

48. Cardona, Fulop, and Pray, op. cit., p. 3.

49. D. A. Revzan, "Trends in Economic Activity and Transportation in the San Francisco
     Bay Area," Real Estate Research Report No. 6, University of California, Berkeley, 1954.

50. Wendt, op. cit., p. 49.

51. Oakland's Form and Appearance, op. cit., pp. 36-37.

52. Ibid., pp. 72-73.

53. Oakland Tribune Yearbook, 1928, p. 205.

54. Tunnard, op. cit., pp. 90-91.

55. Available at the office of the City Clerk of Oakland.

56. Cordona, Fulop, and Pray, op. cit., p. 1.

57. Pacific Telephone Directories for 1930 and 1940 (East Bay Cities).

58. 1936 Real Property Survey, Works Progress Administration, Volume 1, Oakland City Planning Commission, November, 1937.

59. Preliminary Marketability Study of the Lower Broadway Area," prepared for the City of Oakland by EBASCO Services, Inc., January, 1962, p. 12.

60. Hayes, op. cit., p. 55.

61. Ibid., p. 56.

62. Wendt, op. cit., p. 5.

63. Appraisal Records, Alameda County Assessor's Office (filed).

64. Walter Firey, "Sentiment and Symbolism as Ecological Variables," Amer. Soc. Rev. (April, 1945).

65. Oakland Tribune (February 12, 1953).

66. Appraisal Records, Alameda County Assessor's Office (filed).

67. Assessment Rollbooks, Alameda County Assessor's Office, 1973 (open for public use).

68. A Survey of Retail Trade in Oakland, prepared for the City of Oakland by Stanford Research Institute (Menlo Park, 1966) p. 3.

69. Nicholls and Babbie, op. cit., p. 6.

70. A Survey of Retail Trade in Oakland, op. cit., p. 13.

71. Hayes, op. cit., p. 108.

72. Ibid., p. 112-113.

73. William Alonso, "Cities, Planners, and Urban Renewal," in James Q. Wilson, Urban Renewal: The Record and the Controversy (Cambridge, 1966) p. 438.

74. Ibid.

75. Hayes, op. cit., pp. 116-119. See also Judy May, Struggle for Authority: A Comparison of Four Social Change Programs in Oakland, California (Ph.D. dissertation, Department of Political Science, University of California, Berkeley, 1973) for an indepth analysis of this conflict.

76. "A Plan for Planning, An Analysis of City Planning Progress, 1932-1952, and a Program for Planning Its Future," City Planning Commission, staff report, 1952, pp. 17-20.

77. Oakland Central District Plan, op. cit., pp. 62-63.

78. Vance, op. cit., p. 66.

79. Jobs, People and Land, op. cit., pp. 133-134.

80. Oakland Central District Plan, op. cit., p. 56.

81. "Peralta College," Brochure, Redevelopment Agency of the City of Oakland (May, 1967).

82. "Summary of Oakland Redevelopment Projects," Oakland Redevelopment Agency, 1973, Pt. 3, p. 3.

83. Oakland Tribune (February 12, 1967).

84. Fortune (advertisement) (December, 1972) p. 49.

85. Charles Abrams, The City is the Frontier (New York, 1965) pp. 78-79.

86. "Private Enterprise: The $150 Million Urban Gamble," California Business (March 21, 1974) p. 14.

87. Based on interviews with Redevelopment Agency officials on the changing character of federal guidelines.

88. Survey and Planning Application: Oakland Chinatown Survey Area, Redevelopment Agency of the City of Oakland, October 18, 1966.

89. Oakland Tribune (January 10, 1966).

90. "Preliminary Marketability Study of the Lower Broadway Area," op. cit., p. 28.

91. "Oakland Chinatown Redevelopment Project," prepared by Warren Jones and Associates, Okamoto/Liskamm, Ribera and Sue (November, 1965) p. 10.

92. Oakland Tribune (February 13, 1962).

93. U.S. Census of Housing and Census of Population data.

94. Oakland Tribune (February 18, 1966).

95. Survey and Planning Application (1966), op. cit., Section R104.

96. Survey and Planning Application: The Chinatown-Old City Urban Renewal Project, Redevelopment Agency of the City of Oakland, June 14, 1968, Section R102.

97. Oakland Tribune (June 24, 1970) p. 37.

98. "Chinatown Redevelopment Questions and Answers," Oakland Redevelopment Agency, June, 1974, pp. 2-3.

99. "Chinatown Offering 1," Invitation for Proposals, Neighborhood Development Program, Oakland Chinatown Redevelopment Project, Oakland Redevelopment Agency, February, 1974, pp. 9-10.

    "Summary of Three Proposals," Agenda for Community Meeting, Oakland Chinatown NDP Project, Chinese Community Center, October 28, 1973, Oakland Redevelopment Agency.

100. Economic Market Analysis and Transient Housing Study: Chinatown NDP Area, prepared for the Oakland Redevelopment Agency by Larry Smith & Company, Inc., and Willis Research, Inc. (January 17, 1973) p. 35.

101. Oakland Tribune (June 24, 1970) p. 37.

102. Alonso, op. cit., p. 445.

103. Oakland's Form and Appearance, op. cit., p. 23.

104. James E. Vance, Jr., "Focus on Downtown," Community Planning Review (Summer, 1966).

105. Chris Godchaux, "The $140 Million Urban Gamble," California Business (March 21, 1974) p. 18.

106. Alonso, op. cit., p. 452.

107. Economic Market Analysis and Transient Housing Study, op. cit., p. B-2.

108. Ibid., p. 7 (cover letter).

109. J. B. Jackson, "The Stranger's Path," Landscape, Vol. 7, No. 1 (1957) p. 11.

110. Survey of Chinese Households in the East Bay Suburbs (see Appendix).

111. Vance (1966) op. cit.

112. Wallace Smith, Housing: The Social and Economic Elements (Berkeley, 1970) p. 483.

CHAPTER SIX

CITY PLANNING VERSUS SELF-DETERMINATION

Introduction

The reemergence of the Inner City as a middle-class housing, shopping, and cultural area was achieved at tremendous social cost and without much thought as to the implications of systematic community displacement. Oakland's city fathers were bent upon saving the Central Business District, which had suffered with the outmigration of mass appeal retail establishments since World War II. Inner City land values, once bolstered by racial segregation, sagged in the shadow of Fair Housing as ethnic families dispersed into outlying areas. The profitability of real estate investments in the Inner City was at stake. Slum clearance seemed to be the only way out. Socially useful but no longer lucrative structures were condemned as "blighted." Chinatown and the surrounding quarter stood in the way of economic progress and civic pride. Chinese residents who could not afford the higher rents of the redeveloped quarter would have to seek housing elsewhere. This chapter will examine the plight of foreign-born Chinese being displaced from the Inner City and community efforts to meet their needs.

The problems of Chinese newcomers in Oakland have been accentuated by narrow minded attitudes toward the significance of physical deterioration in the Chinese quarter. Those who led the charge against its blight were the ones who stood to gain the most from its transformation. Not until they became financially unattractive were Oakland's slums either removed or brought up to code. Perceptions of the Inner City shifted as its value to those in power began to change. According to the geographer Yi-Fu Tuan:

> Our tastes are those of well-educated middle-class adults who wield
> expensive cameras. These tastes are not necessarily shared by
> children, nor by the country's minorities.[1]

City planners, swayed by their physical orientation and misconception about the workings of ghetto life, did not hesitate to join the campaign against slums. What could be more American than the City Beautiful? Professing the righteousness of their beliefs and the altruism of their motives, planners failed to recognize that redevelopment was essentially a means of renewing the fortunes of landowners and developers.[2] Environmental quality is actually a moral and ecological issue, not a question of aesthetics.[3] According to the geographer Pierce Lewis, visual blight in America often persists when it is technically feasible, financially profitable, and institutionally permitted.[4] Oakland is a case in point.

Requiem for a Gilded Ghetto

The settlement of Chinese newcomers in the area east of Lake Merritt was necessitated during the 1960's by the redevelopment of the Chinese quarter. Although the Chinese population of Oakland climbed by 48 percent between 1960 and 1970, the number of Chinese in the quarter decreased during this period from 1554 to 1507.[5] Residents displaced by the construction of the Grove-Shafter Freeway west of Broadway and Bay Area Rapid Transit District facilities near Madison Square moved into the Peralta Heights and Clinton Park districts of East Oakland. The proximity of residential districts along Park Boulevard to Chinatown made them relatively convenient, especially by local bus service. Acculturated Chinese families had settled in the single-family houses of the Peralta Heights and Highland districts ever since World War II. Chinese families, who comprised about eight percent of the population of these two districts in 1960, paved the way for the influx of newcomers.[6]

Scattered apartment houses and old single-family dwellings, built in the neo-classic style, between Park Boulevard and East 14th Street accommodated the needs of low-income residents. Tracts 4054 and 4055 supported only 209 Chinese residents in 1960 but

OAKLAND'S CHINESE POPULATION, 1970

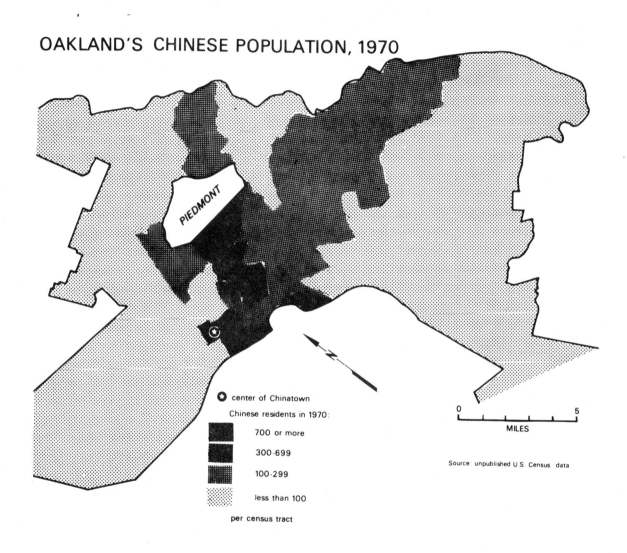

PIEDMONT

center of Chinatown

Chinese residents in 1970:

700 or more

300-699

100-299

less than 100

per census tract

0   MILES   5

Source: unpublished U.S. Census data

1239 in 1970. Fair Housing made it possible. Urban Renewal made it mandatory. Cultural bonds kept the foreign-born and established Chinese together east of Lake Merritt. Yet class differences kept them apart in different neighborhoods. Middle-class Chinese families tended to move north into Trestle Glen, farther east into Skyline, or closer to Chinatown along the shore of Lake Merritt.

Chinese investors, well aware of the lack of housing for Chinese newcomers, acquired small apartments in response to the relaxation of immigration restrictions after 1962. Of the 33 multi-unit properties (parcels with five or more units) held by Chinese owners within a 90 block sample area of the Clinton Park district in 1973, 15 were purchased between 1962 and 1966.[7] Out-of-towners, however, made up only about six percent of the Chinese owners in the sample area. The availability of multi-family housing serviced by Cantonese-speaking landlords drew newcomers into the area. Few could afford single-family dwellings. About 87 percent of the single unit properties owned by Chinese in the sample area were owner-occupied. Chinese investors, quick to take advantage of immigrant needs, eased the process of their relocation.

In contrast to Chinatown, however, Chinese settlement east of Lake Merritt was neither concentrated nor highly visible. Variations in the availability of suitable low to moderate rent apartments among neighborhoods remained small until the late 1960's. The community had no focal point, no center of sentimental, symbolic, or practical value. Chinese residents, especially the foreign-born, looked to Chinatown Oakland for direction, assistance, and opportunity. "Chinatown East" was merely a place in which to reside in 1960. By 1970 its lack of neighborhood facilities and services for Chinese newcomers, ousted from the Inner City, had become a source of unrest. In no census tract outside of Chinatown did the Chinese comprise more than nine percent of the population in 1960. In 1970 the Chinese made up between nine and seventeen percent of the population in five census tracts east of Lake Merritt.

The dispersal upset traditional patterns of both community and public assistance. Too few to warrant special treatment, but too many to be ignored by neighborhood social service agencies, the Chinese have challenged the efficacy of small-scale neighborhood institutions as a vehicle for acculturation. Special bi-lingual programs and personnel, which were easy to furnish in a concentrated ethnic community like Chinatown, were more difficult to fund and administer in mixed ethnic neighborhoods inhabited by Chicanos, Blacks, Chinese and Caucasians. The economies of scale in ethnic acculturation had either been overlooked or disregarded. Public agencies, although aware of the increasing number of foreign-born Chinese residents east of Lake Merritt, were reluctant to reorganize their programs and adjust to new needs. "Chinatown East was difficult to identify and slow to complain. Officials could always fall back on the proverbial "the Chinese take care of their own."

Geared to meeting the middle-class needs of acculturated Chinese residents, public agencies in East Oakland were unprepared for the influx of newcomers. City planners, preoccupied with designing the City Beautiful and manipulation in a milieu of political games, were too busy to attend to the social implications of their schemes. Higher rents in East Oakland required longer working hours. Greater distance from work and stores in Chinatown meant more time devoted to commuting. Parents had less time to spend with their children, whose problems in school stemmed in most cases from their bilingual background. The problems of foreign-born Chinese youth in East Oakland have festered in a sea of good intentions but shallow commitments. Community elders and public officials expressed their desire to help but complained of lack of money to fund special programs.

The battle for community control in the Chinese community of Oakland intensified as it became apparent that Chinatown businessmen were unable to fulfill their social obligations. Chinese merchants, landlords, and employers, who reaped the benefits of immigration, were reluctant to take responsibility for the needs of newcomers. Chinese merchant-businessmen had to struggle for success. Why should recent immigrants be treated with such deference? Chinatown, which had facilitated the settlement and acculturation of

TABLE 10

CHINESE OWNED PROPERTY IN THE CLINTON PARK RESIDENTIAL DISTRICT IN A 90-BLOCK SAMPLE AREA OF EAST OAKLAND IN 1973

Type of Land Use	Residence of Chinese Property Owners						Total
	Owner-Occupied		Owner Residing Elsewhere in Oakland		Owner Residing Out-of-Town		
	Number	Percent	Number	Percent	Number	Percent	
Single Unit Residential	96	67.7	11	13.4	3	20.0	110
2-4 Unit Residential	27	19.0	38	46.3	6	40.0	71
5 or More Unit Residential	9	6.3	20	24.4	4	26.6	33
Commercial	10	7.0	13	15.9	2	13.3	25
Total	142	100.0	82	100.0	15	99.9	239

TABLE 11

PERIOD IN WHICH THE PROPERTY WAS ACQUIRED

Type of Land Use	Before 1960	1960-1964	1965-1966	1967-1969	1970-1972
Single Unit Residential	40	18	15	25	12
2-4 Unit Residential	25	19	7	11	9
5 or More Unit Residential	6	10	10	2	5
Commercial	8	6	5	1	5
Total	79	53	37	39	31

Chinese immigrants in the past, no longer functioned in this capacity. The transformation of the Inner City into a middle-class area challenged the validity of old assumptions and the wisdom of old solutions.

Mainsprings of Community Control

The fight for community control in Chinatown Oakland erupted in the late 1960's as new groups rose to impugn the legitimacy of traditional community institutions. "The future of (San Francisco) Chinatown's century-old organizations, spawned by the bachelor society, adapted to the family society, and now confronting the needs and life style of new working-class immigrants, hangs in the balance."[8] Oakland Chinatown's merchant-businessmen, like those of San Francisco Chinatown, have come under attack by radical and liberal Chinese groups, outraged at their unwillingness to share the reins of community power.

The demand for community control is neither new nor radical. As political scientist Alan Atshuler has pointed out:

The aspiration toward more meaningful democracy, of which these demands are the latest extension, has in successive guises been a key item on the political agenda throughout American history.[9]

An outgrowth of the Poverty and Model Cities Programs, on one hand, and the Civil Rights and Black Power Movements, on the other, community control was envisioned as a means for self-government and territorial sovereignty.[10] The vulnerability of the ghetto to outside interests was dramatized by redevelopment. The colonial nature of Chinatown, exploited by local businessmen and perpetuated by immigration, became blatantly clear.[11]

The battle for control of Chinatown Redevelopment is being waged on several fronts. At one level it is a political struggle among Chinese business leaders, who have been heavily involved in the redevelopment process; liberals representing Chinese social agencies, who have been allowed to participate in a superficial way; and radical youth groups, who have been left out. Radicals, like conservatives, sought the spoils of political victory. At another level, it is part of an institutional schism. Although both conservative and liberal leaders claim to speak for the whole community, liberals did not really organize until the late 1960's and did not voice their opposition to conservative leadership until 1970.[12] Generational differences, divisiveness over the two Chinas, and conflicting views of the Chinese community to be served provided ample grounds for friction. The legitimacy of community institutions and the relevance of traditional values were finally opened to question.

For the foreign-born Chinese youth thrust into the working-class neighborhoods of North and East Oakland, gangs offered ways of venting their frustrations, asserting their identity, and exerting at least some control over their destiny. Disdained by community elders and spurned by traditional institutions, many turned to gangs, which flourished in San Francisco under similar conditions. The Suey Sing, the largest of Oakland's Chinese youth gangs, was originally the name of one of Oakland's early tongs. Both emerged out of a deep sense of frustration with existing institutions which purported to serve the needs of disadvantaged Chinese but failed. In the words of Gordon Yow:

> Kids join for protection from other groups, backed up by sheer numbers and fire power, for a sense of security, and for social needs. . . . Much of the hostility between foreign-born and American-born Chinese youth comes out of "scapegoatism"--directing their frustrations and energy toward each other, rather than at the institutions and society that perpetuates their condition.[13]

The lack of bilingual programs and teachers in outlying schools hindered the academic progress of foreign-born Chinese students, whose affinity for study had been a matter of record. Educational achievement, a major avenue for Chinese occupational mobility in the past, was no longer open for an increasing number of foreign-born Chinese youth. The Oakland Public Schools, beset with more explosive problems among its Black and Chicano students, failed to meet their needs. Oakland's chronic unemployment rates and discriminatory hiring practices in certain trades heightened their sense of frustration. The violent and underhanded tactics of Chinese gangs, reminiscent of past times when the tongs ruled Chinatown, elicited the attention but not the sympathy of community leaders who had previously ignored their demands.

Traditional community institutions (family associations, fraternities, service clubs, churches), which had worked so well in the past to facilitate the process of Chinese settlement and acculturation, had become obsolete.[14] Dedicated to preserving Chinese identity, customs, and values, traditional institutions had failed to meet the needs of the foreign-born and the expectations of the American-born. Community elders pointed to their hard work, sacrifice, and self-reliance as examples for the young to follow. Family associations continued to adhere to the traditions of mutual assistance and to the promotion of clan, and not community, interests. Historic rivalries and obligations, which ripened in a bachelor society, had little meaning to foreign-born working-class families in a period of unprecedented public assistance.

Broadening the community's base to include Japanese and Filipinos was bitterly resisted by elders despite its advantages in seeking outside assistance. Special public programs for Chinese newcomers would be justifiable in terms of numbers only if grafted onto an Asian identity. Liberals argued that Chinese problems, rooted in the colonial character of the Chinatown, could only be solved by drastic political restructuring. Liberals insisted that sacrifice was not the price of immigration, as merchant-businessmen alleged, but rather a manifestation of societal injustice. Elders fought to retain their control over outside assistance and their position as spokesmen for the Chinese community. The issue of Chinatown Redevelopment, originally contemplated as an Asian Cultural Center, inflamed old wounds as its implications for the community were finally recognized.

In Pursuit of Community Based Planning

Chinese settlement east of Lake Merritt required few special services by either public agencies or community organizations until the 1960's, when newcomers from Hong Kong flocked into the area. Prior to this time, most of its Chinese families settled by choice. Established families, ready to relinquish the security, low rents, and convenience of Chinatown, arrived in increasing numbers as restrictive covenants and real estate practices began to fade during the 1950's. Chinese families dispersed, although small concentrations built up where accessibility to Chinatown was best. The students at Cleveland Elementary School, east of Lake Merritt, were 38 percent oriental in 1963, for example.[15] The Inner City still functioned as the reception area for working-class immigrants. Lincoln Elementary School in the heart of Chinatown remained 90 percent oriental in 1962. Since the Japanese population of Oakland was widely scattered, variations in oriental population from year to year provide a reliable indicator of Chinese settlement patterns.

Foreign-born working-class immigrants who settled east of Lake Merritt in the last half of the 1960's did so by necessity. Only partially acculturated and unfamiliar with Oakland, most relied on relatives for assistance. The availability of multi-family housing at moderate rents and the prospect of Cantonese-speaking neighbors and nearby relatives made the area attractive. Its dearth of special neighborhood facilities and programs would have to be endured. The Clinton Park, Fruitvale, Peralta Heights, Highland, 23rd Avenue, and San Antonio Park districts of East Oakland into which they filtered were heavily populated by Black and Chicano as well as White residents. The Chinese were a minority within a minority, an unenviable position.

Lack of bilingual educational programs in public schools east of Lake Merritt prompted many parents to seek other solutions. Lincoln Elementary School, renowned for its bilingual programs, began to accommodate an increasing number of Chinese students, many of whom lived outside the Inner City.[16] Its student body reached 68 percent oriental in 1971. Special bilingual programs, sponsored by the Bay Area Bi-Lingual Education League, cater to the needs of Cantonese and Spanish speaking students. Effective bilingual programs have not been launched in elementary schools outside the Inner City, even though oriental youngsters comprised nearly 46 percent of students at Cleveland in 1971. Oriental students, who made up about 20 percent of the student bodies of Westlake and McChesney Junior High Schools, have not received serious attention.

Problems rooted in the invisibility of working-class Chinese needs, hidden by the success of established middle-class Chinese and by the demands of Blacks and Chicanos, have yet to be addressed. Special classes for Chinese students with limited English skills at Oakland High School, 19 percent Oriental in 1971, have been ineffective. Bilingual programs at Oakland Technical High School, 15 percent oriental in 1971, have been more successful but have been plagued by administrative uncertainties.[17] Even Laney College, situated at the edge of the Chinese quarter, has been reluctant to meet the special needs of its foreign-born Chinese students, even though Asians constitute its second largest ethnic minority. Public education in Oakland remains entrenched in outdated assumptions. Officials have failed to adjust their programs to the reemergence of the Inner City. Administrators were either insensitive to or out of touch with the implications of the transformation.

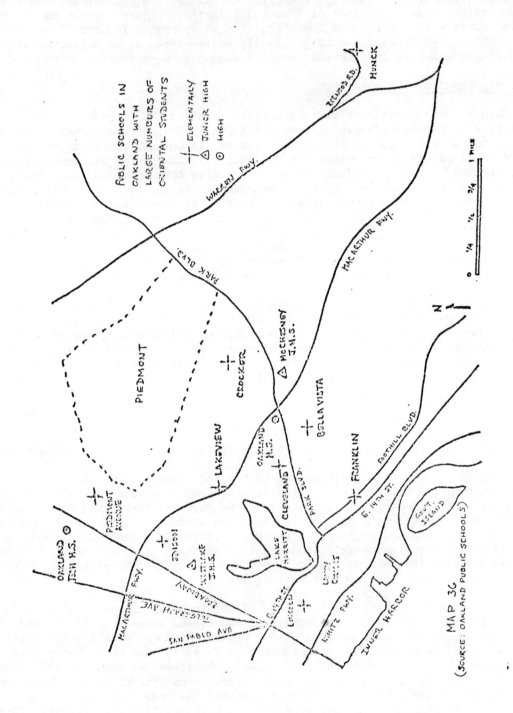

PUBLIC SCHOOLS IN
OAKLAND WITH
LARGE NUMBERS OF
ORIENTAL STUDENTS

+ ELEMENTARY
△ JUNIOR HIGH
⊙ HIGH

MUNCK

REDWOOD RD.

WARREN FWY.

PARK BLVD.

MACARTHUR FWY.

PIEDMONT

MCKENLEY J.H.S.

CROCKER

BELLA VISTA

LAKEVIEW

OAKLAND H.S.

CLEVELAND

FRANKLIN

FOOTHILL BLVD.

PARK BLVD.

PIEDMONT AVENUE

EDISON

WESTLAKE J.H.S.

LAKE MERRITT

E. 14TH ST.

GOV'T. ISLAND

OAKLAND TECH H.S.

MACARTHUR FWY.

TELEGRAPH AVE.

BROADWAY

SAN PABLO AVE.

E. 14TH ST.

LINCOLN

UNION POINT

NIMITZ FWY.

INNER HARBOR

N

0   ¼   ½   ¾   1 MILE

MAP 36
(SOURCE: OAKLAND PUBLIC SCHOOLS)

132

TABLE 12

PERCENTAGE OF STUDENTS ORIENTAL IN PUBLIC SCHOOLS SERVING DISTRICTS
WITH LARGE CHINESE POPULATIONS

	March 1962	March 1963	March 1964	March 1965	March 1966	March 1967	March 1968	October 1969	October 1970	October 1971
Bella Vista Elementary	25	16	15	14	14.0	14.2	12.9	12.4	11.3	10.5
Cleveland Elementary	50	38	38	35	34.5	36.8	37.8	42.8	43.7	45.6
Crocker Elementary	11	11	12	11	11.7	11.4	10.7	9.7	9.3	8.8
Edison Elementary	15	16	11	12	13.6	13.3	12.6	11.4	8.9	9.4
Franklin Elementary	10	11	9	10	8.3	9.0	9.1	8.9	6.8	5.9
Lakeview Elementary	15	13	17	15	16.8	16.9	16.3	17.6	15.6	18.6
Lincoln Elementary	90	65	60	59	55.0	59.0	64.3	64.5	66.3	68.2
Munck Elementary	6	1.5	2	5	5.2	6.9	5.8	10.6	13.8	15.8
Piedmont Ave. Elementary	8	10	0	10	6.0	5.0	5.4	6.8	9.2	8.1
McChesney Jr. High School	20	20	20	21	20.0	19.9	19.8	21.9	22.3	22.7
Westlake Jr. High School	28	29	31	29	25.4	25.4	21.7	22.0	20.0	19.2
Oakland High School	5	11	13	17	18.6	20.0	21.2	20.9	18.5	18.6
Oakland Tech. High School	6	7	8	10	14.9	17.5	15.9	11.7	9.6	14.7

School officials were not the only ones to be caught in the transition. Special public health programs for Cantonese speaking newcomers were likewise unavailable. Medically speaking newcomers were likewise unavailable. Medically indigent Chinese were forced to go to the West Oakland Health Center, where there were no Chinese doctors, to Highland Hospital in East Oakland, or all the way to Chinese Hospital in San Francisco.[18] The importance of familiar neighborhood medical facilities for ethnic patients has been well stated.[19] Cantonese speaking legal service for disadvantaged Chinese is available through the Legal Aid Society. Assistance is confined, however, to part-time student help in West Oakland, on San Pablo Avenue near 23rd Street, far away from areas of Chinese settlement.[20]

Traditional community institutions were willing to support the Chinese Community Center, the East-West Institute, and other self-help organizations under their influence. Assistance to the disadvantaged in the form of information, classes, jobs, recreational activities, and welfare aid was made available but in small doses. Family associations, churches, and service organizations were established to promote the well-being of their members. Community needs were of secondary importance and could be met by the Chinese Community Center. The influx of foreign-born Chinese into Oakland during the 1960's taxed the capacity of community facilities, which had been so effective in the 1950's.[21] Community elders, unwilling to draw upon resources over which they had no control, were unable to meet new demands.

The Chinese Community Council, incorporated in 1969, expanded to fill the gap. Geared to the needs of Chinese residents in the East Bay who do not speak, read, or write English fluently, it has become a major force in the community. Only recently have social service organizations, except for the International Institute, attempted to solve problems with bilingual staff working directly in the community.[22] Most agencies preferred to channel their aid through Chinatown business or professional leaders who claimed to speak for the community. Not until 1972, for example, was the Oakland Chinese Community Council supported by the United Bay Area Crusade, which now contributes a third of its annual budget.

Although the Council offers a wide range of services, including information and referral, educational, cultural, and recreational programs, and interpretation for non-English speaking Chinese, its vocational training and job placement program deserves particular attention. Funded by the City of Oakland's Concentrated Employment Program, it is aimed at heads of immigrant households. Even more importantly, however, is the Council's evolving role as a social planning and coordinating agency. Staffed by professionals and located in unpretentious accommodations in the heart of Chinatown, it at last furnishes both immigrants and outsiders a viable alternative to traditional community institutions. If adequately financed, the Council holds tremendous promise.[23]

Arrangements for the placement of bilingual personnel in public agencies and for the creation of bilingual programs in schools serving dispersed ethnic communities can only be coordinated by community-based social planning agencies sensitive to the needs of the disadvantaged. The efficacy of traditional community institutions, designed in the past to meet the needs of sojourners in a racist society, can no longer be presumed. City planners, who paved the way for redevelopment, can hardly be trusted to look out for the needs of the disadvantaged. The needy, whose difficulties stem from their non-English background, cannot be expected to hold their own in the urban game. Advocacy planning has failed to make much headway despite its heroic claims.[24] Social planning agencies run by professionals, staffed by bilingual personnel, periodically evaluated, and funded by public agencies are a step in the right direction.

Planning for the City Solvent

Oakland's fiscal crisis, revealed in a series of articles by Bill Martin in the Oakland Tribune in May of 1974, was said to be part of a national trend.[25] Oakland, like other core cities, has been plagued by an eroding tax base and skyrocketing demands for public services, especially for public safety. According to Arnold J. Meltsner of the Graduate School of Public Affairs at the University of California, Berkeley, the city's predicament is the product of rising operating costs and not the result of greater attention to the needs of Oakland's deprived population.[26] Public safety expenditures, for fire and police, took up only 34.6 percent of the city's budget in 1964-65 but soared to 41.4 percent in 1974-74.[27] Still unclear, however, are the reasons for greater public safety needs.

The need for increased police and fire protection in Oakland emanates from two sources. The rising cost of labor, as Meltsner has shown, is certainly one reason. Increasing social instability, which encourages anti-social behavior, is another. Much of the instability in Oakland is an outgrowth of public, but largely national, policy. The persistence of high rates of unemployment, especially among minority workers, is certainly a contributing factor. The cost of low wage levels, which benefit the city's employers, is ultimately borne by property owners. Firms which are not labor-oriented have flocked to southern Alameda County, where they feel less encumbered. The cycle becomes self-perpetuating unless broken at some point. The shallowness of Oakland's commitment to attacking its unemployment problem has been well documented.[28]

> Oakland's approach, based on stabilizing big business for training
> programs, did nothing to increase the total job supply and avoided
> any buildup of a small business or poor people's political base of
> opposition to existing elected officials.[29]

Urban renewal, which uprooted communities and upset neighborhood bonds, is another contributing factor to the city's social instability. The "anomie" hypothesis contends that "disturbances or disruptions of the collective order, the external regulating force which defines norms and goals and governs behavior," lead to criminal behavior.[30] Although only one explanation among many theories, it seems to operate well at the neighborhood scale. Massive environmental changes, like freeway construction and redevelopment projects, accelerate the process of invasion and succession. Ecologically stable communities lose their identities and communal aspirations under rapid social transformation. In doing so, they become vulnerable.

Inner City residents displaced by urban renewal projects sought refuge in Fruitvale, East and South Central Oakland.[31] It is not surprising that robbery in other parts of Oakland is a relatively rare event. A study by the Center on Administration of Criminal Justice at the University of California, Davis, based on reported crimes from 1966 to 1968, disclosed that robbery was concentrated on a few major streets.[32] East 14th Street, MacArthur Boulevard, Foothill Boulevard, San Pablo Avenue, and Telegraph Avenue were ranked at the top. Heavily patrolled Inner City streets, like Broadway, were relatively safe in terms of reported robberies.

The problem of providing police and fire protection for a rapidly expanding "zone in transition" has accelerated the costs of public safety. Surveillance in East Oakland and North Oakland has been a seething issue. Helicopter surveillance, conceived by officials as a means of cutting costs, is construed by many residents as an invasion of privacy and an instrument of suppression. Oakland's Home Alert Program, in stark contrast, has been much more effective. Promoted by the Oakland Police Department since 1970, it stresses the need for community vigilance. According to Patrolman William Lovejoy, "in blocks that are set up - not in name only - and actually are functioning, they've knocked the crime down to nothing."[33] The value of community stability, difficult to estimate in fiscal terms, is usually omitted in benefit-cost calculations.

The cost of urban renewal to cities has been grossly understated. Federal subsidies for redevelopment, which cover the expense of physical and economic planning, do not cover the cost of social planning. Social planning agencies, which mitigate the impact of redevelopment, could be funded by Federal subsidies. The cost of resettlement far exceeds the cost of relocation, which is now subsidized by the Federal government. The costs of attending to problems caused by redevelopment might alternatively be charged to those who stand to gain most by the transformation. Urban renewal promised to broaden the city's tax base by raising property values in the Inner City. Property taxes, which contributed to 42.8 percent of municipal revenues in 1964-65, dropped to cover only 34.7 percent in 1973-74, as many had predicted.[34] Mayor Reading, who in real life is a corporate executive, has pushed for a wage tax to be assessed against those who work in Oakland. Less regressive alternatives, proposed by Oakland Citizens Committee for Urban Renewal (OCCUR) include raising property taxes, a gross receipts tax, an admissions tax on entertainment, tapping Port of Oakland revenues, and a real estate transfer tax.[35] The City Council has sided with Mayor Reading.

Planning for fiscal solvency is not simply a matter of political leverage or budgetary discipline. It is also a matter of dissolving social stresses and incompatibilities. Preoccupied with an eroding tax base, city fathers have failed to realize that core cities function as a seedbed for new industry and not a greenhouse for those with established political roots. Relocation is often inbred in the life cycle of a firm. Property tax rates, important for land-intensive or building-intensive industries, may not be as crucial to other industries. The core city's drawing power is not its tax rates but rather its labor force, transportation, services, and other externalities. Threats to business, residential, and personal property which stem from social instability raise the cost of insurance as well as police and fire protection. Planning for the City Solvent entails minimizing costs and not maximizing revenues.

Conclusion

The fate of the Chinese community, stable for decades within Oakland's zone of discard, is being determined by forces outside the control of its residents. Burdened by the immigration of working-class Chinese, displaced by redevelopment, and hindered by the legacy of obsolete institutions, it has been sacrificed in the name of both middle-class and traditional values. Like so many other inner city communities, Chinatown has been transformed to save the Central Business District and to perpetuate the customs and values which its elders espouse. Confucian precepts, which guided the community for nearly a century, no longer inspire the young in either China or the United States. Filial piety, which laid the basis for mutual assistance in a period of intense racism and gave dignity to suffering in the family interest, is no longer such an appealing moral value. According to Dr. Lin Yutang, the modern scholar and philosopher, "all Chinese are Confucianists when they are successful and Taoists when they are failures."[36]   The failure of Chinatown's successful community leaders to facilitate the acculturation of Chinese newcomers may be rationalized on philosophical grounds. The failure of Oakland's city fathers to anticipate the consequences of their plans cannot.

The shift toward "comprehensiveness" in city planning did not get under way until the past decade. The case of redevelopment in Oakland illustrates what can happen when social planning is not built into the planning process. Oakland's experience with redevelopment, in comparison to that of most American cities, has been a mixed blessing. Planning in Oakland has come a long way. The experience of Chinatown, relative to that of West Oakland, has been mild. Yet even the Chinese have had tremendous problems with the re-emergence of the inner city. Planners, who are supposed to anticipate as well as foment change, have yet to recognize the social costs of community displacement.

The conflict between local neighborhoods and city officials over redevelopment has also been raised by other programs involving social change. Political scientist Judy May, whose study of four social change programs traced the origins of increasing citizen participation in Oakland between 1955 and 1968, concludes that:

> Citizen participants attacked features of American politics--political legitimacy based upon conformance to procedures rather than performance, political authority delegated to experts, and governmental policy directed toward economic growth at the expense of economic redistribution--which now repress disadvantaged groups; and in doing so, they participated in a new period of institutional reform.
>
> Both city officials and citizen participants believe that it is the city's responsibility to promote the economic welfare of its citizens, but each advocates different means to that end. Whereas city officials allocate public funds to projects intended to make the city more attractive to potential investors, citizen participants seek leverage over projects supported with public funds in order to reduce the costs and increase the benefits of these projects to the low-income and minority communities.
>
> . . . . Whereas city councilmen trust administrative officials to operate their agencies in conformance with council policies, citizen participants distrust both the policies and their administrators.
>
> Uniting in neighborhoods as clients of public services, they have organized to share responsibility for allocating scarce resources among programs and to hold professionals accountable for the manner in which they perform their services.[37]

Footnotes to Chapter Six:

1. Yi-Fu Tuan, "Visual Blight: Exercises in Interpretation," in Lewis, Lowenthal, and Tuan, "Visual Blight in America," Resource Paper No. 23, Assn. of Amer. Geog., 1973, p. 25.

2. Charles Abrams, The City is the Frontier (New York, 1965) p. 108.

3. Tuan, op. cit., p. 26.

4. Pierce Lewis, "The Geographer as Landscape Critic," in Lewis, Lowenthal, and Tuan, "Visual Blight in America," Resource Paper No. 23, Assn. of Amer. Geog., 1973, pp. 2-3.

5. Unpublished census tract data, U.S. Census, 1960 and 1970.

6. Ibid. (see Chapter Four).

7. Assessment Rollbooks, Alameda County Assessor's Office, 1973.

8. Victor G. and Brett de Bary Nee, Long-Time Californ' (New York, 1972) p. 254.

9. Alan Atschuler, Community Control: The Black Demand for Participation in Large American Cities (New York, 1970) p. 13.

10. Charles Abrams, The Language of Cities (New York, 1972) p. 61.

11. Robert Blauner, "Internal Colonialism and Ghetto Revolt," Social Problems, Vol. 16, No. 4, pp. 393-408.

12. Oakland Tribune (June 24, 1970) p. 37.

13. Gordon Yow, "Crime in Oakland Chinatown," unpublished manuscript, Criminology 141B (Street), University of California, Berkeley, Spring, 1972, pp. 41-45.

14. For a cursory update, see "The Changing Face of City's Chinatown," Oakland Tribune (March 2, 1974) p. 17E.

    For deeper insight into the controversy, see Jane Yee Armstrong, "Oakland Chinatown: A Study of Social Conflict" unpublished manuscript, Political Science 197, University of California, Berkeley, Spring, 1974, pp. 18-28.

15. Data based on the following reports by the Oakland Public Schools:

    "Racial Composition of Student Bodies, Nov. 1962-March 1966"
    "Racial Composition of Student Bodies, Mar. 1965-Oct. 1968"
    "Report on School, Region and District Racial-Ethnic Composition of Students, Oct. 1971"

16. Information from interviews within the community.

17. Jane Yee Armstrong, op. cit., p. 16.

18. California's Health (February, 1970) p. 3.

19. See Count D. Gibson, Jr., "The Neighborhood Health Center: The Primary Unit of Health Care," Amer. Jrn. of Pub. Health, (July 1968) pp. 1188-1191.
    Pierre de Vise, "Misused and Misplaced Hospitals and Doctors," Resource Paper No. 22, Assn. of Amer. Geog., 1973, pp. 45-46.

20. Jane Yee Armstrong, op. cit., pp. 29-30.

21. For an interesting appraisal of the impact of immigration on Chinatown and the Mission District of San Francisco, see "Babel in Bagdad by the Bay," San Francisco Planning and Urban Renewal Association, (August, 1970).

    San Francisco District Office data (U.S. Immigration and Naturalization Service) for January 1969 suggests that Alameda County accommodates about 17 percent of the Chinese aliens living in the San Francisco Bay Area.

22. Jane Yee Armstrong, op. cit., p. 5.

23. Oakland Chinese Community Council "Agency Profile" (November, 1973) gives a brief run-down of its activities and structure.

24. See Michael Brooks, "Social Planning and City Planning," Special Report No. 261, Planning Advisory Service, American Society of Planning Officials, pp. 39-44.

    Roger Kasperson and Myrna Brietbart, "Participation, Decentralization, and Advocacy Planning, Resource Paper No. 25, Assn. of Amer. Geog., 1974, pp. 48-49.

25. Bill Martin, "Oakland is on the Brink of Bankruptcy," Oakland Tribune (May 12-15, 1974).

26. Cited in Martin, ibid. (May 12, 1974); for more detail see Arnold J. Meltsner, The Politics of City Revenue (Berkeley, 1971).

27. Data for 1973-1974 from Martin, op. cit. and for 1964-1965 from City and County Data Book, U.S. Bureau of the Census, 1967.

28. Edward C. Hayes, Power Structure and Urban Policy (New York, 1972) pp. 131-184.

29. Ibid., p. 167.

30. Keith Harries, The Geography of Crime and Justice (New York, 1974) p. 78; for insight into gangs see John Bryan, "Inside the Chinese Gangs of San Francisco," San Francisco Phoenix, Vol. 1, No. 16 (April 19, 1973) pp. 5, 24.

31. William L. Nicholls II and Earl R. Babbie, Oakland in Transition: A Summary of the 701 Household Survey, Survey Research Center, University of California, Berkeley (June, 1969) pp. 62-67.

32. Fran Dauth, "The Geography of Oakland Crime Areas," Oakland Tribune (June 6, 1973).

33. David Kleinberg, "Neighborhood Organized Against Crime," San Francisco Chronicle (May 14, 1974).

34. Same sources as note 27.

35. Martin, op. cit. (May 12, 1974).

36. Cited in The World's Great Religions, Time Incorporated (New York, 1963) Vol. 1, p. 91.

37. Judy May, Struggle for Authority: A Comparison of Four Social Change Programs in Oakland, California, Ph.D. dissertation, Department of Political Science, University of California, Berkeley, 1973, pp. ii-iii.

CHAPTER SEVEN

THE LESSONS OF CHINESE SETTLEMENT

Introduction

The lessons of Chinese settlement, acculturation, and dispersal in the East Bay Region deserve wider application than might at first be expected. Contemporary models of inner city settlement, based largely on the interaction of European immigrants with Black Americans, have been more concerned with the racial than the ethnic nature of ghetto life. Not until recently have city planners come to realize that the American dream of a house in the suburbs is neither universal nor feasible. The case of the Chinese in American cities, whose ties to Chinatown persist even during a period of civil rights and occupational mobility, illustrates the ethnic foundations of Inner City settlement. A century of immigration restrictions and racism, by compounding the dependence of newcomers on ghetto institutions, undermined their acculturation. The lifting of immigration and racial obstacles eased their acculturation but did not make Chinatown any less attractive for low-income foreign-born Chinese newcomers. Not until threatened by the process of redevelopment, however, has the value of the ghetto to immigrant families been recognized. The costs of ghetto displacement have yet to be anticipated. It is not surprising that, having mistaken its origins, we have failed to deal with the problems of inner city settlement which have been generated by immigration. If the central city is to continue to function as a reception area for disadvantaged immigrants, then national policies must provide for their support.

The systematic nature of inner city evolution in the United States is evident in the plight of oppressed minority communities in most American cities. Solutions to the ills of the central city have been bred in a culture of misconceptions about how they function as social, ecological, and physical communities. National efforts to redeem the city, beset by the arrogance of physical planners, did not begin to shift toward strategies for social change until the late 1960's when the Model Cities Program began to roll. If the American city is to weather the burdens and uncertainties of social change, then new institutions must be devised to facilitate the process of acculturation and adaptation. This chapter will attempt to rectify some of the misconceptions which have clouded our thinking in hopes of building more realistic models for testing new solutions to old problems.

Two Versions of Urban Settlement

Behavioral assumptions about the dynamics of inner city decay and development spring from middle-class perceptions. Faith in the sanctity of the nuclear family, belief in the impartiality of the market place, and trust in the efficacy of the political and judicial arenas permeate the art and taint the practice of city planning in the United States. Research on the American city by social scientists remains wedded to narrow assumptions about how people perceive their environments and rely on their communities. Implicit in most theories on the structure of cities is the notion that ethnic status is either short-lived or permanent, depending on the existence of racial barriers. Ethnicity, according to the middle class model of urban settlement, is regarded as an obstacle to be overcome in pursuit of assimilation.

Residents are usually divided into independent decision-making units, nuclear family households, with varying sizes and incomes but similar ideals and environmental aspirations. Households are sorted into different ecological areas, which have distinctive values in terms of convenience, aesthetic appeal, and architectural suitability. Those with large incomes and small families have greater rent-paying ability and thus get first choice of residence. The rules of the middle-class game presume that all households share similar needs, tastes, and capabilities. Community institutions, such as neighborhood associations and rotary clubs, exist to encourage property maintenance and improvement and to mobilize resources in quest of political spoils, like schools and parks. The more attractive the environment, the more powerful its population, the more stable and prestigious the community.

For ethnic communities, these assumptions do not apply. Members of immigrant groups have widely varying needs, tastes, and capabilities, depending upon the extent to which they have acculturated. Partially acculturated city dwellers tend to prefer residence in an ethnic quarter, where extended family obligations, familiar customs of doing business, and traditional institutions offer them security within a more complex metropolitan world. Communal needs and limited linguistic capabilities draw newcomers together, despite differences in income and generation. Community institutions, such as churches and clan associations, exist to perpetuate the customs, obligations, and facilities on which newcomers, landlords, and local businessmen rely. The less attractive the environment, the less prestigious and more stable the community, the greater the possibilities for rapid although not necessarily complete acculturation.

Overcrowding and undermaintenance due to massive immigration, racial restrictions in housing and hiring, or demolition of housing by public agencies retard the rate of acculturation in ethnic neighborhoods. Inner city communities operate in an open system, subject to forces well outside their control. Middle-class communities usually operate in a partially closed system, insulated from most of the forces outside their influence. Most people and their politicians attribute the physical deterioration of the inner city to the unwillingness or at least to the inability of its residents to maintain their neighborhood. Slums are thought to emanate from the poverty and values of their residents, according to the middle-class model of urban settlement. Chinatown Oakland, like so many other ethnic communities, remains vulnerable to the threat of immigration and public land-use policies, as it has for over a century.

FIGURE 3

A MIDDLE-CLASS VERSION OF URBAN SETTLEMENT

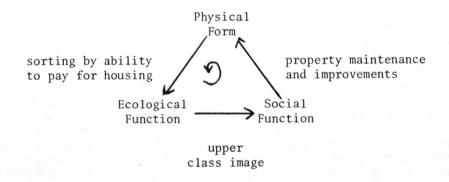

FIGURE 4

AN ETHNIC VERSION OF URBAN SETTLEMENT

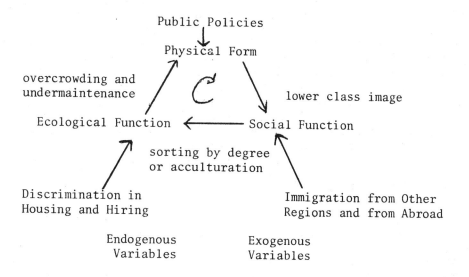

Public Policies

Physical Form

overcrowding and
undermaintenance

lower class image

Ecological Function ← Social Function

sorting by degree
or acculturation

Discrimination in
Housing and Hiring

Immigration from Other
Regions and from Abroad

Endogenous
Variables

Exogenous
Variables

Middle-Class Prescriptions

The crux of the problem with the Oakland Inner City in middle-class terms was its concentration of low-income residents. Plans to upgrade the physical environment of Inner City neighborhoods and to relocate disadvantaged residents "elsewhere" in subsidized housing units seemed well-meaning. However, few subsidized rental units have in fact been built. Prospects for more rental housing for Oakland's lower-income residents appear dim. Massive improvements have attracted higher income residents into the Inner City, forcing partially acculturated residents into outlying neighborhoods of East and South Oakland. Redevelopment, advanced in the name of slum clearance and civic progress, has worked to the advantage of property owners at the expense of ethnic residents. Too many low income residents would after all hinder efforts by city planners to turn the Inner City into a mixed income, multi-racial ecological area.

The combination of rent subsidies and housing the disadvantaged in suburban areas struck a responsive chord, especially among those who felt that integration was the ultimate answer. To suburban communities, which have struggled to insulate themselves from precisely this kind of invasion, the idea was an anathema. Central city fathers and civil rights advocates who favored such a strategy for the East Bay failed to recognize the limited capabilities and communal needs of disadvantaged eithnic newcomers. Rent subsidies, designed to equalize differences in rent-paying capacity, would not meet the immediate social needs of immigrant residents. The lack of special public as well as mutual assistance programs outside of Chinatown Oakland inhibited Chinese acculturation in outlying neighborhoods, where they are treated no differently from other residents. The issue of special programs for special needs among non-English speaking minorities continues to be confused and distorted by the bugaboo of racial segregation.

Middle-class rules, which call for competition among ecological areas for the spoils of political leverage, have made separate but equal a cruel hoax. The dispersal of ethnic groups into the suburbs, which leads to integrated but inferior conditions for disadvantaged residents, avoids the issue of special needs altogether. If communities with distinct needs are to be served by special institutions, then they will have to make their needs known and their identities clear. Some degree of self-segregation is essential. The concept of community without propinquity is a middle-class ideal, which works only if members are mobile, independent, and assimilated. Those with ethnic or communal aspirations,

141

forged either by necessity or by desire, who once found a home in the Inner City have been forced to seek refuge in traditionally middle-class residential areas.

Increasing disenchantment with the nuclear family, the free market system, and the judicial and political arenas during the past decade suggests that the applicability of the middle-class model of urban settlement is shrinking in cities well entrenched in the counter-culture, women's liberation, and the "third-world" movement. Conflicts between sorting by single family income and sorting by acculturation (see Figures 3 and 4) have even surfaced in upper-class neighborhoods of the San Francisco Bay Area, where "communes" of rent-earning adults have brought their way into expensive homes. The ability of established middle-class communities to insulate themselves from forces outside their control has rested heavily on zoning ordinances and building codes. Yet, like inner city communities, they have also become more vulnerable during the past two decades. A recent decision by the United States Supreme Court to rule on the constitutionality of local zoning regulations may mark the dawn of another period of changing land-use controls in this country.

Perspectives in Model Building

The reemergence of Oakland's Inner City as a middle-class habitat is part of a national transition. The suburbanization of American life, which flourished after World War II, continues undaunted by the volleys of "liberal" intellectuals. More Americans now live in suburbs than in either central cities or rural communities. Physically sound and ecologically stable, the suburb has undermined, solely by its popularity, traditional notions about the form and function of cities. The abandonment of the central city in the face of a suburban expansion was construed as a sign of urban decay instead of suburban attractiveness. City planners probed for ways to make the central city more beautiful and more efficient. Three models surfaced to represent the city and to dramatize its plight.

Physical models of urban structure envision the city as a work of art, an expression of metropolitan ideals. The style of Oakland's buildings, texture of its structures, majesty of its skyline, picturesqueness of its neighborhoods, continuity of its edges, color of its streets, and flow of its traffic were all indicative of its quality of life. A symbol of civic pride, the physical heart of Oakland is not merely a manifestation of capital improvements. It is an expression of power, status, innovation, vitality, efficiency, and achievement. Investments in the City Beautiful paid off in rising property values and an enriched tax base, as new residents sought accommodations in its well designed quarters. Threats to the visual harmony of Oakland would be protected against, or so it was believed, by zoning ordinances and restrictive covenants.

The incompatibility of blighted structures and Central Business District renovation could be resolved by physical means. The demolition of old structures and the construction of new commercial and residential accommodations was a popular answer. The disadvantaged would have to be relocated in areas of Oakland, where they would be less visible and detrimental to the city's precious image as a place to shop, visit, and do business. The value of physical improvements had to be protected if past investments were to yield dividends and future investments were to be forthcoming. Oakland's Inner City, like the suburban shopping center, would have to be made safe, clean, and convenient.

Ecological models of urban structure treat Oakland as a set of economic opportunities, a market place of real estate. Varying in relative accessibility as well as structural endowments, the city game pits each player or actor against the other in a battle for stability or change. Winners realized soaring property values at little expense to themselves. Urban habitats compete as places to work, reside, play, or make transactions. The value of land for different uses depends on its proximity to other activities, from which owners may derive external benefits or bear external costs. Owners upgrade or downgrade their structures to conform to the rent-paying capacity of their tenants. Habitats differ in stability, depending on the ability of their owners to sway public improvements, zoning variations, and other forces in their favor. The formation of merchant associations and neighborhood associations was one means of acquiring political leverage in Oakland.

Involvement in the redevelopment process is another.

Overcoming the resistance of inner city residents displaced by redevelopment projects was part of the urban game. Blighted structures, less profitable in a period of Fair Housing, became obsolete in light of the inner city's improved accessibility and brand new facade. The disadvantaged, who could not afford higher rents, could be housed in East Oakland. Rent subsidies would allow them to improve their accommodations and allow city planners to disperse the negative externalities of low-income housing. Inner City housing for low-income residents, like inner city wholesaling and light industry, had supposedly outlived its usefulness, if only to the Central Business District. The winners were inner city landowners, who had mobilized federal, state, and local agencies in a massive effort to save Oakland's Central Business District from the imperatives of supply and demand. The losers in this game were property owners in East Oakland whose investments stagnated as low-income residents filtered into nearby areas. The promise of rent subsidies has yet to be fulfilled in Oakland. The rules of the City Practical do not compensate for broken promises.

Social models of urban structure regard Oakland as a center of cultural ferment and communal resilience. The pageantry of city life, its ethnic folkways, tapestry of traditions, rural customs, and distinctive institutions give the landscape its vitality and exuberance. The tolerance, wealth, and diversity of the City Flexible furnish incentives for social interaction and community cohesion. Oakland is a stepping stone to acculturation and communal aspirations. Mixed land uses, dreaded in the City Beautiful and scrutinized in the City Practical, are an integral part of the City Flexible. Wholesale and light industrial operations offered Oakland's ethnic communities at least some measure of insulation for nearly a century due to their depressing effects on residential property values. Seclusion within a zone of discard was an advantage for those who could not afford higher rents, as long as structures are profitable to maintain and safe to occupy. Streets, playgrounds, churches, schools, and other community centers provided places where partially acculturated people could meet, exchange information about jobs and other opportunities, enjoy recreation, and seek assistance. For acculturated middle-class families, much of this took place in the home or in central offices or areas explicitly designated for such purposes.

Survival in an open system, with so many outside forces at work to determine the fate of the community, required more than vigilance. It was a matter of reducing uncertainties either by spatial or by institutional adjustment. Gravitation to the zone of discard reduced the threat of encroachment. The creation of community institutions which could compete in the ecological arena also lowered the risk of intrusion. The experience of Chinatown Oakland, as opposed to Chinatown San Francisco, is a matter of record. The danger of reliance on spatial alternatives for Chinatown Oakland was redevelopment. The danger of institutional fortitude is that those who control the institutions may also own much of the land. Landowners in the urban game have always tended to collude in the interest of rising land values.

At least two institutions will be necessary to sustain the vitality of ethnic communities in Oakland's Inner City. Community-based and federally financed social planning agencies will be needed to insure that social as well as physical and economic needs are recognized by public agencies and that communities are warned and advised of events which threaten their destiny. Federal assistance will also be needed to finance the acquisition and rehabilitation of deteriorated inner city structures by incorporated neighborhood or community organizations in order to avoid the pitfalls of the urban game. Only if insulated from the opportunism of ethnic as well as non-ethnic landowners and only if informed as well as represented in the political arena do Oakland's ethnic communities stand a chance of survival in the Inner City.

The importance of federal funding for community planning, ownership, and rehabilitation stems from the role of the inner city in absorbing the shocks of national economic growth. If the economy is to be responsive to shifts in technological change and transport innovations, then regional adjustments are inevitable. The movement of people from areas of high unemployment to areas of low unemployment is a national necessity. The inner city has served as a lubricant for facilitating this transition for over a century. Its transformation into a middle-class habitat is more than a personal tragedy. It is a national loss brought about by our apparent disregard for the spatial implications of ethnic immigration.

Not until both legislators and planners come to grips with the reality of inner city life will its problems be addressed. Misled by its form, observers have condemned its function as a reception area for ethnic residents. In the case of Oakland, the causes of inner city blight originated with the owners of Inner City property, who were entitled to profit from undermaintained structures. National policies must perceive the inner city as a vehicle for acculturation and national economic adjustment as well as a work of art and an expression of internal functional shifts.

Emerging Patterns of Chinese Settlement

Chinese settlement in the United States originally took three basic forms: Chinese camps, Chinatowns, and Chinese centers. Chinese camps, once common in frontier America, began to fade as Chinese railroad workers, miners, fishermen, farm laborers, laundrymen, and shopkeepers were driven out of many rural communities by racial violence during the last three decades of the 19th century. Many Chinese sought refuge in large cities like San Francisco, where traditional institutions had provided for their security and employment. Chinatown social enclaves emerged to serve the everyday needs of displaced and oppressed newcomers, who were confined by local laws and customs and by their own communal needs. Those Chinese who wished to venture beyond the obligations and restrictions of Chinatown headed for other cities like Oakland and Berkeley, where loosely knit community centers grew to meet the periodic needs of a dispersed Chinese population. Chinese community centers, although much less colorful than the Chinese camps of the Old West and the Chinatowns of San Francisco and New York, were nevertheless the most pervasive form of Chinese settlement in this country. The term "Chinatown," which refers to small as well as large Chinese quarters, fails to differentiate between the functions of the two places.

Unlike San Francisco Chinatown, which was protected by clan, district, and Six Companies institutions, Oakland Chinatown has been susceptible to displacement and encroachment by outside activities. Encroachment, first by wholesaling and light industry and then by high-rent housing, retailing, and public (governmental, recreational, educational) activities have been almost impossible to stop. The inherent vulnerability of Chinese community centers like Oakland Chinatown to outside forces has become even more apparent in the aftermath of redevelopment. In contrast, San Francisco Chinatown's problems have stemmed not from redevelopment but from massive immigration, which also accelerated during the 1960's.

The rebuilding of the Central Business District, the growth of high-rent housing, and the construction of civic projects in Oakland's Inner City began at the very time when foreign-born families arrived to help revive the sagging economy of the Chinese quarter. No longer propped up by practice of racial discrimination in the East Bay housing market, sub-standard Inner City dwellings were abandoned by those who could afford to move into better accommodations. The reemergence of the inner city as a middle-class residential and commercial area was envisioned as a means of raising Inner City property values during a period of Fair Housing. Although allegedly an effort to combat urban blight, redevelopment in Oakland has made it increasingly difficult for low-income residents to settle in the Inner City. Removing low-rent housing in Chinatown Oakland has diverted newcomers into East Oakland and into other cities.

Already plagued by financial troubles, Oakland's city fathers hoped to shift some of the burden of accommodating the poor to suburban communities. Planners argued that the Central Business District had to be accessible and evoke a feeling of security if it were going to draw business from the suburbs. Chinatown businessmen thought that redevelopment would turn the quarter into a regional center serving the entire East Bay Chinese community. The dispersed pattern of Chinese settlement in the East Bay is an outgrowth of redevelopment as well as previous tendencies. In contrast Chinese settlement in San Francisco is far more concentrated, reflecting the institutional resilience (districts, clans, Six

144

Companies) and scale of immigration into the community.

The Future of Ethnicity in the Inner City

The future of ethnicity in the inner city will hinge on both local land-use policies and national migration policies. The impact of any combination of these two policies on inner city ethnic settlement may be sorted into four possibilities, based on the history of Chinese settlement in the East Bay Region of the San Francisco Bay Area. Only two variations are specified for each policy: decreasing or increasing immigration, and redevelopment or no redevelopment. There may, of course, be other variations. Although redevelopment may proceed with or without federal or suburban subsidies to central cities for meeting the needs of ethnic newcomers, it is assumed for analytical purposes that such subsidies would reduce the fiscal burden and thus the political pressures on a city to redevelop. If this assumption is valid, then federal subsidy programs and metropolitan tax schemes may really be the policy variables being examined:

(A) A possible decrease in immigration into cities without redevelopment would probably lead to immediate reduction in the size and density of large Chinatowns, which depend upon immigration for their economic and political strength. Less dramatic declines would be felt in smaller Chinese centers, which rely less on the local immigrant community and more on the patronage of dispersed Chinese families. The drop in Chinese immigration in Oakland from 1880 to 1906 and from 1910 to 1940 revealed such a trend.

(B) A possible decrease in immigration in cities with active redevelopment programs would most likely be followed by a rapid decay in Chinese community centers due to their inherent vulnerability to outside pressures, such as urban renewal. This pattern seemed to occur in Oakland from 1950 to 1965. Large Chinatowns would suffer to a much lesser degree due to their more substantial political and economic roots.

(C) A possible increase in immigration in cities without redevelopment programs would encourage the growth of both Chinatowns and Chinese centers. Large Chinatowns would be especially prone to expand because of heightened immigration. Chinese community centers would have space in which to grow in the absence of redevelopment. Chinatown Oakland exhibited this tendency from 1906 to 1910 and 1940 to 1950.

(D) A possible increase in immigration in cities with intensive redevelopment would result in the rapid growth of large Chinatowns and in a leap-frog form of expansion in smaller Chinese community centers, which are unable to resist displacement by urban renewal. The experience of Oakland Chinatown since 1965 is a manifestation of such a trend. Changes in both local and national policies will be needed to break this trend.

FIGURE 5

FOUR ALTERNATIVES FOR PUBLIC POLICY

| | | National Migration Policies | |
		Decreasing Immigration	Increasing Immigration
Local Land Use Policies	No Redevelopment (federal subsidies or metropolitan taxation)	A	C
	Redevelopment (no subsidies and no metropolitan taxation)	B	D

145

As suggested in Chapter One, the future of inner city ethnic communities will be governed by immigration restrictions, public land-use policies, and variations in racial discrimination practices. The above analysis does not include racial discrimination as an independent variable, since it concerns the future, and not the historic, evolution of Chinese settlement in the inner city. For other ethnic groups in the United States, however, the role of racial discrimination may continue to be crucial. Both the physical form and spatial pattern of inner city settlement have crystallized out of these three exogenous forces, to which inner city residents have had to adjust. It is hoped that this study has given some insight into the process of this adjustment. Public policies designed to further national, metropolitan, and municipal interests at the expense of ethnic communities will undoubtedly continue. To attribute the consequences of these policies to the ethnic residents, themselves, however, can no longer be justified in theory or condoned in practice. New ways must be implemented to anticipate and compensate for the consequences of these policies if the lessons of Chinese settlement are to have any practical significance. And it should be emphasized, in closing, that far more cities have the easily encroached-upon type of Chinatown found in Oakland than have the more durable type found in San Francisco.

APPENDIX

A SURVEY OF CHINESE IN THE EAST BAY SUBURBS

Much has been written about Chinatown, but little is known about the rapidly growing Chinese suburban community in the American city. About 26 percent of the Chinese in the East Bay Region, for example, resided in the suburbs in 1970, compared with only 15 percent in 1960. A questionnaire was designed, tested, and mailed to Chinese households in El Cerrito, Kensington, Orinda, Moraga, Walnut Creek, Concord, and Hayward. The names and addresses were selected from East Bay telephone directories. Unlisted Chinese households and Chinese households in other suburban communities were not included in the sample. Special care was taken to avoid questions which might be misleading, confusing or construed as frivolous or offensive by the recipient. A letter, a questionnaire, printed on bright red paper, and a stamped, self-addressed return envelope were mailed in October of 1973.

Of the 243 questionnaires to be mailed out, only 18 were invalidated as either "not at this address" or "not Chinese." Of the 225 remaining (valid) questionnaires, 93 were completed and returned. Most questions (of the single response type) were appropriately answered by 70-80 households. The results are presented in the following tables.

The response rate ranged from 18.7 percent in Kensington to 55.4 percent in El Cerrito. Most mail surveys of Asian Americans have been fortunate to elicit a 15 percent rate of return. The overall response rate for this survey was 41.3 percent. No attempt has been made to draw general conclusions from the data, except as they help to support the arguments specified in this dissertation. Much more can and should be said about how the data pertain to other questions of practical as well as theoretical interest. It is hoped that this survey will begin to broaden our understanding of the reasons behind and the consequences of residential dispersal in a major Chinese-American Community.

(Cover Letter)

Government officials have seldom shown much concern for the culture and
aspirations of Chinese-Americans in the East Bay. To be more responsive,
they must recognize what you have experienced and how you wish to perpetuate your heritage.

Your help in completing the enclosed questionnaire will contribute much
to our understanding of the past and to our planning for the future of
the Chinese community in the East Bay. Please take this opportunity to
help make the East Bay a better place for future generations.

Please contact me or use the back of the questionnaire if you have any
questions, criticism, or suggestions. This survey is part of a Ph.D.
research project at the University of California at Berkeley. Your
answers will remain confidential and will be used only for statistical
purposes. A self-addressed, stamped return envelope is enclosed for
your convenience.

Sincerely,

Willard Tim Chow
Faculty Sponsor
Chinese Student Assn.
 of Laney College
Phone: 843-5740 x 294

SURVEY OF THE CHINESE IN THE EAST BAY REGION

1. Where were you born? _____ husband _____ wife _____ single

2. To what generation do you belong? (first-born in China, second-parents born in China, third-grandparents born in China, etc.)
   _____ husband _____ wife _____ single person

3. What is your present occupation? _____ male _____ female

4. In what city do you work? _____ male _____ female

5. Indicate highest level of education completed (M - male, F - female):
   _____ less than high school graduate _____ four year college graduate
   _____ graduated from high school _____ more than four years college
   _____ some college/junior college (advanced degree)

6. In what city did you live before moving into this area?

7. In what year did you move? _____ Why did you leave that location?

8. Why did you select your present area of residence?

9. Do you rent or own your home?
   _____ rent from Chinese owner _____ own (bought from Chinese)
   _____ rent from non-Chinese owner _____ own (bought from non-Chinese)

10. Did you experience any racial discrimination in your search for a home?
   _____ from landlords _____ from realtors _____ from others (please
   _____ from sellers _____ from banks or other specify)
   _____ from neighbors lending institutions _____ no discrimination
   at all

11. Describe the most common type of discrimination experienced in your search:

12. Have you experienced any racial discrimination since moving into this area?
   _____ no discrimination _____ occasionally _____ regularly from 19__ to
   19__

13. Describe the most common type of discrimination experienced since you moved in:

14. What are the most common reasons for you and your family's going into Oakland China-town?

15. Describe the nature of your family's participation in the activities and programs of the Oakland Chinese community:

16. Have there been any attempts to organize the Chinese in your residential area to participate in any local activities or programs? If so, please describe such efforts and your reaction to them:

THANK YOU FOR YOUR ASSISTANCE. Please mail to Willard Chow, Laney College, 900 Fallon, Oakland.

TABLE A

RESPONSE BY SUBURBS

Suburb	Number Mailed	Number Valid	Number Not Returned	Number Returned	Response Rate in Percent*
El Cerrito	110	110	50	60	55.4
Orinda	11	7	4	3	42.8
Moraga	9	6	4	2	33.3
Walnut Creek	22	16	11	5	31.2
Concord	42	37	26	11	29.8
Hayward	33	33	24	9	27.3
Kensington	16	16	·13	3	18.7
Total East Bay	243	225	132	93	41.3

*Response Rate = $\frac{\text{Number Returned}}{\text{Number Valid}}$ x 100

TABULATIONS (Part I)

TABLE B

PREVIOUS RESIDENCE

Q. 1(a) In what city did you live before moving into your present home?

Origin	El Cerrito Kensington	Orinda Moraga Walnut Creek Concord	Hayward	Total East Bay Suburbs
Berkeley	20	0	0	20
Oakland	8	3	6	17
San Francisco	13	3	0	16
Rest of Bay Area	4	6	2	12
Rest of California	1	2	0	3
Out of State	5	4	1	10
Subtotals by Area	51	18	9	78

150

TABLE C

YEAR OF MOVE

Q. 1(b) In what year did you move?

Year of Move	El Cerrito Kensington	Orinda Moraga Walnut Creek Concord	Hayward	Total East Bay Suburbs
1945-1956	4	0	0	4
1957-1960	8	1	2	11
1961-1964	10	4	5	19
1965-1968	12	7	1	20
1969-1972	18	8	1	27
Subtotals by Area	52	20	9	81

TABLE D

TENURE

Q. 1(c) Do you rent or own your home?

Tenure	El Cerrito Kensington	Orinda Moraga Walnut Creek Concord	Hayward	Total East Bay Suburbs
Own	37	16	9	62
Rent	4	1	0	5
Subtotals by Area	41	17	9	67

TABLE E

SEARCH PROCEDURES

Q. 2 How did you learn about your present area of residence?

Source	El Cerrito Kensington	Orinda Moraga Walnut Creek Concord	Hayward	Total East Bay Suburbs
Realtors	21	5	2	28
Friends	17	5	3	25
Relatives	6	2	2	10
Community Contacts	5	0	2	7
Newspapers	2	3	0	5
"Riding Around"	2	1	2	5
"Fellow Employees"	0	4	0	4
Other Means	4	1	0	5
Subtotals by Area	57	21	11	89

TABLE F

SCOPE OF SEARCH

Q. 3 What other residential areas in the Bay Area did you seriously consider in searching for your home?

Other Area	El Cerrito Kensington	Orinda Moraga Walnut Creek Concord	Hayward	Total East Bay Suburbs
Berkeley	16	3	0	6
Oakland	3	3	2	8
Rest of Alameda Co.	4	3	4	11
San Francisco Co.	3	3	0	6
Contra Costa Co.	15	12	0	27
San Mateo Co.	3	1	0	4
Marin Co.	3	2	0	5
Santa Clara Co.	1	1	0	2
None	15	4	3	22
Subtotals by Area	65	29	10	104

TABLE G

REASONS FOR SELECTION

Q. 4 Why did you select your present area of residence over the other areas?

Reason	El Cerrito Kensington	Orinda Moraga Walnut Creek Concord	Hayward	Total East Bay Suburbs
Closer to Good Schools	33	10	4	47
More Stable Neighborhood	24	10	5	39
More Relaxing Surroundings	19	13	4	36
Greater Visual Attractions (View)	23	5	1	29
More Reasonably Priced Houses Available	11	5	4	20
Parks & Recreation Facilities	15	3	1	19
"Closer to Work"	10	5	1	16
Closer to Friends	11	2	2	15
Closer to Relatives	12	0	2	14
Lower Property Taxes	6	0	2	8
Closer to other Chinese People	6	0	1	7
Other Reasons	6	7	1	14
Subtotals by Area	176	60	28	264

TABLE H

RACIAL DISCRIMINATION

Q. 5 Are you aware of any Chinese residents who have experienced any racial discrimination by realtors, lenders, sellers, landlords, or neighbors in your residential area?

Response	El Cerrito Kensington	Orinda Moraga Walnut Creek Concord	Hayward	Total East Bay Suburbs
Yes	7	0	3	10
No	44	20	6	70
	51	20	9	80
If so, how long ago?				
6-10 years ago	2	0	0	2
10-20 years ago	5	0	3	8
Subtotals by Area	7	0	3	10

TABLE I

ACTIVITIES FOR CHINESE FAMILIES

Q. 6(a) Would you strongly support more activities for Chinese families?

Response	El Cerrito Kensington	Orinda Moraga Walnut Creek Concord	Hayward	Total East Bay Suburbs
Yes	22	14	4	40
No	22	4	4	30
"Maybe"	2	0	1	3
Subtotals by Area	46	18	9	73

TABLE J

PREFERRED PROGRAMS

Q. 6(b) If so, what programs would you prefer?

Type	El Cerrito Kensington	Orinda Moraga Walnut Creek Concord	Hayward	Total East Bay Suburbs
Cultural, Educational, Language	6	10	2	18
Social, Recreational, Youth	7	2	0	9
Church	1	0	1	2
Political	0	1	0	1
Subtotals by Area	14	13	3	30

TABULATIONS (Part II)

TABLE K

FREQUENCY OF CHINATOWN TRIPS

Q. 1 About how often do you or your family go to Chinatown Oakland?

Frequency	El Cerrito Kensington	Orinda Moraga Walnut Creek Concord	Hayward	Total East Bay Suburbs
Once a week or more	11	1	4	16
Once or Twice a Month	23	11	3	37
3-6 Times a Year	6	2	0	8
Once or Twice a Year	2	3	0	5
Rarely or Never	4	3	1	8
Subtotals by Area	46	20	8	74

TABLE L

REASONS FOR CHINATOWN TRIPS

Q.2 Why do you or your family go to Chinatown Oakland?

Reason	El Cerrito Kensington	Orinda Moraga Walnut Creek Concord	Hayward	Total East Bay Suburbs
To shop for groceries	47	13	8	68
Lunch or dinner at a restaurant	42	11	7	60
To visit relatives or friends	5	2	5	12
Community celebrations and events	5	0	2	7
Other commercial services	5	0	1	6
Religious Activities	4	0	1	5
To work or do business	1	0	0	1
Subtotals by Area	110	26	24	160

155

TABLE M

REDEVELOPMENT

Q. 3 Would you move to Chinatown Oakland if it were improved through redevelopment?

Response	El Cerrito Kensington	Orinda Moraga Walnut Creek Concord	Hayward	Total East Bay Suburbs
Yes	3	0	2	5
No	47	21	6	74
Subtotals by Area	50	21	8	79

TABLE N

PRESENT CENTER

Q. 4 Do you feel that Chinatown Oakland is now the center of the East Bay Chinese Community?

Response	El Cerrito Kensington	Orinda Moraga Walnut Creek Concord	Hayward	Total East Bay Suburbs
Yes	30	7	6	43
No	13	7	3	23
Subtotals by Area	43	14	9	66

TABULATIONS (Part III)

TABLE P

PLACE OF BIRTH

Q.1 In what city were you born?

Place of Birth	El Cerrito Kensington	Orinda Moraga Walnut Creek Concord	Hayward	Total East Bay Suburbs
S. F. Bay Area	34	13	10	57
Elsewhere in California	10	5	1	16
Elsewhere in U. S.	17	11	3	31
China	29	5	4	38
Taiwan, Hong Kong or Macao	9	5	0	14
Elsewhere in the World	5	1	0	6
Subtotals by Area	104	40	18	162

TABLE Q

PLACE OF WORK

Q. 2 In what city do you work?

Workplace	El Cerrito Kensington	Orinda Moraga Walnut Creek Concord	Hayward	Total East Bay Suburbs
San Francisco	25	6	1	32
Berkeley	19	0	0	19
Oakland	6	1	1	8
Elsewhere in Alameda Co.	2	2	11	15
Contra Costa Co.	12	12	0	24
Elsewhere	4	0	0	4
Subtotals	68	21	13	102

TABLE R

LEADING OCCUPATIONS

Q. 3 What is your occupation?

Occupational Group with Three or more Members	El Cerrito Kensington	Orinda Moraga Walnut Creek Concord	Hayward	Total East Bay Suburbs
Housewife	19	10	3	32
Engineer	23	1	0	24
Secretary or Clerk	11	2	1	14
Educator or Teacher	5	3	0	8
Pharmacist or Optometrist	4	2	1	7
Nurse or Medical Technician	5	0	1	6
Physician or Dentist	1	2	2	5
Chemist or Scientist	3	0	0	3
Accountant	2	1	0	3
Salesperson	2	1	0	3
Retired	1	0	2	3
All other Occupations	23	11	6	40
Subtotals by Area	99	33	16	148

TABLE S

GENERATION

Q. 4 To what generation do you belong?

Generation	El Cerrito Kensington	Orinda Moraga Walnut Creek Concord	Hayward	Total East Bay Suburbs
Born in China (1st)	22	5	2	29
Parents born in China (2nd)	25	7	5	37
Grandparents born in China (3rd)	2	7	1	10
Great Grandparents born in China (4th)	4	1	0	5
Subtotals by Area	53	20	8	81

TABLE T

CHILDREN

Q. 5 How many children do you have?

Number	El Cerrito Kensington	Walnut Creek Concord	Hayward	Total East Bay Suburbs
None	6	2	0	8
One	6	3	0	9
Two	21	9	2	32
Three	12	4	3	19
Four or more	7	2	3	12
Subtotals by Area	52	20	8	80

TABLE U

EDUCATION

Q. 6 Which of the following best describes your educational background?

Education	El Cerrito Kensington	Orinda Moraga Walnut Creek Concord	Hayward	Total East Bay Suburbs
High School	7	3	3	13
Some College/Junior College	5	4	2	11
College Graduate	19	5	1	25
Advanced College Degree	21	7	2	30
Subtotals by Area	52	19	8	79

WITHDRAWN

THE REEMERGENCE OF AN INNER CITY: THE PIVOT OF CHINESE SETTLEMENT IN THE EAST BAY REGION OF THE SAN FRANCISCO BAY AREA

BY WILLARD T. CHOW

WITHDRAWN